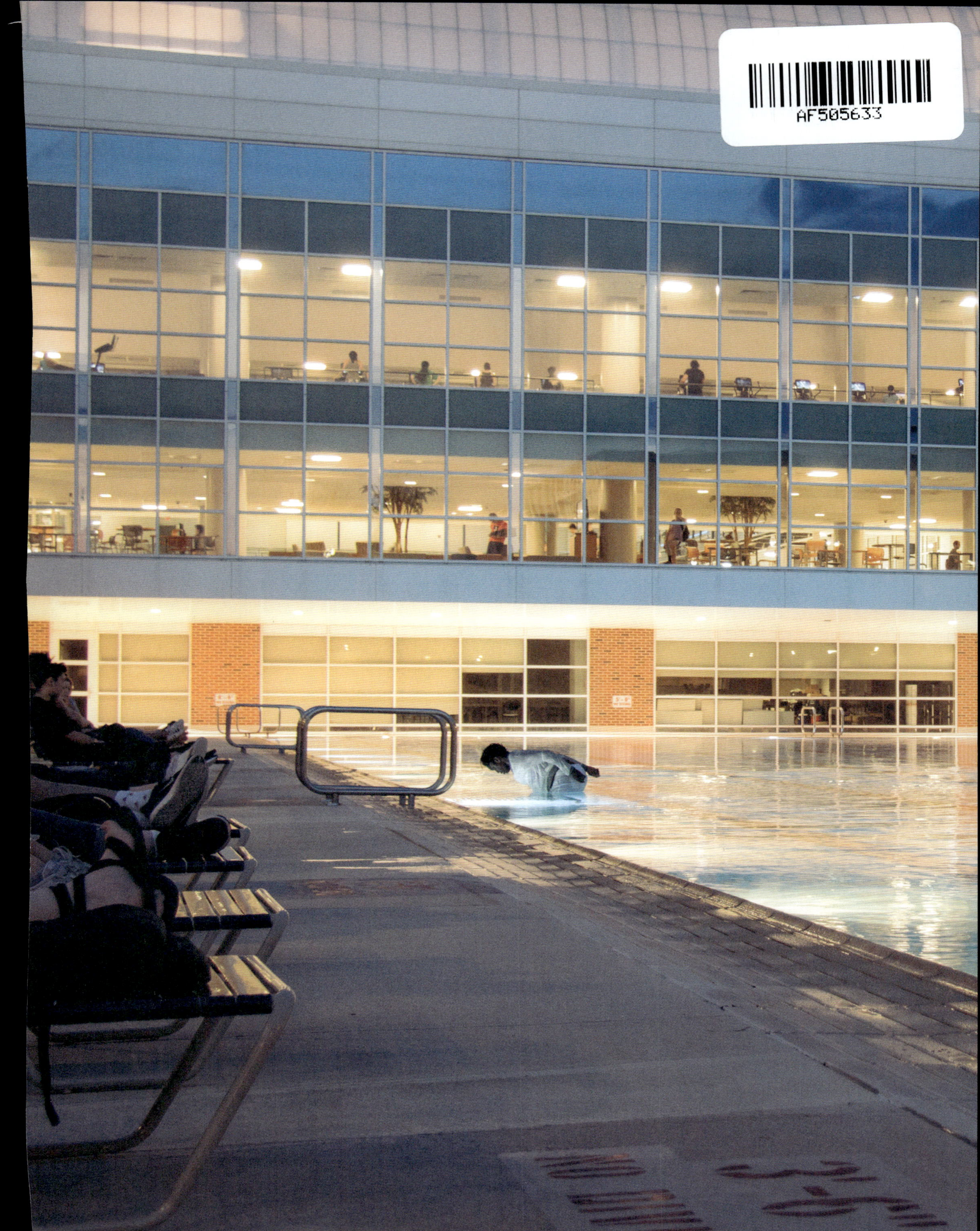
AF505633

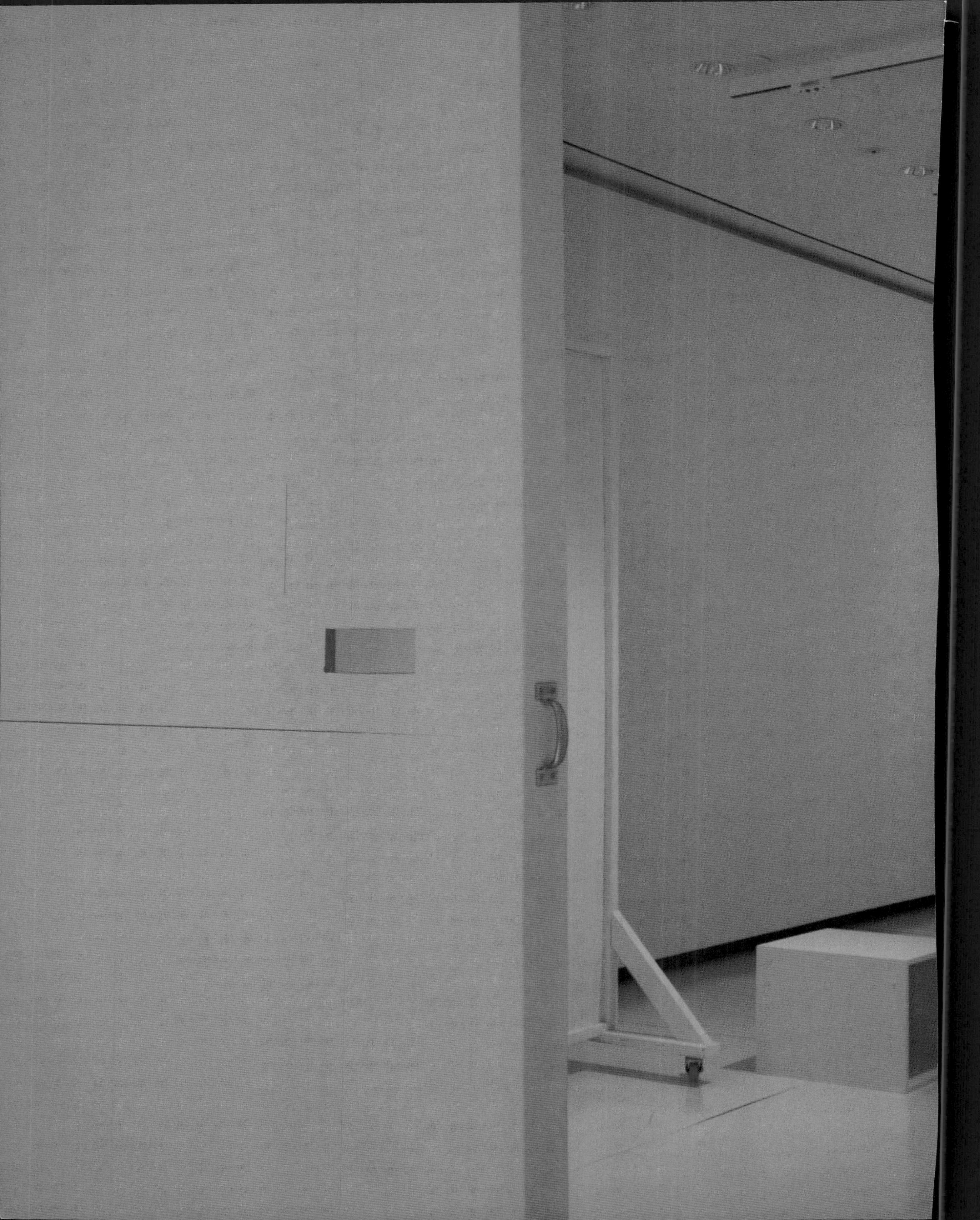

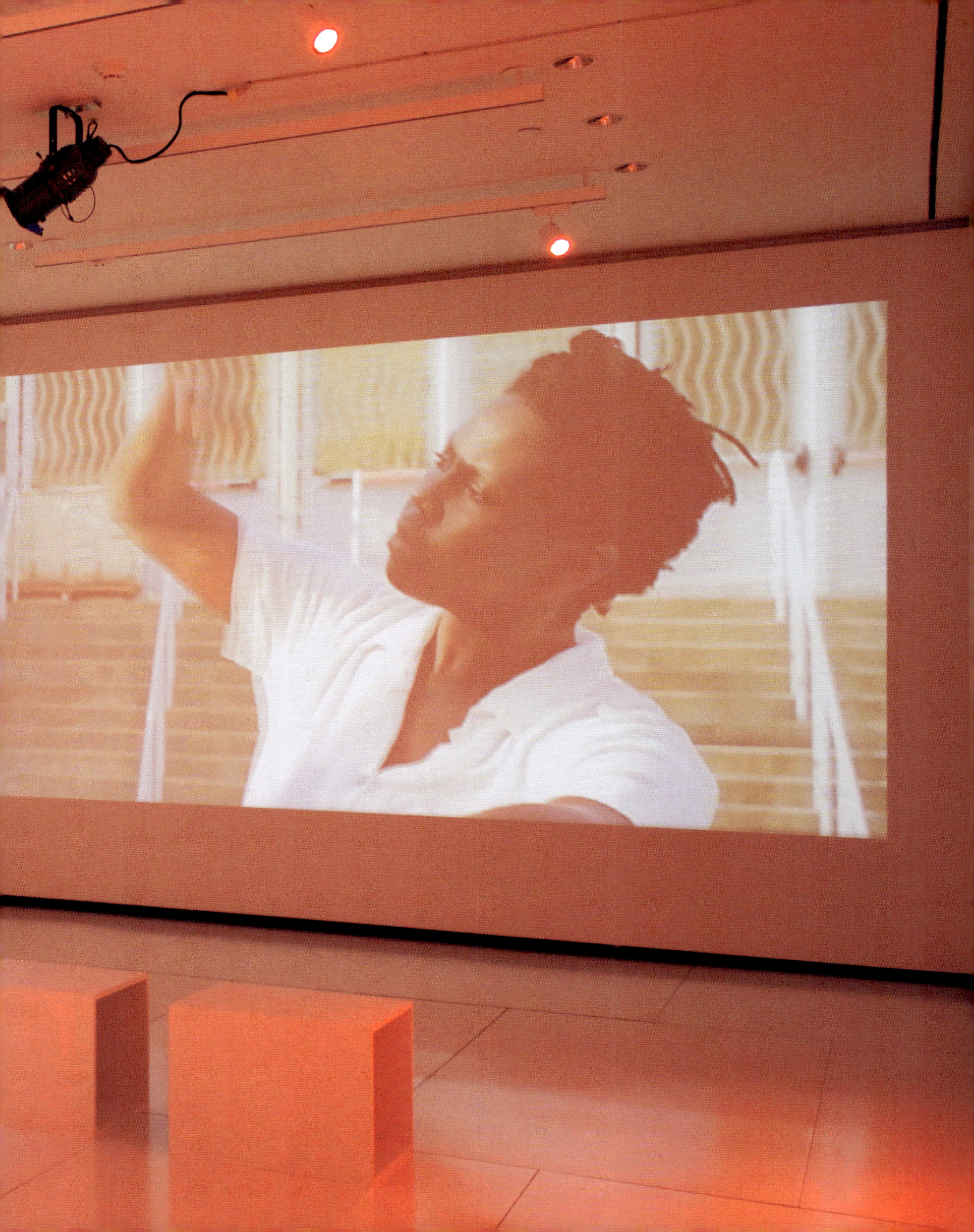

Krannert Art Museum
with Project Row Houses

Contributors

Ryan N. Dennis
Jennifer Doyle
Cynthia Oliver
Amy L. Powell
Sandra Ruiz

Autumn Knight

In

Rehearsal

This publication accompanies the exhibition
Autumn Knight: In Rehearsal, organized by
Krannert Art Museum and Kinkead Pavilion,
University of Illinois at Urbana-Champaign,
on view January 27–July 8, 2017. This
publication has been made possible in part by
The Andy Warhol Foundation for the Visual
Arts with additional funding provided by the
College of Fine + Applied Arts Matching
Funding Program, University of Illinois at
Urbana-Champaign.

Curator: Amy L. Powell
Copyeditor: Maria Bailey
Production Manager: Kathryn Koca Polite
Design: Practise
Type: Merkury (Radim Peško, 2003–13)
Lithography: Colour & Books, the Netherlands
Print: Wilco Art Books, the Netherlands

Library of Congress Control Number:
2018948979
ISBN: 978-1-883015-50-3

Published by
Krannert Art Museum and Kinkead Pavilion
with support from Project Row Houses

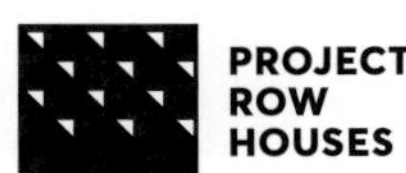
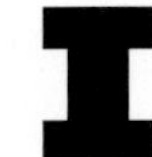

Distributed by ARTBOOK | D.A.P.
75 Broad Street, Suite 630
New York, NY 10004
artbook.com

Krannert Art Museum and
Kinkead Pavilion
University of Illinois at Urbana-Champaign
College of Fine + Applied Arts
500 East Peabody Drive
Champaign, Illinois 61820 USA
kam.illinois.edu

Front cover: Rehearsal view of *El Diablo y
Cristo Negro*. Krannert Art Museum,
Champaign, January 25, 2017

Inside front cover: Rehearsal view of
Lament, with Abijan Johnson. University
of Illinois Stock Pavilion, Urbana,
April 11, 2017

Page 1: *An experimental freezing of a room through
metaphorical means*, with Autumn Knight. University of
Illinois Activities and Recreation Center, Champaign,
April 19, 2017

Pages 3–4: Installation view of *Autumn Knight: In
Rehearsal*. Krannert Art Museum, Champaign, January
27–July 8, 2017

Contents

Forewords

Project Row Houses (PRH) is pleased to sponsor the publication of *Autumn Knight: In Rehearsal*, celebrating the work of emerging artist and native Houstonian Autumn Knight. As an artist whose work often highlights African Americans and their lack of inclusion in art, academic, and medical institutions, we find that Knight's work is a beautiful illustration of the PRH model: empowering individuals and communities through collective creativity and cultural preservation.

By extending her work outside of the studio and into a social context, Knight finds creative solutions to address issues of race, gender, and authority that engage her community and her audience alike. As PRH celebrates its 25th anniversary, we are proud to uplift Knight, a resident of our community and member of the PRH family. Her contribution to social practice as a means of igniting important dialogues helps us see ourselves and others differently, thus evidencing new ways of bringing people together.

Appreciation extends to all who have contributed both directly and indirectly to this publication and related programming, with special acknowledgement to PRH's Curator and Programs Director, Ryan N. Dennis, and Krannert Art Museum's Curator of Modern and Contemporary Art, Amy L. Powell.

It is our hope that this work will inspire artists to use their platform to empower people and enrich communities through art, engagement, and direct action.

Eureka Gilkey
Executive Director
Project Row Houses

Autumn Knight's catalytic performances claimed space on the Illinois campus for black female artistic practice to flourish aesthetically and as a critical, pedagogical tool. "Taking blackness as a starting place," as Autumn stated in a public panel discussion in 2017, remains a vital political act. "I put black women first—then move forward from there. If I didn't ask for a black woman cellist, I wouldn't have *gotten* her. But I did." And in doing so, Autumn set the stage, quite literally, for *In Rehearsal*, a succession of performances that both galvanized and implicated audiences in engagements with difference, vulnerability, and the eternal immediacy of racial violence and misrecognition.

To prepare for *In Rehearsal*, KAM curator Amy L. Powell spent nearly a year with Autumn traversing Illinois's campus—mining departmental resources, igniting conversations, and imagining sites that Autumn would activate with her daunting provocations. Performing works in vast and unconventional spaces—the Stock Pavilion and the Activities and Recreation Center's outdoor Olympic pool—as well as in the museum defied the structures that rank and isolate domains of learning on a university campus. These spaces were animated not only by Autumn, but also by her avatars when she was not present—students S. Bianca Bailey and Holly Garrett and dancer Abijan Johnson. These extraordinary young women followed Autumn's scripts and directional cues. They dedicated their talents, undisciplined their disciplines, and subjected themselves to stagings that ranged from the absurd to the sublime; emotionally wrought, technically difficult (e.g., playing a cello while lying on your back), and tedious yet consuming acts of sorting and assembling came together in ways that revealed a certain kind of pathos in the everyday.

Though ephemeral and rooted in the moment of their enactment, Autumn's performances endure through the illuminating writings collected in this volume, two of which have been generously sponsored by Project Row Houses. Thank you, Ryan N. Dennis, Jennifer Doyle, Cynthia Oliver, and Sandra Ruiz, for your attentive and compelling reflections. Even the bones of Autumn's performance—her scripts, annotations, directional notes—are reproduced here, offering us wonderful entry into the artist's behind-the-scenes ruminations. But none of this would be possible without Amy L. Powell, whose rigor and vision have transformed KAM into a site for critical interdisciplinary conversation and experimentation. We thank her for bringing Autumn to campus, for this extraordinary volume, and for her dedication to realizing the capacity of art to provoke discussion, unsettle convention, and inspire socially engaged action. And to Autumn Knight, who touches so many of us so deeply, a final word of gratitude: your humor, warmth, and gravitas electrify us, and leave us renewed in your wake.

Allyson Purpura
Senior Curator and Curator of Global African Art
Krannert Art Museum

Rehearsing Knowledge

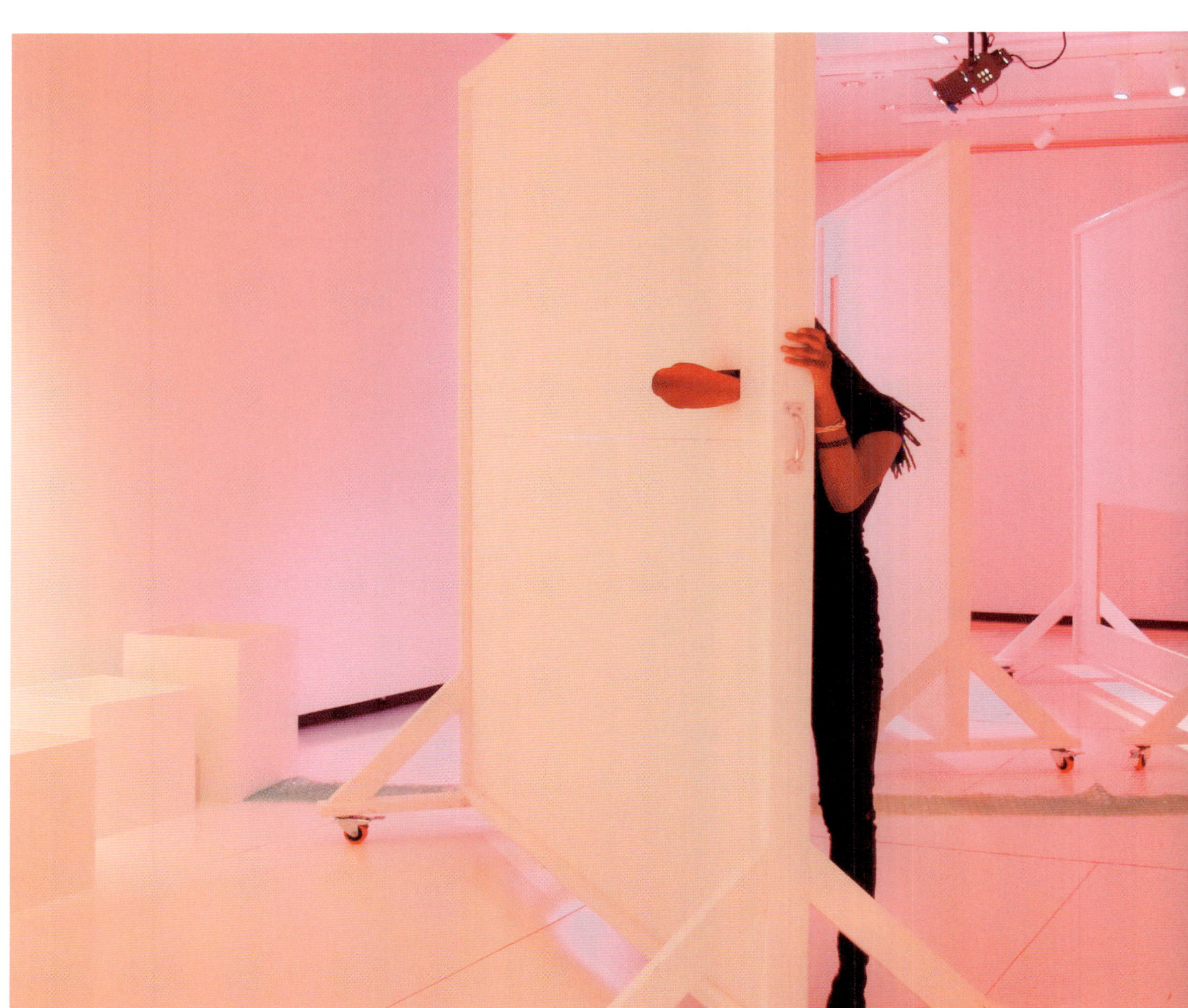

Amy L. Powell

in
the

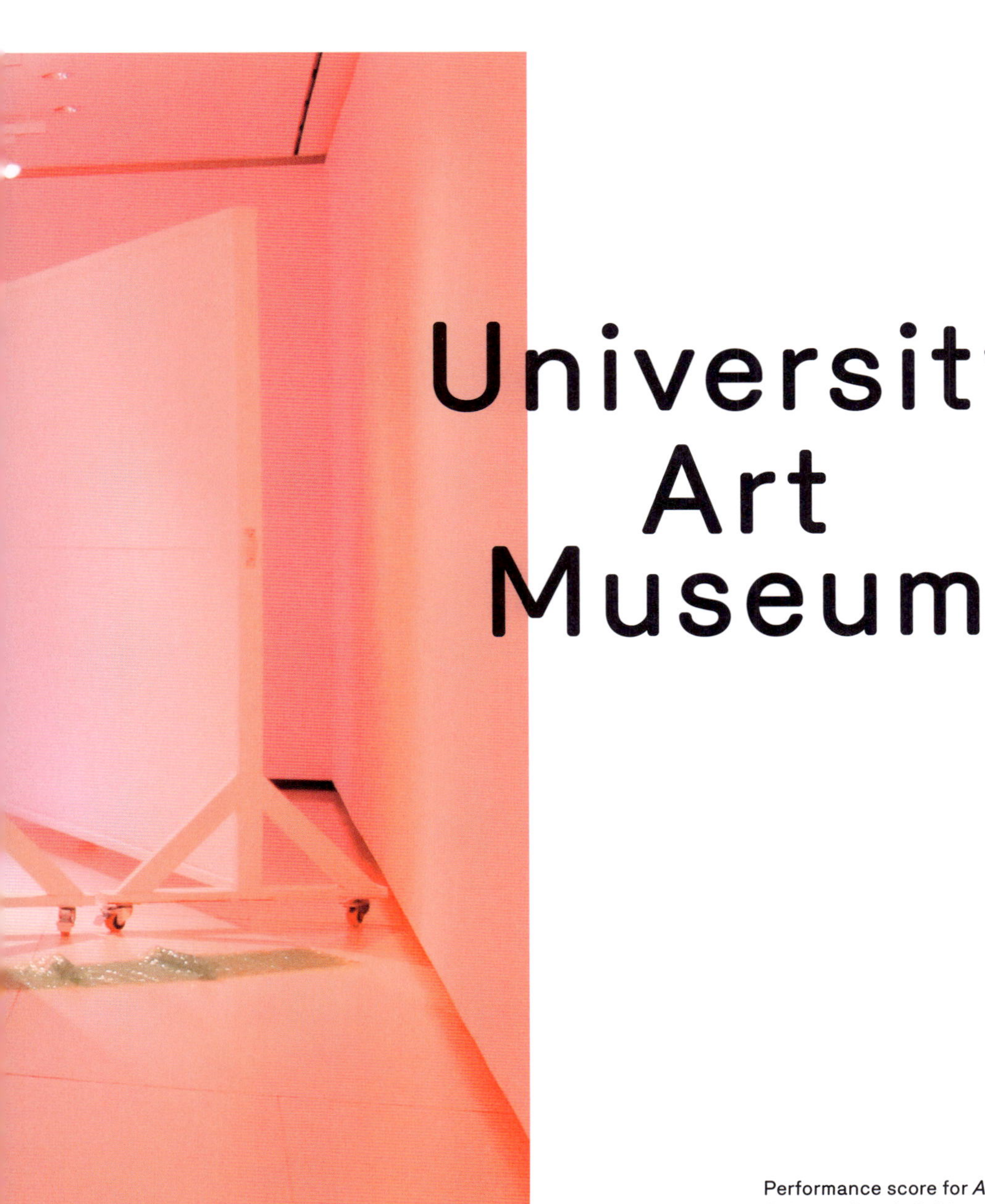

University
Art
Museum

Performance score for *Autumn Knight: In Rehearsal*, with S. Bianca Bailey. Krannert Art Museum, Champaign, February 2, 2017

"Perhaps diversity workers aim to transform the wall into a table, turning the tangible object of institutional resistance into a tangible platform for institutional action."[1]

What knowledge is produced, and for whom, when a black woman is at the center of a university art museum? In her research on diversity work, Sara Ahmed asserts that institutions shore up their "happiness" by inviting people of color to join the fold, which demonstrates good faith practice and ostensibly diverse outcomes. Embedded in the question of service as Ahmed outlines it—to whom diversity work addresses and what it enables and disallows—are barriers and performance, walls transformed into tables which become devices to adjust ways of seeing.

Ahmed's metaphor is fitting for the tensions of authority, race, and gender that propelled Autumn Knight's solo exhibition *In Rehearsal* at Krannert Art Museum (KAM) in the spring semester of 2017 at the University of Illinois. Four performances comprised the project's main events, with companion pieces Knight scripted for every week of the exhibition that the artist wasn't present (because she lives in New York). A gallery installation with pink and blue lights overhead, glossy white floorboards below, and three videos projected into corners designated a space for performance to unfold, marking the gallery as a distinctive container within the museum with every surface altered. Each of Knight's three videos showed clips the artist montaged from her digital archive.[2] Showing disparate topics and time periods, these were characteristically Knight, full of edgy humor and physical movement (e.g., Whoopi Goldberg as Fontaine, a scholarly drug addict describing her visit to the Anne Frank House in Amsterdam, in *Direct from Broadway*, 1985; Mya Taylor exclaiming the beauty of transgender talent; Hazel Scott playing two pianos; an egg yolk passed between lovers' mouths in Itami Juzo's film *Tampopo*, 1985). Four white panels on wheels with rectangular cutouts of various sizes moved around the gallery each day, and residual objects from live performances accumulated over time: orange tape on the floor marking a spatial boundary, a bag of Styrofoam peanuts, a ghost light.

While Knight is reflected in all aspects of the exhibition—her live performances, the companion pieces, and the gallery installation—her primary avatar is consultant and worker.[3] Knight's background is in theatre and drama therapy with a focus on the psychology of group dynamics. Qualified as a therapist but without license or interest in that career path, Knight stages widely varied performances united by their aim of self-awareness and growth, both for the artist and her audiences. Encountering Knight's work entails some wrestling with difficult questions—one's perceptions of race, gender, and class; one's participation in structures of authority that Knight radically reimagines; and the possibilities and blind spots that come up when empathic relation is solicited. Challenging worldviews and complicity in order to shape new possibilities is common enough in good performance art, which Tavia Nyong'o describes as "dredging the unconscious zones of culture and exposing them to dramatic, often emotional upheaval."[4] For Knight, such questions take on renewed charge by making blackness and femininity the essential and yet shifting ground from which everything unfolds.

The transformative implications of this live work assume particular valences in the context of the university art museum, an interdisciplinary hub in the knowledge production factory of higher education.[5] Knight's graduate training followed the Tavistock method and British psychoanalyst Wilfred Bion's theories of group relations, which establish several premises for analyzing the behavior of individuals when they act in groups.[6] Institutions are comprised of people performing in given roles, and together they bring assumptions and other hang-ups that may prevent the group from accomplishing the task at hand. When groups systemically exclude and discriminate, the work of examining oneself to grow more self-aware, to modify and manage behavior over time, becomes structural and

Powell

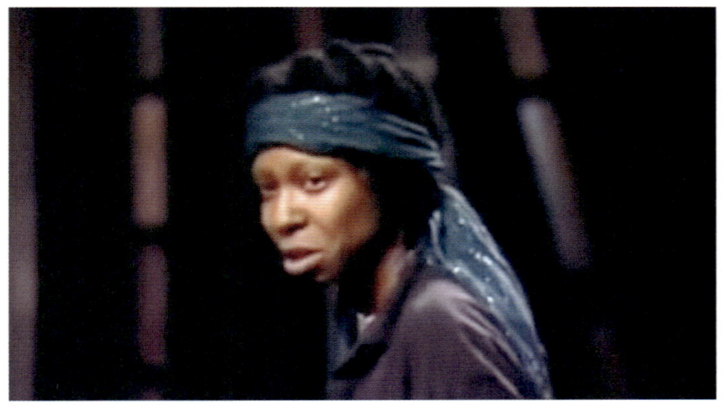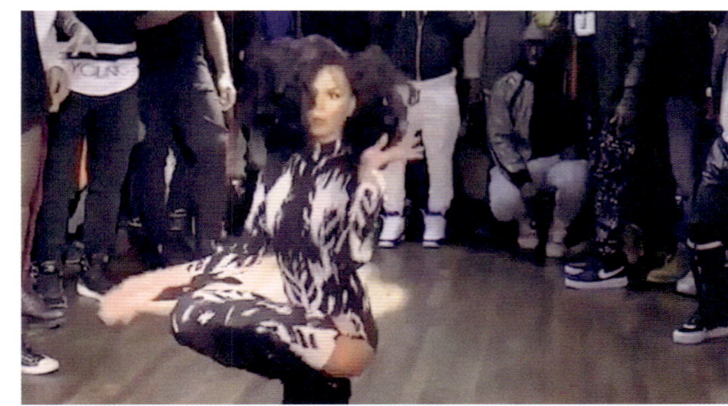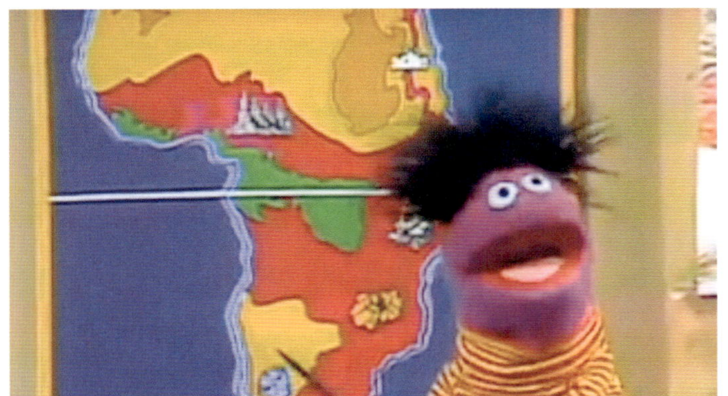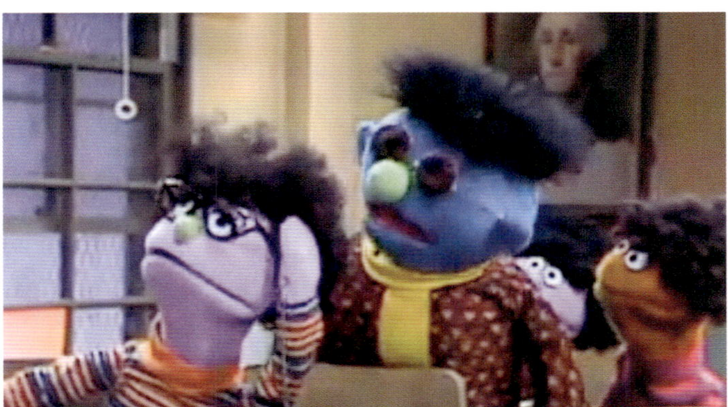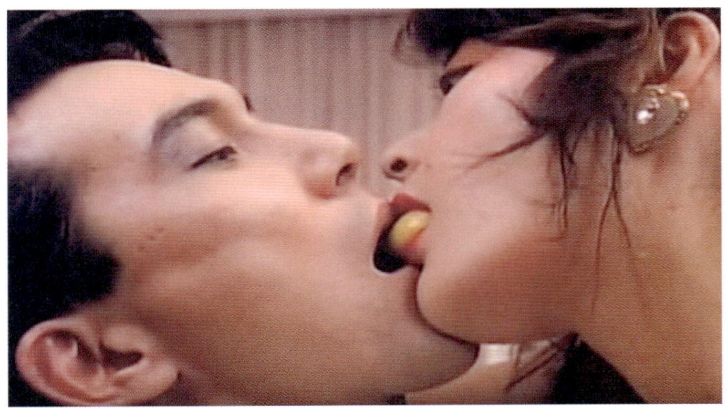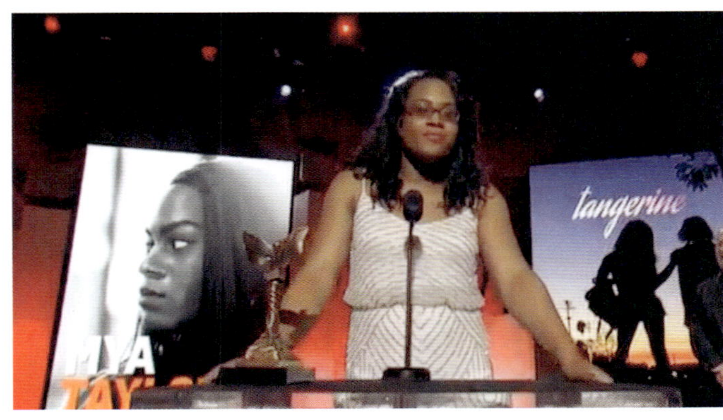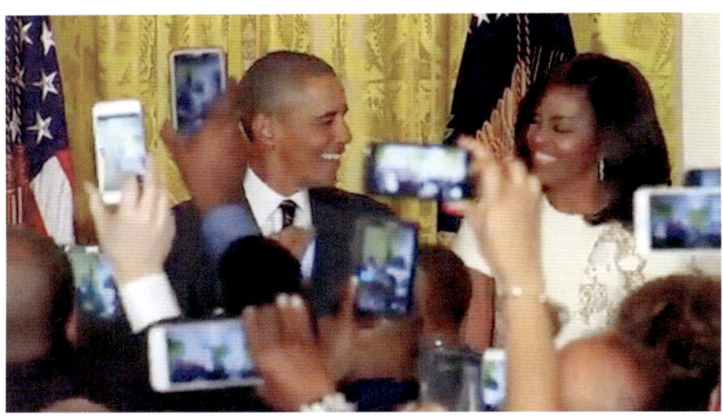

From left to right, top to bottom:
Film still from *Direct from Broadway* with Whoopi Goldberg, 1985, dir. Thomas Schlamme; Still from *Vogue Knights* with Leiomy Maldonado, November 24, 2016; Stills from *Sesame Street*, Episode 0666, November 4, 1974; Film still from *Tampopo*, 1985, dir. Juzo Itami; Mya Taylor accepting Best Supporting Female for *Tangerine* at Spirit Awards, February 27, 2016; President Barack Obama and First Lady Michelle Obama during a press conference for reception celebrating Black History Month, February 18, 2016

Rehearsing Knowledge

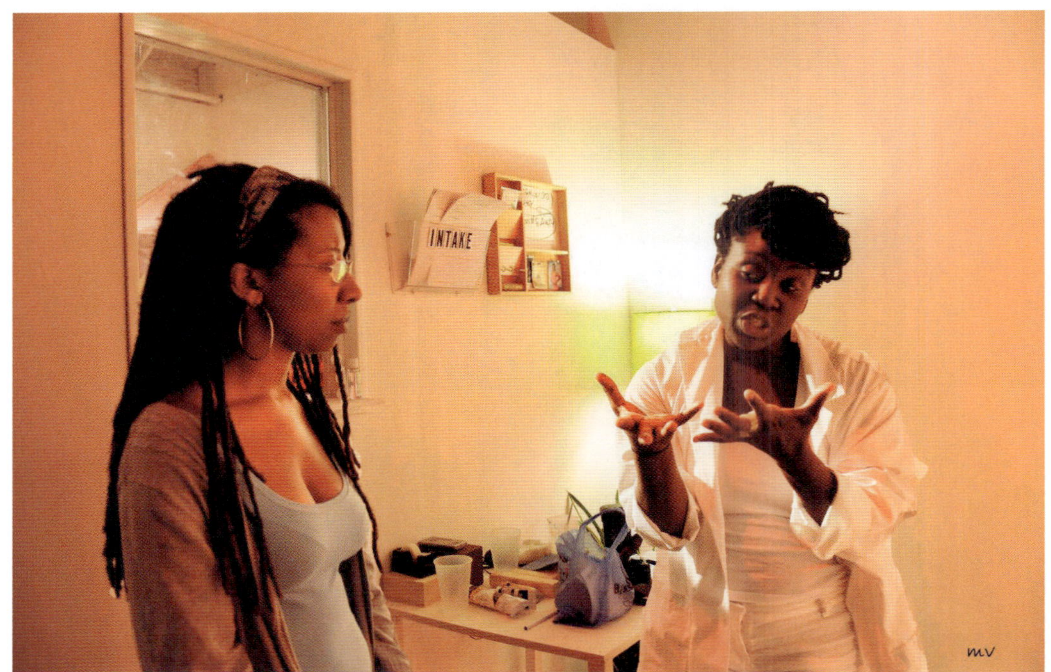

Performance Prescriptions in *State Fair*, with Autumn Knight.
DiverseWorks, Houston, September 9–October 29, 2011

political. Since 2011, when she set up a "performance pre-scriptions" booth at DiverseWorks in Houston and assigned specific performance tasks to visitors for their ailments (e.g., Diet Coke addiction, the loss of a mother), Knight has turned clinical dynamics into a performance practice that emerges from her, and yet implicates all audiences and the very structures through which we organize ourselves.[7] The ways that knowledge and knowledge institutions are encoded with racism, gender discrimination, and the (in)appropriateness of humor and insanity, among other things, offer materials for play in Knight's work.[8] Her sce-narios are unexpected and often hilarious, drawn with an actor's ability to make characters believable and with a psychologist's responsibility to resolution and time bound-aries. She balances discomfort with a lingering sense of urgency and personal homework. She draws a metaphorical circle to keep audiences with her in situations that allow for a great deal of improvisation.

Here + Now (p. 40–49) exaggerates the performative elements of a group psychoanalytic context to reveal struc-tures of power and authority and how they reproduce according to deeply ingrained assumptions that organize public life. Knight has performed this work four times to date: at Project Row Houses in Houston in 2013, with a group of Muslim women in Houston in 2013, among the artist residents of Skowhegan, Maine, in 2016, and as part of *In Rehearsal* with university faculty, students, visiting scholars, and other KAM visitors. She adapts the work according to the circumstances of the participants and the institution at hand. People are invited to sit in a configura-tion of chairs that Knight has arranged in advance. The fishbowl formation allows participants to see one another and to get things underway by questioning who sits where—who decides to be at the center versus the periphery? And why does the group allow for such leaders or outsiders? Knight is a consultant to the group along with collaborator Kelley Hershman, a licensed therapist and a former grad-uate colleague of Knight's at NYU. Knight and Hershman give the group their only task: to examine themselves in the here and now.

Here + Now is about the social production of knowl-edge, which the group manifests concretely by providing data in what they say, their body language, and how they react to comments from others. Actual institutional dynam-ics—which in KAM's case included the university and the museum—cannot help but be reflected in how the conver-sation unfolds. Hershman and Knight described to me that the "unconscious flare" of the institution would rear up like

Powell

the bottom of an iceberg (we're more often only at the tip of the iceberg, goes the metaphor) and demonstrate what is unspeakable in day-to-day interactions, those assumptions and feelings people hold at bay in order to work and live.[9] During the session at KAM, Knight and Hershman sat silently with participants and looked at one another or at the floor until their interventions became necessary to set the group back on task. At one point Hershman said, "The question is, is it speakable, because the data as of now says that it's not." Meanwhile, the participants tried to figure out what was happening while also avoiding commentary on the roles they had evidently taken on. A bewildered tension mounted. At another point Knight said, "I can't help but wonder if the group's confusion is due to the identity of the consultant who gave them the task." Inevitably for Knight—and what makes this work resonate with questions she poses in other, very different performances—the group renders her authority contentious, disagreeable, and even invisible (one participant decried "some invisible authority"). I think of Claudia Rankine in her collection *Citizen: An American Lyric*, who wrote, "Apparently your own invisibility is the real problem causing her

confusion. This is how the apparatus she propels you into begins to multiply its meaning."[10]

Knight further pushes the dynamics of visibility and authority by choreographing movement for other performers. Providing scores—written directives open to interpretation—and scripting situations constitutes a major thread in Knight's work. She is interested in what happens when the figure of the artist is dispersed through other bodies, as well as when those performers bring specialized knowledge to the conversation. This is one way that Knight highlights structures of authority while also building new ones, asking who is authorized to speak, from what platforms, and about what subjects.

At KAM such questions merged with the status of the university art museum as a place where knowledge about black women is produced—as objects of desire, subjection, and reclaimed power in the history of art; and in scholarship in a range of disciplines. These dynamics factored into our planning of the exhibition, when Knight and I met with women faculty members for more than a year to discuss the audiences and participants for the project. Each week in the exhibition, a solo performer spent one hour engaging

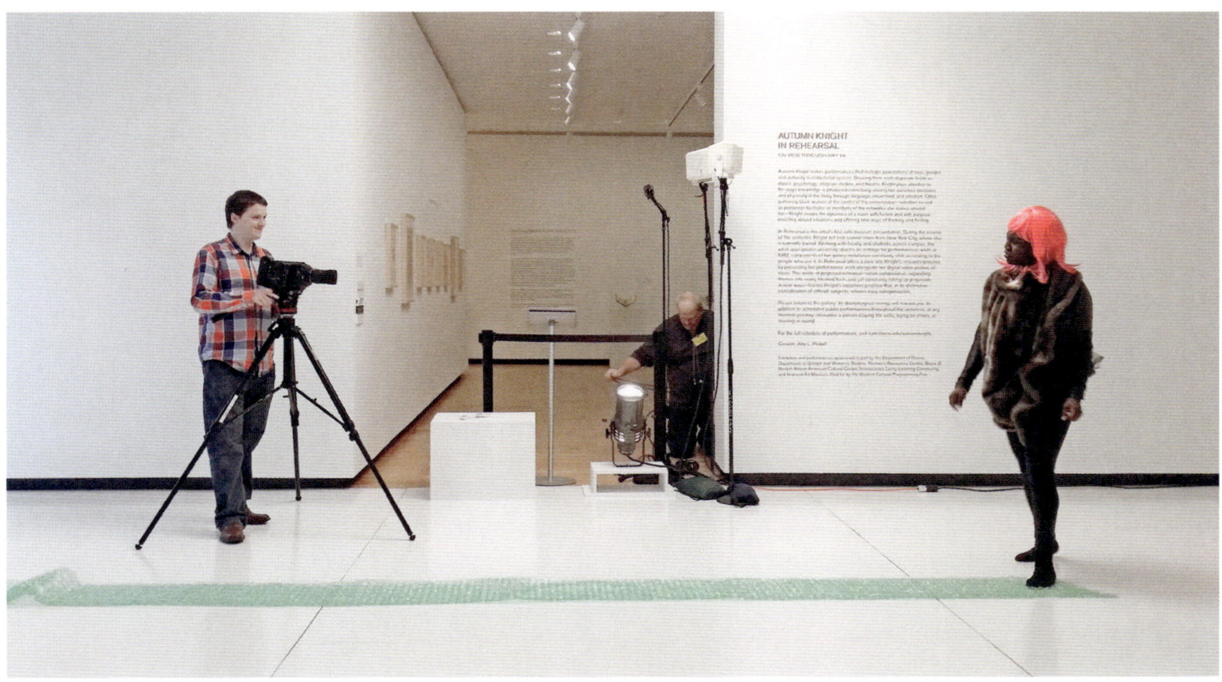

Rehearsal view of *El Diablo y Cristo Negro*, with Autumn Knight. Krannert Art Museum, Champaign, January 25, 2017

15

Rehearsing Knowledge

in tasks Knight assigned (p. 96–111). Holly Garrett, a graduate student in cello performance and literature, performed Knight's instructions to play the cello in various physical positions in the gallery with gold mylar balloons pinned in her hair. She did so on two occasions coinciding with the presentation of *Lament* (p. 60–67)—playing Ernest Bloch's *Schelomo: Rhapsodie Hébraïque for Violoncello and Orchestra* (1915–1916), a George Crumb sonata (1955), and Coleridge-Taylor Perkinson's *Lamentations: Black/Folk Song Suite* (1980). S. Bianca Bailey, a doctoral candidate in engineering, performed Knight's written scores in nine separate weeks. Bailey and Garrett's weekly appointments ensured the consistency of live performance in the gallery and also offered a proxy for the artist—Knight enjoyed that viewers might mistake one of the performers for herself. Bailey's actions made her both an object to be encountered and a speaking subject imparting knowledge from her research on water purification systems in Kenya or from books she brought into the space. In week three she tried on pairs of shoes and told harrowing and inspiring stories about her life. In week five she brought small, cheap objects from home and incessantly rearranged them according to size or color or more idiosyncratic methods. In week six she read entire sections of Suzan Lori Parks's play *In the Blood* (1999). In week seven she filed her nails for one hour without speaking. That visitors could potentially encounter a student performer, a black woman at the center of the university art museum, offered a live platform for Knight to redraw subject/object dynamics and to play with what knowledge is imparted and performed.[11]

Art historian Jessica Santone argues for the distinctive power of Knight's methods that refuse a singularly authored voice, that seek out channels for distributing authority, and that open subtle spaces for "encouraging the capacity for learning how the other feels."[12] We can imagine Knight's work being in demand because this list aligns with efforts of socially engaged museums, as well as of universities facing no shortage of quandaries in public education where teaching intersubjectivity is increasingly fraught. Staging an exhibition of this work requires care. Knight and I talked a lot about how the exhibition would attune to the complexities of institutional dynamics that are already part of her performances. I wanted to ensure that the environment at the University of Illinois would support her and learn from her work in the difficult and generous ways it intends instead of flattening or otherwise distorting it as *only* about race or gender, the artist's identity, or her perceived capacity to help an audience with their feelings.[13]

What I learned is that Knight's background in group dynamics informs how she makes collaborations among her performers and audiences, and how she structures the images or tasks one is left with after a performance. At every turn Knight's work problematizes the artist as the object and subject under consideration. She actively diffuses or takes on multiple strands of authority to point out how her character and position are complex in addition to being self-aware about how they are communicated and received in a given space. In the process, she finds ways forward and accumulates possibilities for multiplicity, nuance, and critical reflection, whether audiences get it—whether they listen—or not.[14]

Another performance, *An experimental freezing of a room through metaphorical means* (p. 76–87), offers a salient image in this regard. Knight developed the work for the Houston iteration of the longstanding exhibition *do it*, a project initially conceived by curator Hans Ulrich Obrist with artists Christian Boltanski and Bertrand Lavier in 1993, in which artists write scores to be performed or concretized in other mediums.[15] Knight's use of performance scores is both established and experimental, referencing decades of artists since the Fluxus movement and layering the shifting dynamics of subjectivity and authority by allowing a form for the artist to choreograph actions for others.[16] For *An experimental freezing*, Knight combined Iñake Bonillas's 2001 score, *Cold Storage Room* ("Keep the temperature of a room at –18°C"), with Shilpa Gupta's untitled score from 2012 ("LOOK STRAIGHT / DON'T SEE"). The first iteration happened on a blazing hot day in Houston in July 2013, one week after the acquittal of George Zimmerman for his vigilante murder in Florida in early 2012 of Trayvon Martin, an unarmed black teenager. Knight manifested a figure of black maternal precarity. Dressed in white, she handed an ice cube to each audience member and asked them to "look straight." She cradled a bag of ice as though it were an infant. She kissed the bag as the ice perished. She bit through a plastic covering hanging overhead filled with ice, which fell all around her. A looped five-minute excerpt from Zimmerman's acquittal hearing was the performance's soundtrack: the all-women panel stating their not guilty finding, the judge outlining special privileges enjoyed by jurors, the return of Zimmerman's weapon ("the evidence will be released").

For *In Rehearsal*, Knight recreated *An experimental freezing* in part to account for multiple other public incidents of police and citizen brutality against black people since 2013. She scaled up the performance for the outdoor pool at the university's main gymnasium. In addition to Zimmerman's acquittal, the soundtrack included Sandra Bland's phone message from Texas to her mother ("I am here"), the voice of a man whose two-year old daughter was killed in a shooting in Detroit, the multiple-count sentencing of Oklahoma City police officer Daniel Holtclaw for his sexual assaults on black women, and the friend of a murdered transgender woman in Cleveland. Certain aspects of the performance remained the same: Knight dressed in white, she began by handing ice to each audience member, a bag of ice stood in for an infant, and ice fell on Knight from overhead after being made to appear as a nipple, nourishing the artist and her diminishing bundle. Viewers lounged on pool deck chairs and visible signs of daily campus life continued all around. Students and faculty hurried past on public walkways while people working out on exercise machines overlooked the proceedings. Knight made swimming motions with her arms, folded her waist over the pool's hand railings, and submerged her head multiple times, all movements that became inscribed, along with the work's emotionally wrenching soundtrack, into the university setting. Or, the work shows these elements to be already present but generally unseen, campuses being a flashpoint for racially motivated aggressions and sexual violence. The soundtrack was LOUD, reverberating throughout the full campus block.

An experimental freezing tests audiences' capacity for rigorous and transformational feeling. It is an emotional work. The performance's soundtrack, the setting, the present moment in which we live—all of these factors frame Knight as a central figure, but one who brings the dynamics of institutions and audiences along with her. Everyone is implicated and yet black women remain at the center, multiple as they are in the soundtrack's examples and at times maternal, animal, and sexual in Knight's movements. As with *Here + Now*, the effects of this performance linger, its duration extending through the indeterminate time of lessons learned and perspectives shaped.[17] Such is the case not only for viewers and collaborators, but for the artist as well. Knight often uses exhibitions to reexamine her work, her networks, and her methods. Perhaps inherent in performance, a medium that lends itself to the effects of varying situations on a given work, the presentation process by design benefits Knight's persistent curiosity. Recalling her formalization of "futzing" as a research method at Project Row Houses in 2012 (see Ryan Dennis's essay in this volume, p. 32–39), where many of these performances were staged for the first time, *In Rehearsal* took a widely recognizable concept from Knight's theatre training and made it a focused element of the entire project. Equally exhibition and protean intervention into the museum's galleries and the campus's status quo, *In Rehearsal* seeks to shore up a body of work while also underscoring how things are continuously rethought depending on the context of each performance. The work is never settled.

The primary medium here is the production of knowledge. As such, Knight's commitment to artistic form is evident from her training in psychology, in which a "safe enough" space and time can be articulated with a beginning, middle, and resolution (troubled as these stages may feel while they are happening). From this conviction, Knight asks: if institutions are to be remade, why not through the images and methods that performance can provide? Above all an observer, Knight centers vulnerability, black cultural histories, and psychological dynamics, generating knowledge of institutions and redrawing lines of authority around us all.

1   Sara Ahmed, *On Being Included: Racism and Diversity in Institutional Life* (Durham, NC, and London: Duke University Press, 2012): 175. See also Ahmed's blog: https://feministkilljoys.com.

2   See http://autumnjoiknight.tumblr.com. In June 2017, after the exhibition was open for roughly four months, we replaced Knight's three video montages with two videos showing performance rehearsals recorded during the exhibition: *Lament* and *An experimental freezing of a room through metaphorical means.*

3   Considering black women performance artists for the avatars they produce that destabilize object- and subject-hood comes from Uri McMillan, *Embodied Avatars: Genealogies of Black Feminist Art and Performance* (New York and London: New York University Press, 2015).

4   Tavia Nyong'o, "Between the Body and the Flesh: Sex and Gender in Black Performance Art," in *Radical Presence: Black Performance in Contemporary Art*, ed. Valerie Cassel Oliver (Houston: Contemporary Arts Museum Houston, 2013): 26.

5   Not to mention the ways that movement-based live work affects museum institutions more generally. For a particularly relevant example, see Doryun Chong, "Fugitive Value: Ralph Lemon and Museums," in *Ralph Lemon: Modern Dance*, ed. Thomas J. Lax (New York: The Museum of Modern Art, 2016): 127–135.

6   See, for example, Solomon Cytrynbaum and Debra A. Noumair, eds., *Group Dynamics, Organizational Irrationality, and Social Complexity: A Group Relations Reader 3* (Jupiter, FL: A. K. Rice Institute, 2004). At KAM, Knight circulated an excerpt from this text to *Here + Now* performance participants who committed in advance to attending the event.

7   Carrie Marie Schneider, "Autumn Knight's 'Performance Prescriptions' at DiverseWorks' 'State Fair'," *Glasstire* (September 30, 2011), http://glasstire.com/2011/09/30/state-fair-at-diverseworks/.

8   *Sanity TV* is a performance styled as a talk show. Playing host, Knight explores the boundary between sanity and insanity by improvising along with her audience-member guests. See "Studio Museum in Harlem Artist in Residence Autumn Knight: Sanity TV Holiday Special," *The Greene Space* (November 7, 2017), http://www.thegreenespace.org/story/studio-museum-harlem-artist-residence-autumn-knight-sanity-tv-holiday-special/.

9   Conversation with the author (March 29, 2017). Much of my understanding of the psychological dynamics of *Here + Now* comes from this conversation and from previous conversations with Knight.

10   Claudia Rankine, *Citizen: An American Lyric* (Minneapolis: Graywolf Press, 2014): 43.

11   In another of Knight's performances, *El Diablo y Cristo Negro*, the characters exhibit self-awareness about these dynamics when they joke about eating excessive black flesh. The reference comes from Nicole R. Fleetwood's theorizing of hypervisibility in performances by black women. See *Troubling Vision: Performance, Visuality, and Blackness* (Chicago and London: The University of Chicago Press, 2011).

12   Jessica Santone, "Otherness and Empathy: Performing Affective Pedagogy," *Gulf Coast: A Journal of Literature and Fine Arts*, 27.1 (Winter/Spring 2015): 211–219.

13   Other artists, perhaps Theaster Gates most notably, have made strident critiques and productive re-framings of institutional invitations to fix race problems. See video documentation of Gates's performance *See, Sit, Sup, Sing: Holding Court*, 2012 (The Studio Museum in Harlem, published April 8, 2014, https://youtu.be/bgv49RuzNWw) and Shannon Jackson, "Utopian Operating Systems: Theaster's Way of Working," in *Entry Points*, eds. Carin Kuoni and Chelsea Haines (New York: Vera List Center for Art and Politics, The New School, 2015): 214–229. See also Jennifer Doyle's scholarship on the problems of critical frames that oversimplify work by minoritarian artists, wanting instead to fully consider the political work of emotion: "Feeling Overdetermined: Identity, Emotion, and History," in *Hold It Against Me: Difficulty and Emotion in Contemporary Art* (Durham, NC, and London: Duke University Press, 2013): 94–125.

14   One effect of Knight's play with visibility and authority that I have seen in her live performances over time is that audience members can feel entitled to speak over her or direct her when she poses questions to the crowd. Knight sometimes leaves such remarks unaddressed or points them out with playful incredulity. Managing both modes of response becomes part of the performance.

15   See Hans Ulrich Obrist, ed., *Do It: The Compendium* (New York: Independent Curators International and D. A. P., 2013). The Houston exhibition took place at Alabama Song and was organized by Max Fields and Olivia Junell.

16   Knight's work invites comparison with Clifford Owens, who has solicited and performed scores written by other African American artists to mark out his place, and the place of black performance more generally, in the canon of art history. Knight is more generous to her audiences. I say this not to reduce the conversation to her gender or to the troubling dynamics one may encounter when watching Owens but to assert that the breadth of Knight's training has prepared her conceptually to consider what it would take to make new institutions real. On Owens, see especially Huey Copeland, "Mal d'Anthologie: Clifford Owens and the Crises of African American Performance Art," in *Clifford Owens: Anthology*, ed. Christopher Y. Lew (New York: MoMA PS1, 2012): 15–30.

17   On the long durations of performance, see Frazier Ward, *No Innocent Bystanders: Performance Art and Audience* (Hanover, NH: Dartmouth College Press, 2012): 12–14. *An experimental freezing* also lingers due to the courtroom dramas the performance cites and their effects on the collective imagination. See Lucy Winner, "Democratic Acts: Theatre of Public Trials," *Theatre Tropics* 15.2 (September 2005): 149–169.

EL DIABLO

Y

CRISTO NEGRO

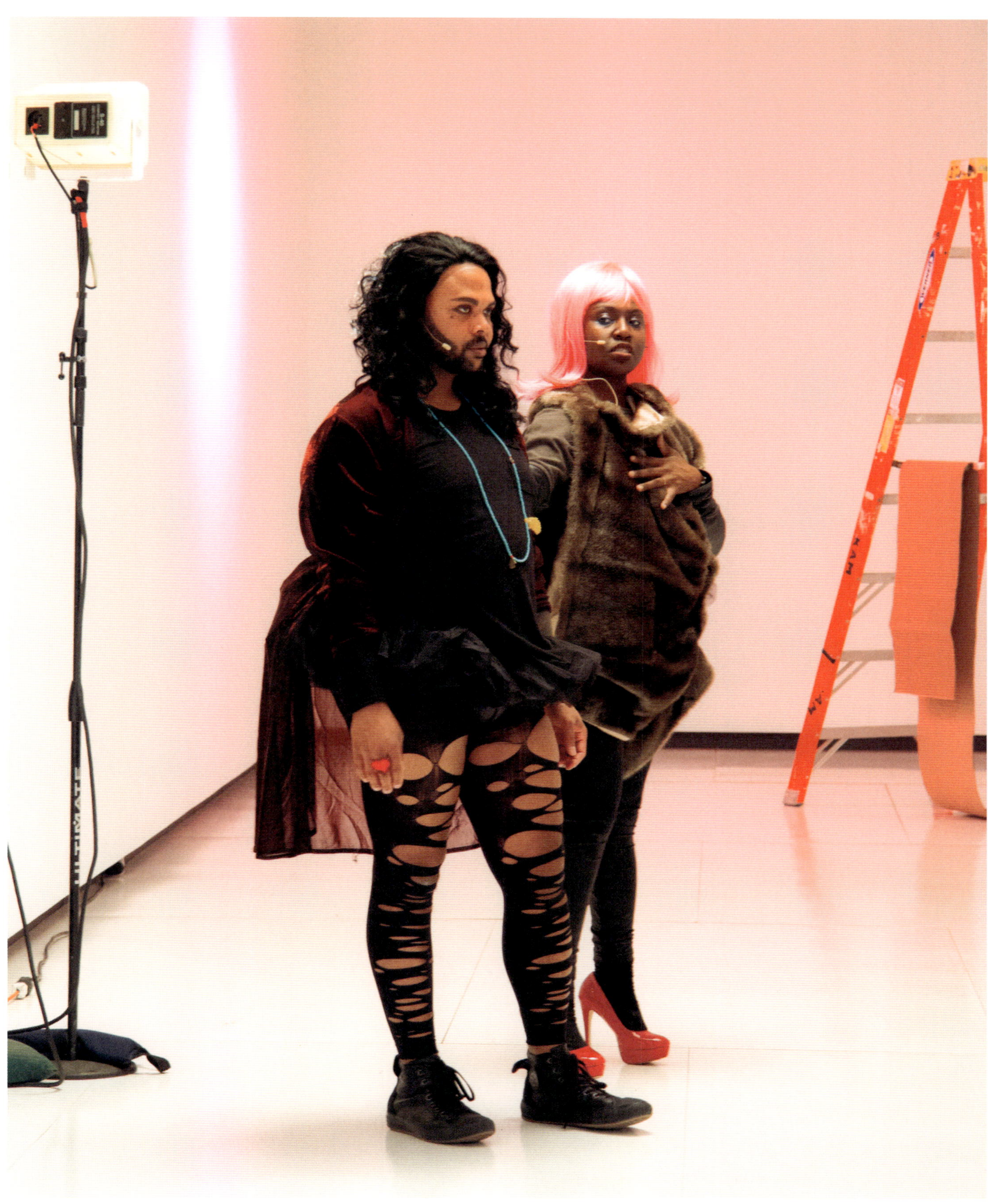

Rehearsal view of *El Diablo y Cristo Negro*, with Autumn Knight and
Chivas Michael. Krannert Art Museum, Champaign, January 25, 2017

El Diablo y Cristo Negro (2012–present) consists of four scripted and improvised comedic dialogues exploring the entwined relationship between good and evil. The Devil and Black Christ are pivotal personas, with appearances by Black Christ's therapist and a flesh-eating monster. This performance is inspired by the Festival de Cristo Negro (Black Christ Festival) and regional mythology in Portobelo, Panama, and asks broad questions about the place of religion and belief in evil among black cultures of the Americas.

SOUNDTRACK

"Devil in a New Dress"
Kanye West

"Hell!"
James Brown

"Down Here In Hell (With You)"
Van Hunt

"Free"
Cat Power

"Waked Up Fucked (In Egypt)"
Caked Up

"Peanut Butter"
RuPaul featuring Big Freedia

"Mind Playing Tricks on Me"
Geto Boys

"Flawless"
Beyoncé

Pages 23–29: *El Diablo y Cristo Negro*, with Autumn Knight, Chivas Michael, and Xavier Roe. Krannert Art Museum, Champaign, January 26, 2017

                    EL DIABLO Y CRISTO NEGRO

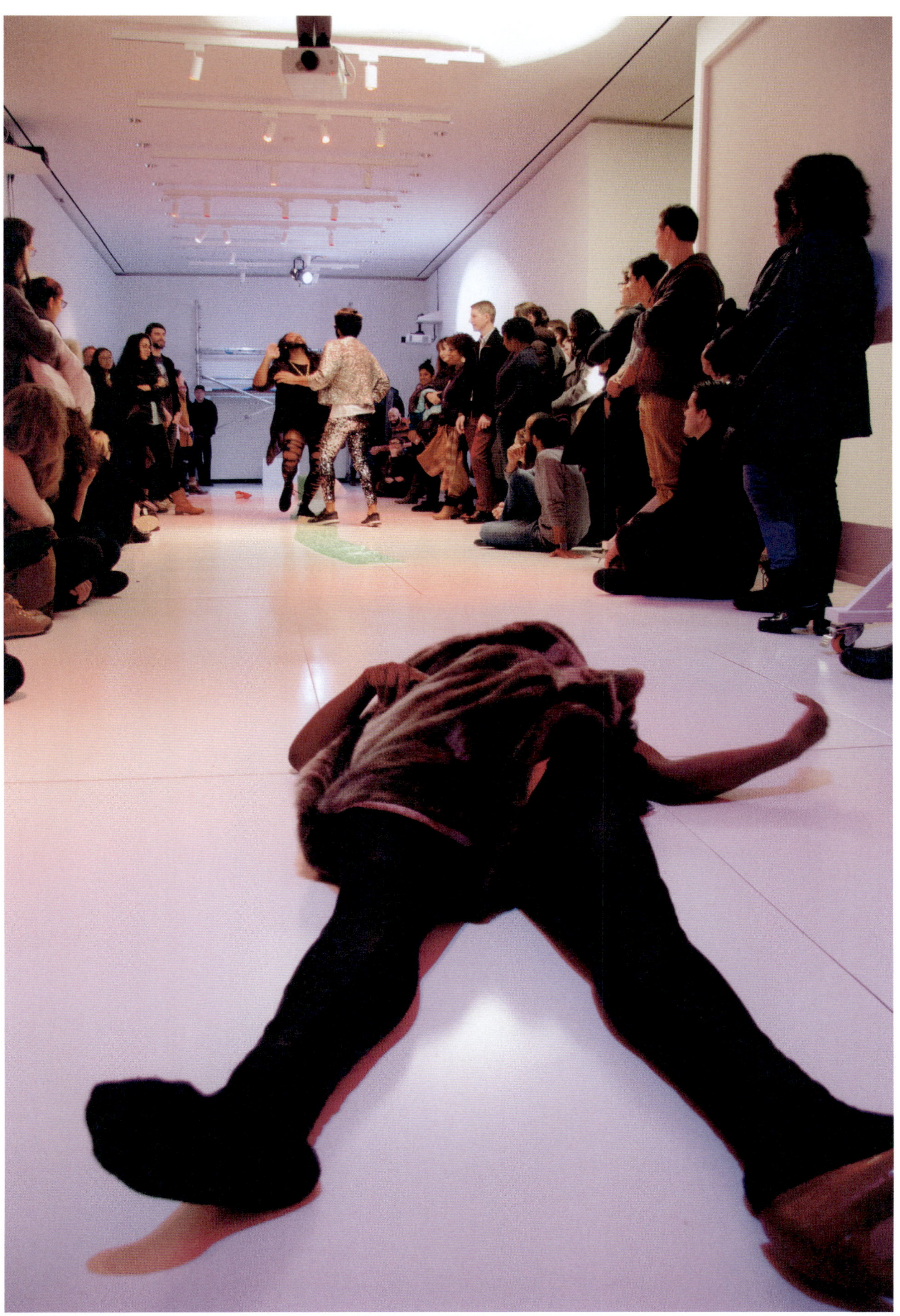

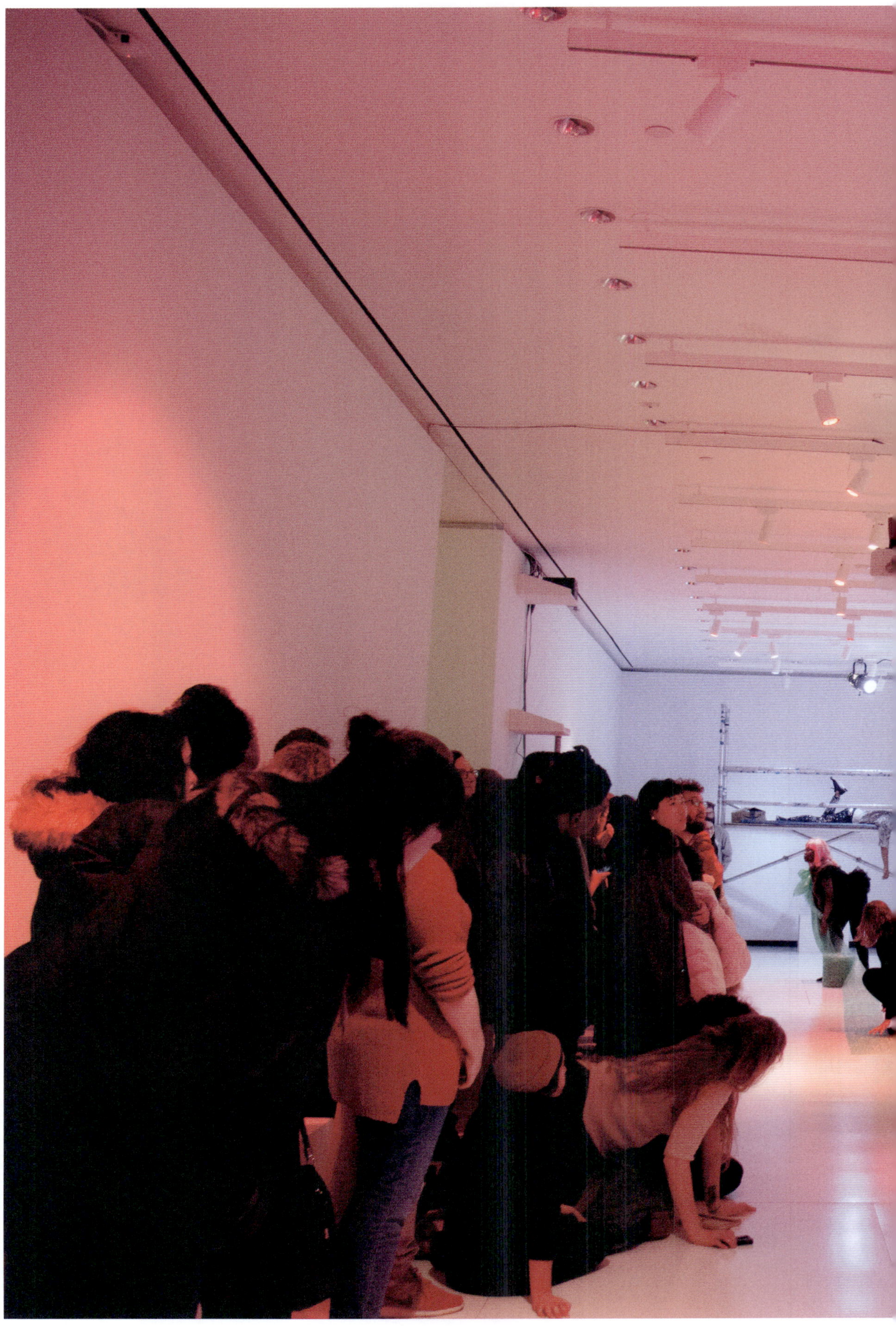

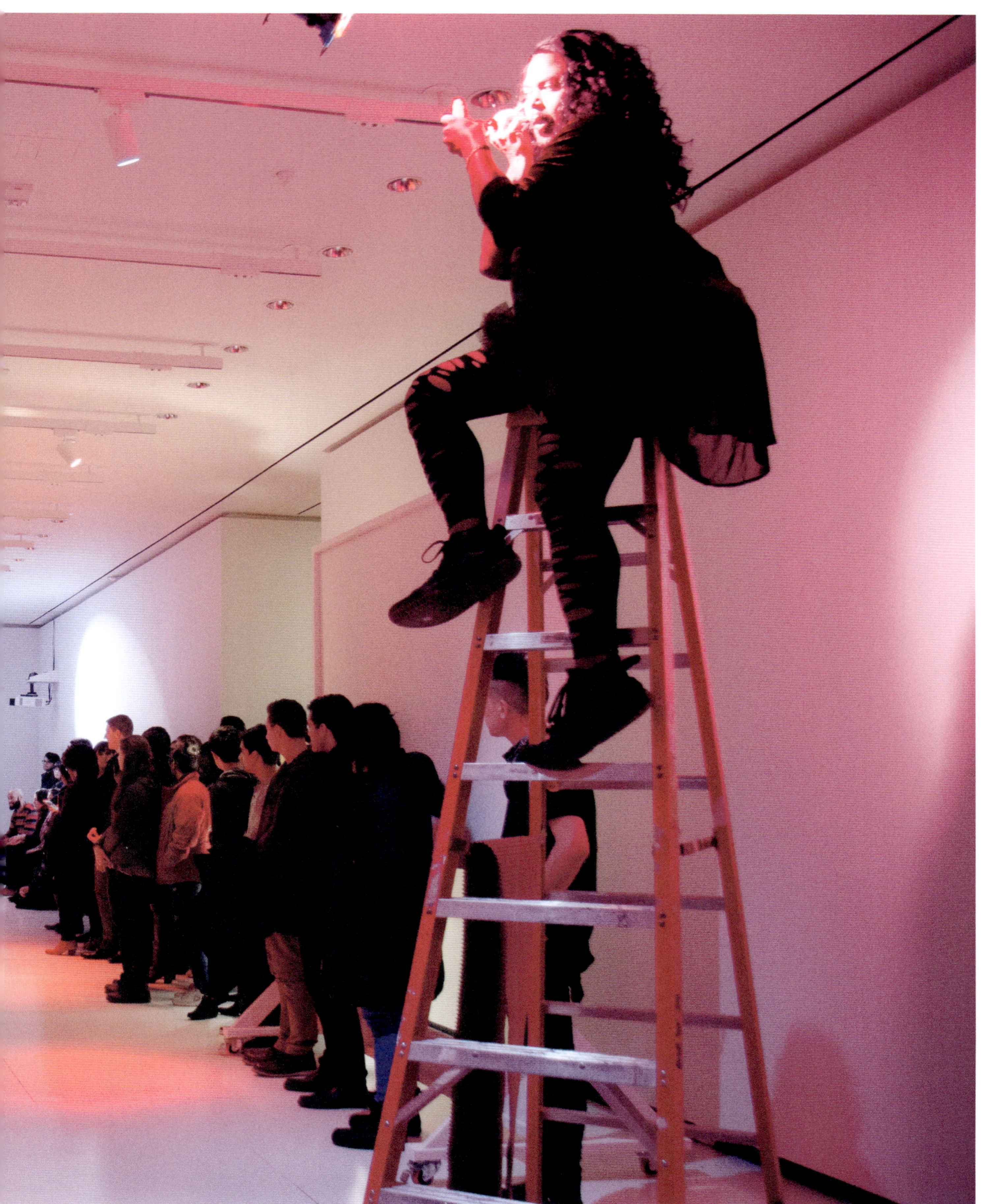

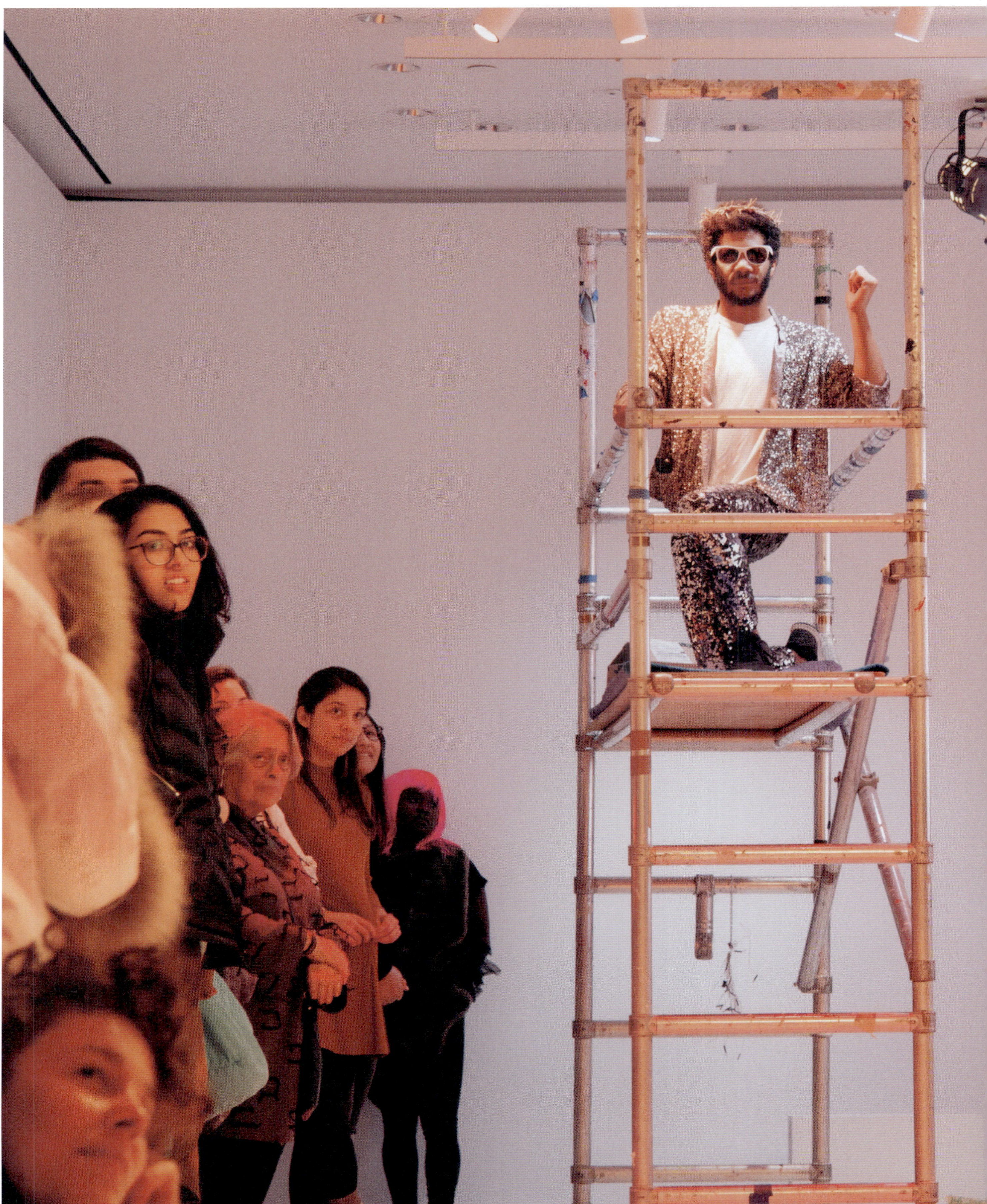

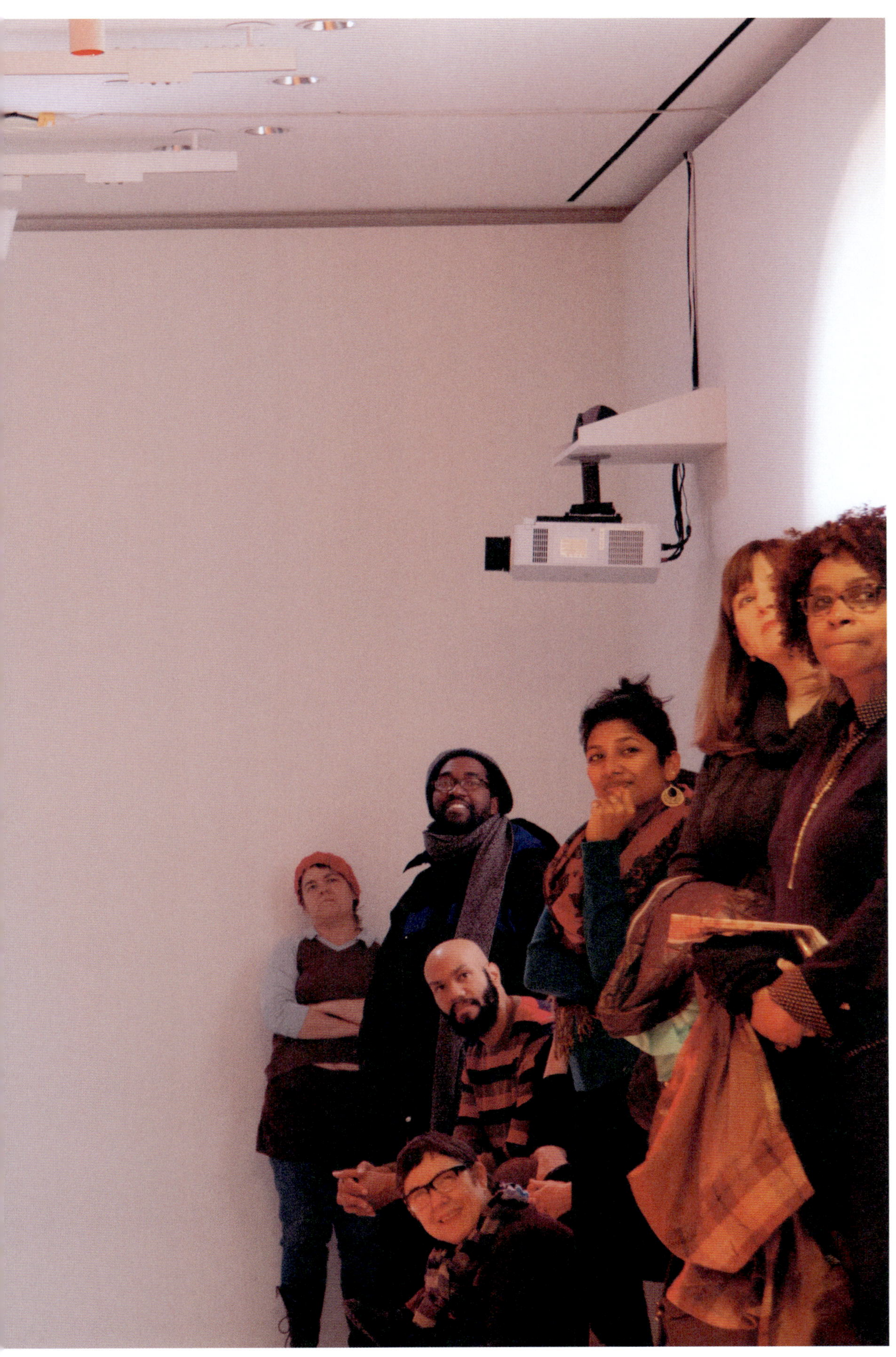

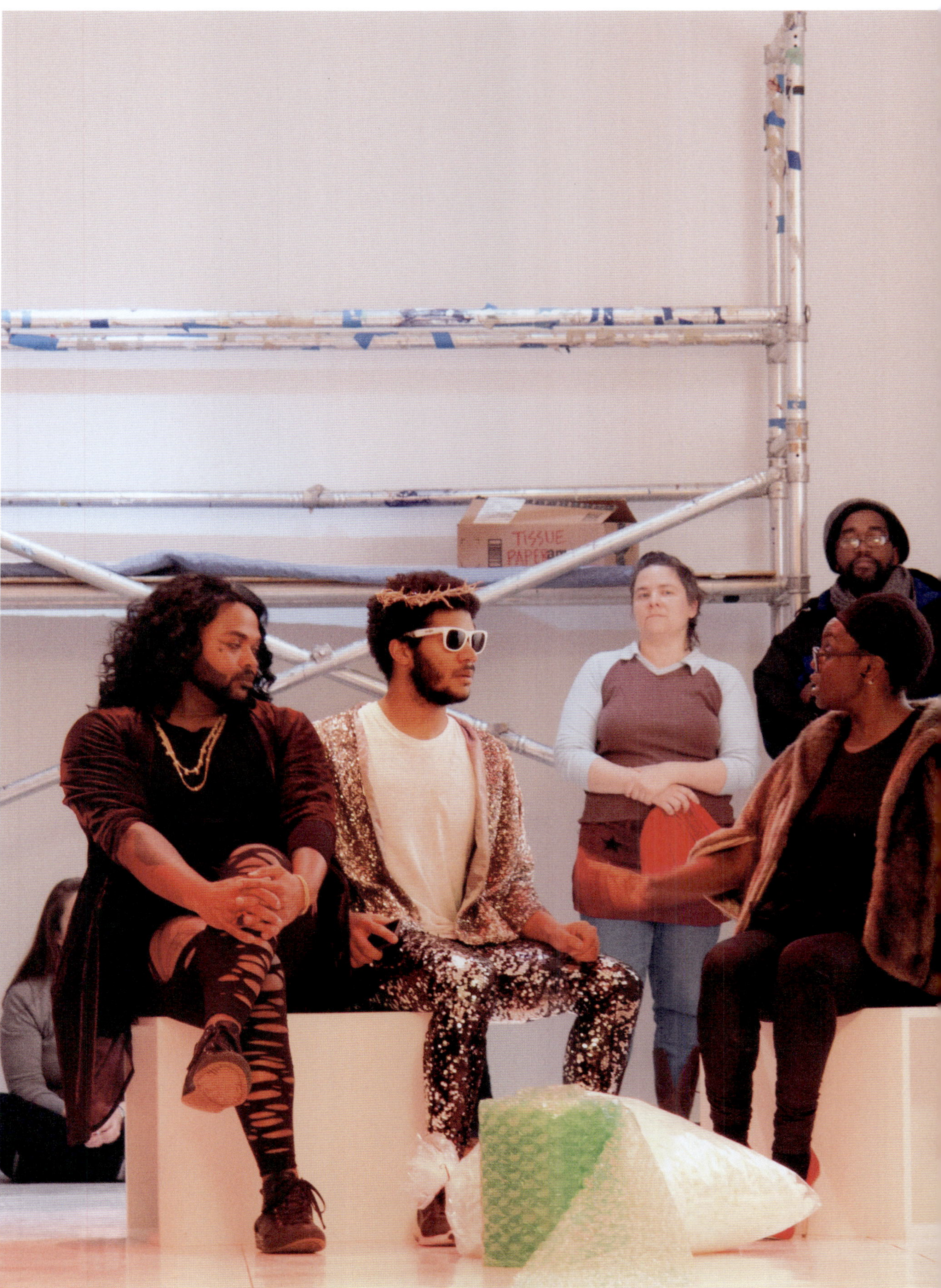

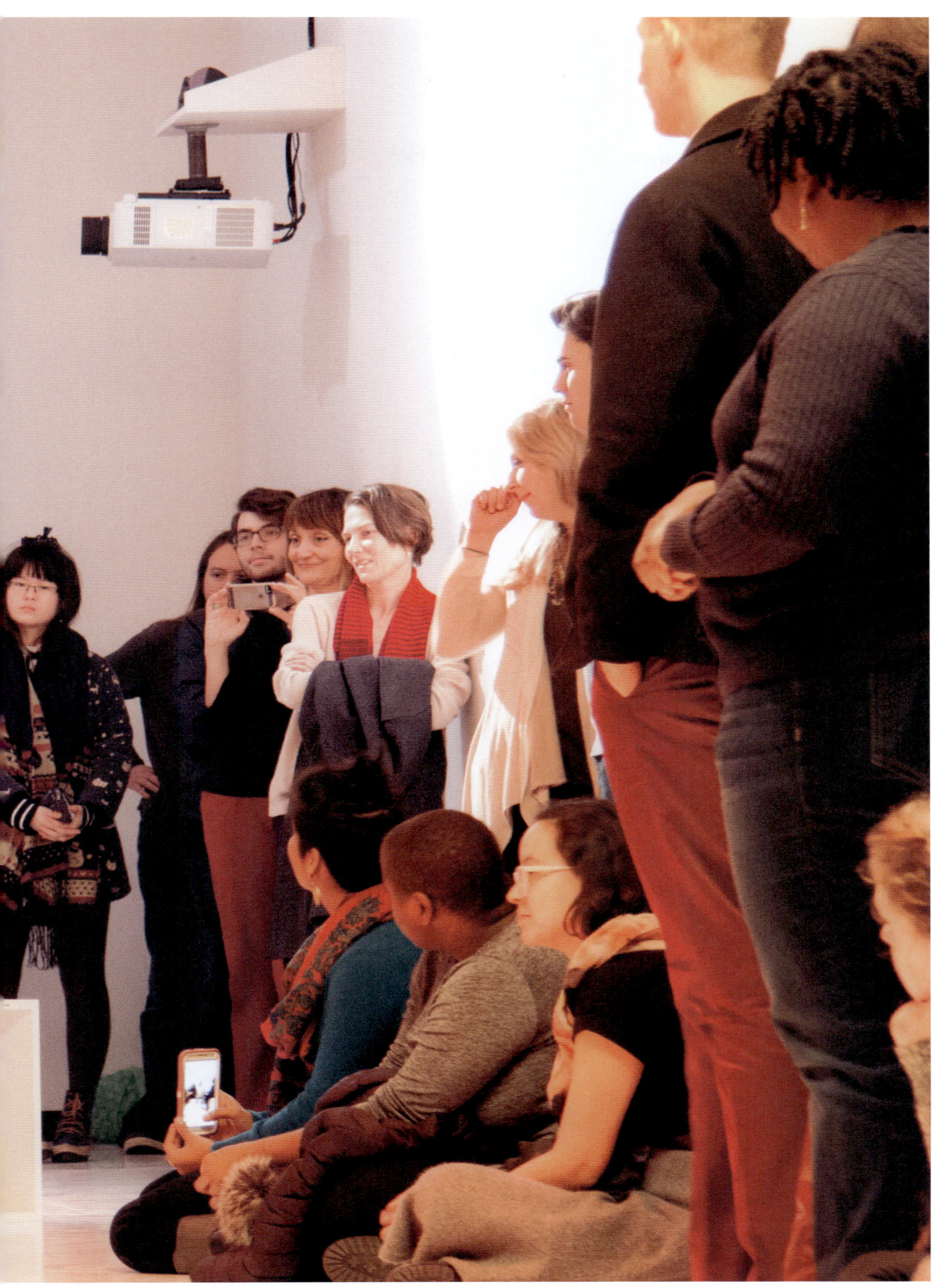

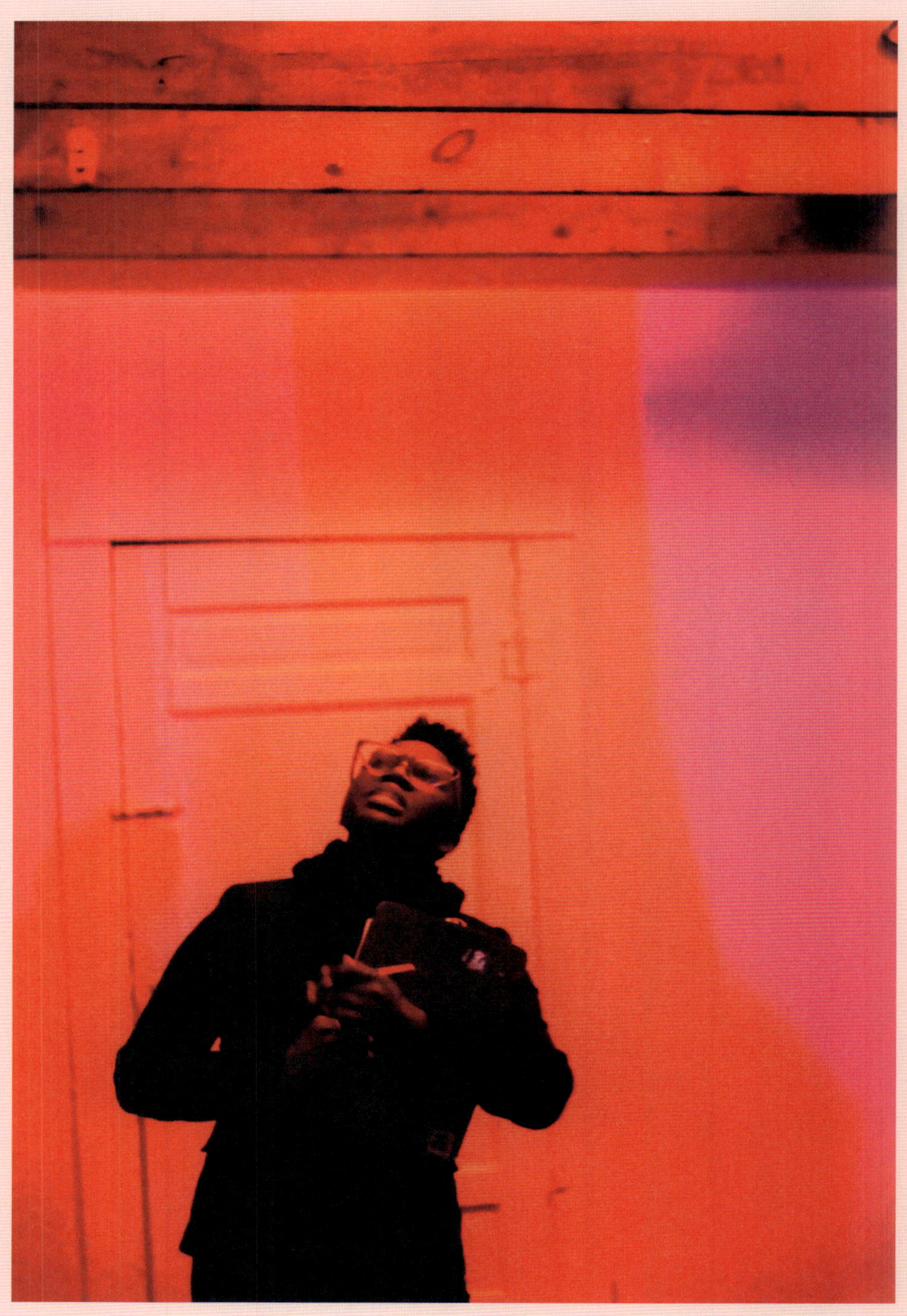

Pages 30–31: *El Diablo y Cristo Negro*, with Autumn Knight, Phillip Pyle, II, and Maurice Duhon. Project Row Houses, Houston, December 28 and December 29, 2012

          EL DIABLO Y CRISTO NEGRO

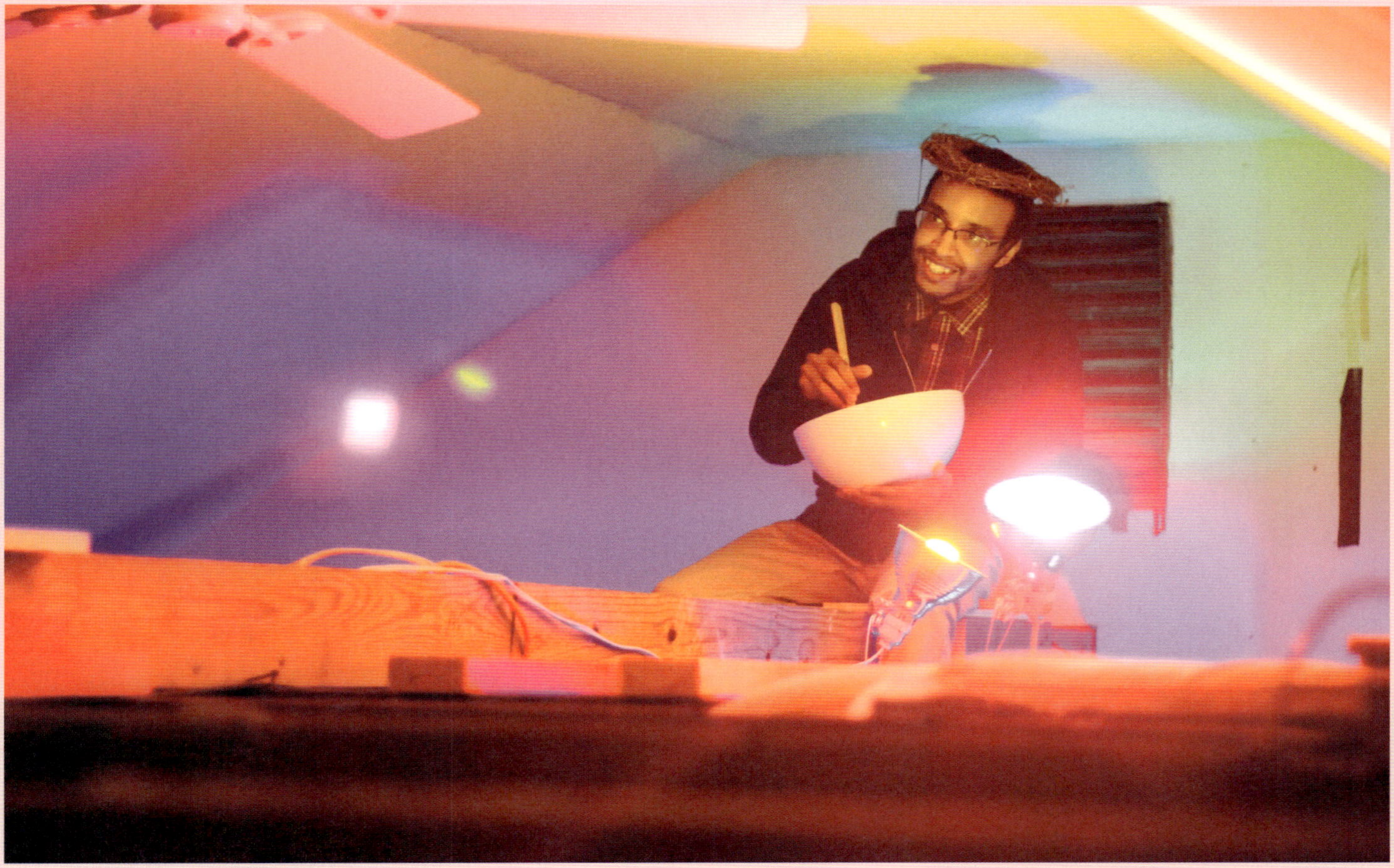

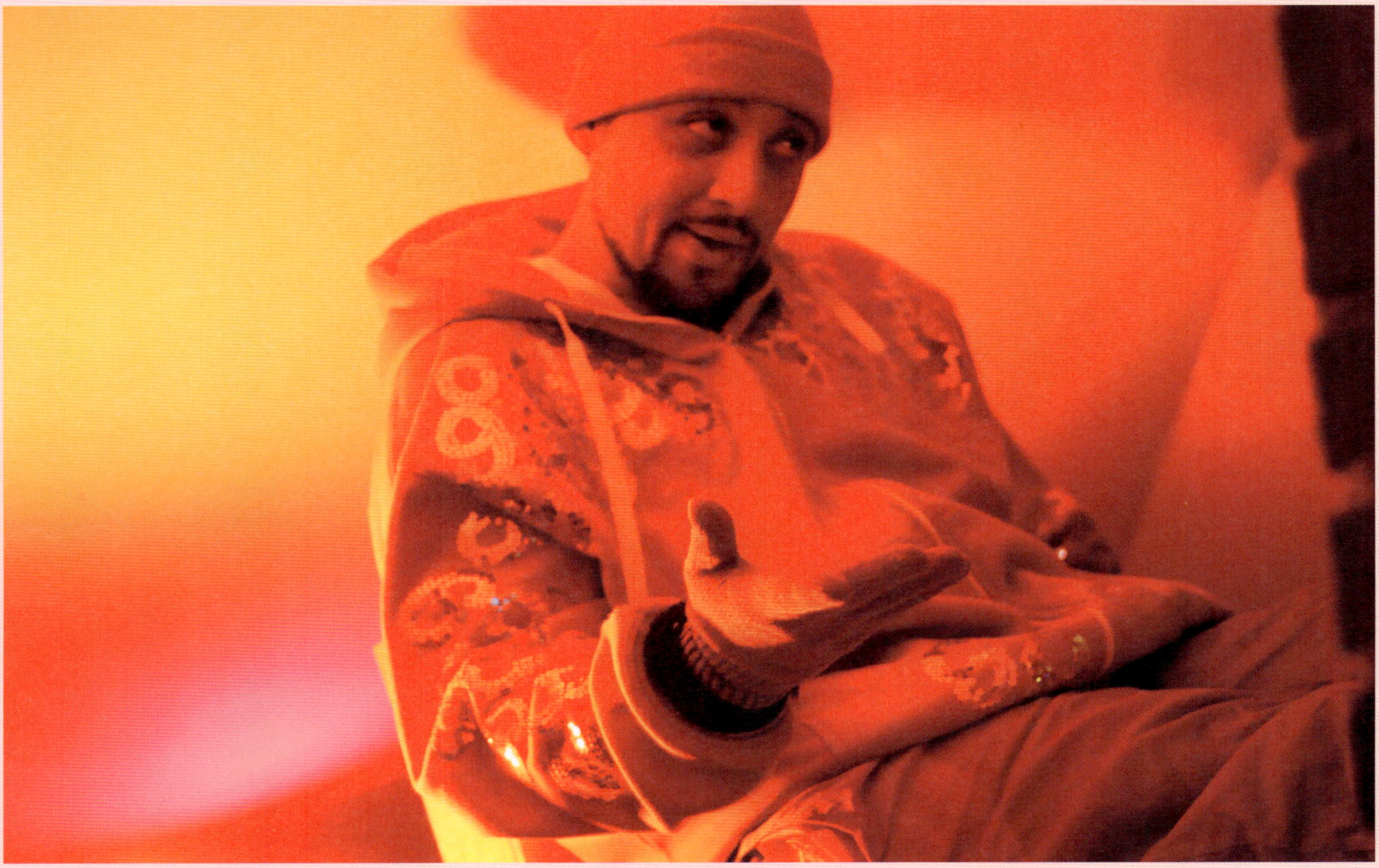

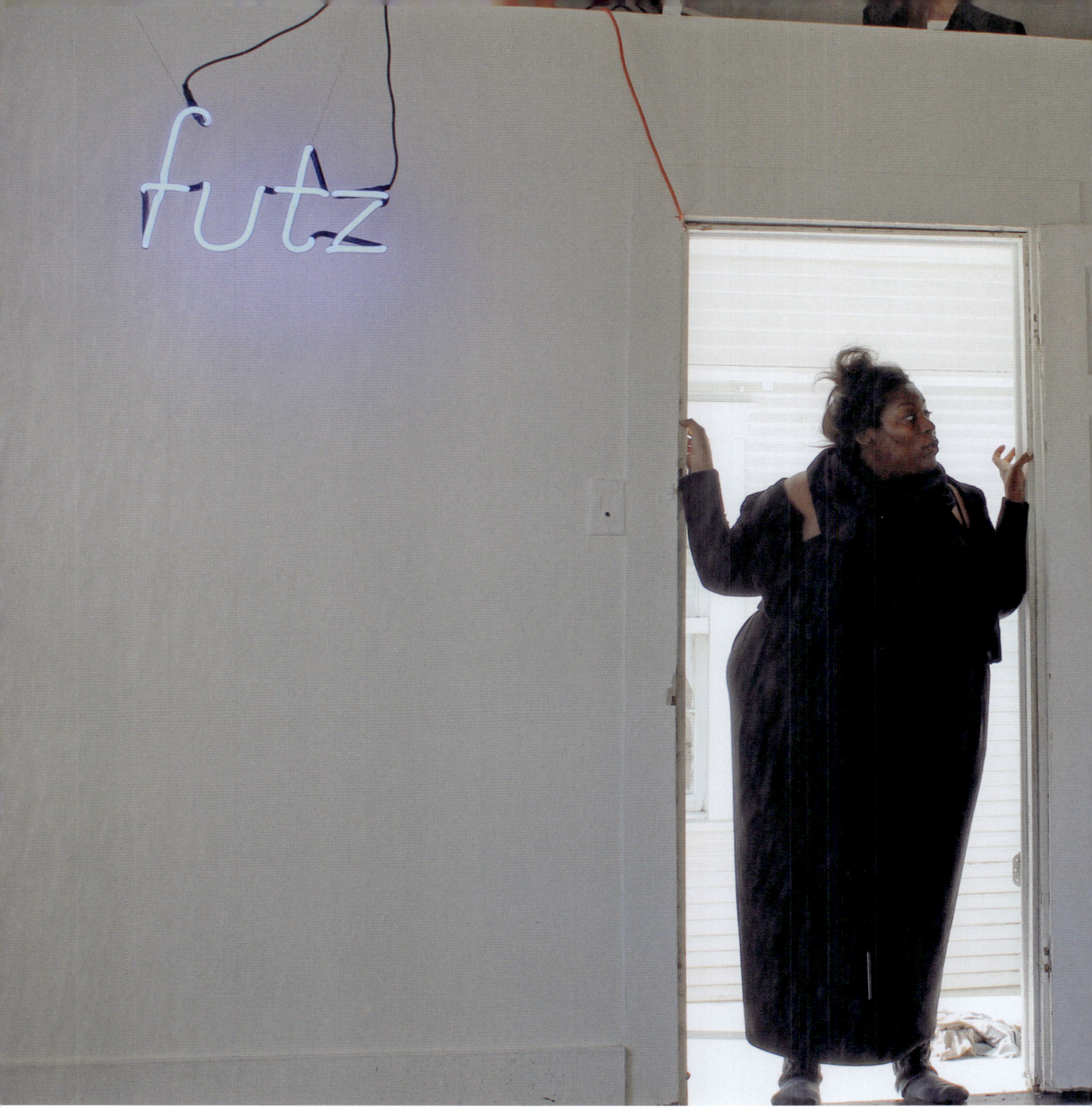

Round 37 | *Futz: A Research Method*, Project Row Houses, Houston,
October 20, 2012–March 3, 2013

Ryan N. Dennis

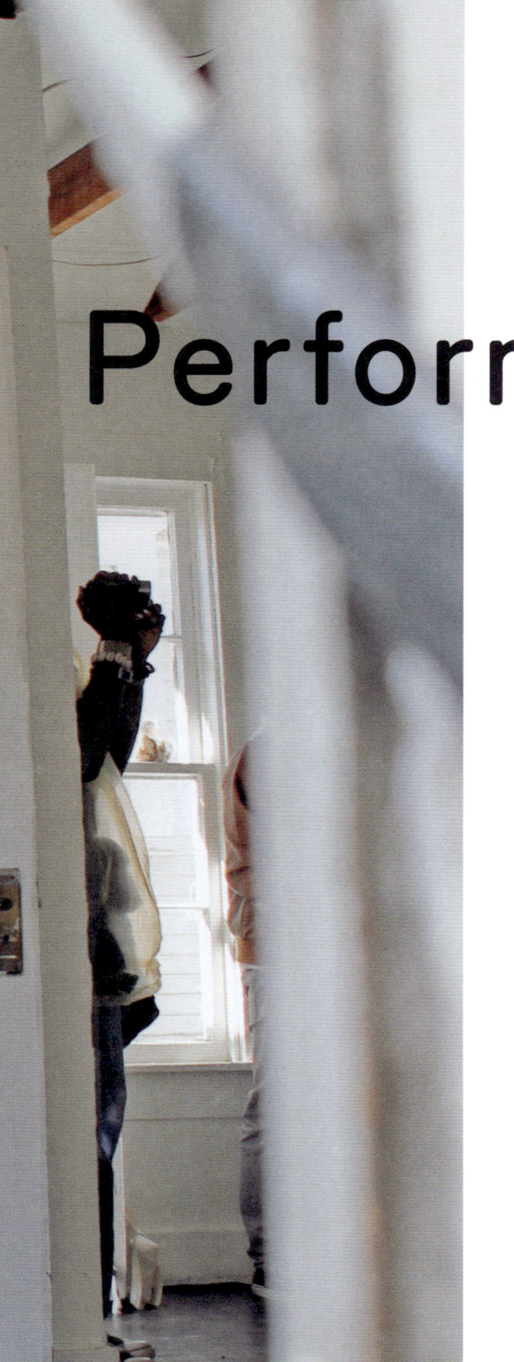

Performance

As

Performance artist Autumn Knight's practice is drawn from her deep well of experience probing the complexities of the human psyche. Employing skills learned from her background in drama therapy, Knight interrogates the thorniest modern-day social issues—race, gender, class, power—in her performances, installations, and text-based work. The absurdity, humor, and sense of play in her art forces her viewers to confront their vulnerability in ways they do not typically anticipate.

Knight taps into her audience's subconscious, allowing viewers to experience new ways of seeing. She creates opportunities for empathy, joy, and questioning, making her audience posit: *What is my role in this space?* With her performances, Knight stage-manages an investigative journey, one taken by the viewer and by Knight herself. Nothing in her work is done without intention. This work is a gift. She, in many ways, has a sixth sense. There is something magical and elevated in her ability to observe; yet her performances are as revelatory for her as they are for the participants.

Project Row Houses (PRH) is a community platform centrally located in the heart of Houston's Historic Third Ward that enriches lives through art with an emphasis on cultural identity and its impact on the urban landscape.[1] The "Rounds" at PRH are not explicitly referred to as "exhibitions" due to their alternative presentation and form. As part of the Public Art Program, the Rounds typically include seven invited artists who activate the 1930s-style shotgun row houses with site-specific installations. I invite artists to respond to the historic architecture of the spaces in ways that engage various contemporary art conversations with a focus on dialogue around hyper-local issues, which include, but aren't limited to: responding to gentrification, investing in small businesses, addressing the Third Ward as a "food desert," and uncovering local activist histories. By presenting a body of work that reflects the Third Ward neighborhood, artists at PRH mirror neighborhoods dealing with similar circumstances in other cities. PRH installations find ways to push artists' practices to new forms that, in turn, create discoveries for them, for those who engage with the work, and for PRH as the institution supporting the work and the artist.

Knight's work is of the boundary-pushing variety. In 2012, Linda Shearer, then Executive Director of PRH, invited Knight to participate in Round 37. I had just been hired and began working closely with Knight to help shape her installation. At the time, Knight was in transition, making what would turn out to be a critical decision to move away from traditional theatre into the world of performance

Dennis

art, the type that employs the artist's body as a central component in the live interaction between artist and audience. Curator Valerie Cassel Oliver describes performance art as temporal and engaging visual elements, whether in documents or with objects that can be shown as part of live performance or in its aftermath.[2] Knight uses interdisciplinary methods to touch on the key components of performance art that connect the performance space, senses of time, the artist's body, and her engagement/exchange with an audience. During an intense period of artistic research and experimentation, Knight proposed *Futz: A Research Method* for Round 37. The project description read:

> Futz: to waste time; idle or busy oneself aimlessly. *Futz* is an experimental performance lab and transmedia installation. Developing a focused art practice is a challenging process to master beyond the walls of a traditionally legitimate art institution. My process has a fumbling and flustered beginning. Depending on the perspective, anyone may appear to be *futzing* around. It remains to be seen when the futzing is done. This series of performances is dedicated to wrestling with futzing as a legitimate strategy in creative processes, lived experiences and beyond. My approach places futzing at the center of this methodology. The performances included are active research that are designed to respond to a series of sub-hypothesis regarding dualism, devils, psychodynamic theory and other hungry ideas. Bi-monthly works featuring dancers, musicians, mental health workers, educators and other performance artists presenting work that is textual, visceral and experimental.

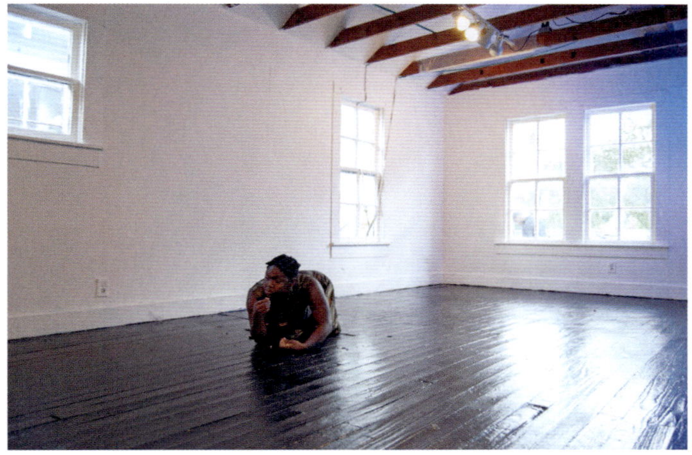

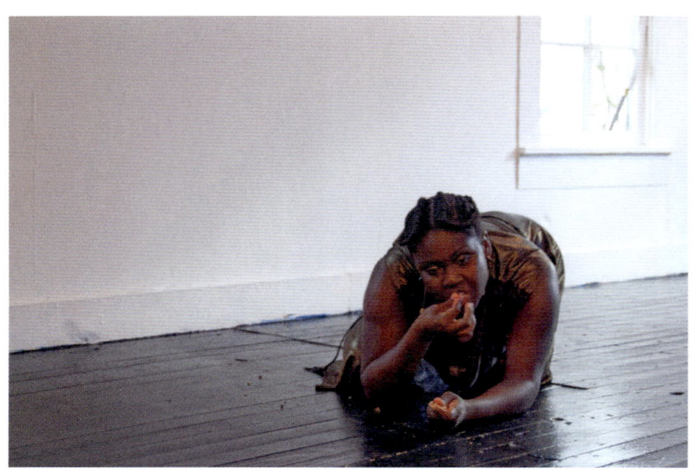

Roach Dance, with Autumn Knight. Project Row Houses, Houston, October 20, 2012

Performance As

Futz: A Research Method marked the beginning of Knight developing her process of experimentation, questioning, and research that would give rise to *In Rehearsal*. Post-*Futz*, Knight continues to shape her practice as a black female performance artist in the world of contemporary art, working both within and outside of institutions and public spaces to critique, inform, and reimagine possibilities that shape the historical tropes of black identity and ultimately create new layers within the performance art landscape.

Performance as Absurdity

Knight uses play and humor to engage her audience. She is an investigator, reading the room to determine how far she can go, even as the viewer is present and seduced by her charm; Knight's presence both captivates and confuses. One of the first works that Knight choreographed as part of her installation at PRH was *Roach Dance*. The performance began as soon as Knight entered the art house, wearing a dark metallic dress that flowed with each movement she made. Her hair was styled in two cornrows, braided forward to look like a roach's antennae. She stared around the room at each audience member, her eyes piercingly intent, and began to twitch. Her head moved in controlled jerks. These movements made members of the audience visibly uncomfortable as the occasional nervous chuckle, looks of concern, and gasps moved throughout the space. There was laughter and bewilderment; the audience was captivated by these gestures as a strange new energy filled the room. There were crackers on the floor. Knight got down on her hands and knees and ate them in a skittish manner, embodying the act as a roach would.

Then she stopped unexpectedly. The audience was experiencing a new phase in the performance. Knight stood up, looked at the audience, and screamed at the top of her lungs. No longer the roach on its knees scurrying around, she became the person *seeing* the roach. Suddenly she was terrified, screaming and running from wall to wall. Knight became all of us who have been taught to fear this insect, to see it as filthy and disgusting, low quality, associated with all things poor and undesirable. According to the description provided by the artist, "*Roach Dance* was a meditation on lack of control and mental health. The subject is nearly driven mad as she shifts between contemplating the roach as an existential symbol and the hopeless fear engendered by perpetually reincarnated pests."[3]

Knight's work draws from the methods executed by performance artist Pope.L, also known as The Friendliest Black Artist in America™, who uses humor to expose conditioned cultural and social conventions. Knight, like Pope.L, works in the "discomfort zone" to open up dialogue about serious issues, in this case mental health and under-resourced communities related to Blackness and the assumptions and perceptions that are often associated with its identity. While absurdism has been a tool used by many artists in the postmodern era, Knight has loosely formalized a process to address myriad issues that are not presented solely for the sake of shock value. There is a means to an end. Knight is committed to framing performances as opportunities for internal questioning from the viewer to break down assumptions and reframe issues that have historically affected disinvested communities and individuals. *Roach Dance* begs us to think about our mental health and

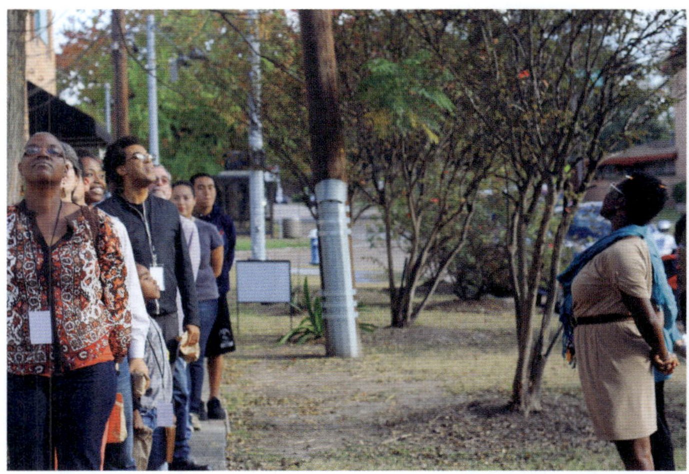

Hands in Your Lap, with Autumn Knight and Megan Jackson. Project Row Houses, Houston, November 24 and November 25, 2012

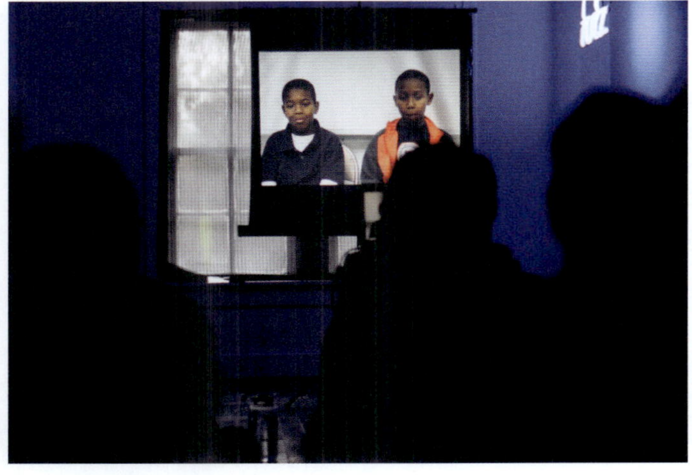

Dennis

the state of mind we enter into when something like a roach, both metaphorically and physically, comes into our homes.

Performance as Pedagogy

Knight approaches the performance arena without a set of answers or preconceived notions on how people will respond to her work and the situations they find themselves in. Typical methods in drama therapy utilize such techniques as improvisation, role play, and storytelling so individuals can express emotions, act out the change they wish to see in the world, develop new skills for empathetic behavior and understanding, and problem-solve in new ways. Knight experiences a performance along with the spectators, becoming a facilitator or, perhaps, a conductor, orchestrating a shared experience between herself and her audience. Her approach allows people to create distance from their patterns and develop actions to gain deeper insights into things that are potentially foreign or from another perspective.

Knight's process can be seen in the extremely thoughtful work *Hands in Your Lap*. This interactive performance created an environment for the audience to become pupils and experience the psychological challenges that are presented within the school system. The use of role-playing comes out of socio-drama, a method that allows for exploring issues involved in complex social situations. Knight and her co-performer, artist Megan Jackson, gathered the audience, forced them to march in a single file line, instructed them to be quiet and listen, not to fiddle, and focus so they could pay attention to the future instruction. The audience went from being spectators to participants who were then given brown bag lunches and ordered to walk into the classroom (the PRH art space for *Futz*) to watch videos of pre-recorded interviews with students answering questions about how art was presented in their schools. Knight's performance reflected on artistic, cultural, and institutional challenges for schools presenting "art" without the care and understanding of its possibilities. *Hands in Your Lap* functioned in similar ways to work by artist and philosopher Adrian Piper, by demanding the viewer's/participant's accountability, both officially (knowing you are coming to perform) and unofficially (attending the performance and then becoming an integral part of the work). While Piper does not rely on role reversal from her audiences, she presents works that "both posit and critique models" of existence and human interaction.[4]

When Knight is not using role-play as a pedagogical practice, she sets a stage for people to enter and actively participate. *Here + Now* was created as an opportunity to explore group relations with co-facilitator Kelly Hershman. The goals of this part-conference, part-experience, part-performance, from Knight's perspective, were to enhance the participants' understanding of how groups function, engage the participants' performative tendencies, and create an experience that one has never had before. *Here + Now* epitomizes Knight's keen sense of play—participants begin the experience believing that they are coming to participate with minimal effort but walk away with the ability to more deeply understand themselves and how they perform exchanges within group settings. The experiential performance has the ability to create a profound sense of awareness, to leave one in a state of shock, or to truly transform oneself. Knight's work dances with reality, makes us question what we know, and then gives us the opportunity to dig a little deeper. We may get nearer to something that looks like an answer. Or, we could walk away, bewildered.

Here + Now was devoted to the study and experience of group behavior and the social, cultural, and economic power dynamics informing the making and consumption of art.[5] In a space with strangers or individuals with whom one is only lightly acquainted, how does one eliminate the fear of communicating freely? Knight wins trust and creates a space that is both safe and daring enough to encompass participants' vulnerability. The effect on the audience is profound. Unlike many performance artists, Knight is not content to merely be watched. Instead, she engages people and involves them—they explore a topic *with* her. The dynamics of power shift in Knight's performances, due to her ability to powerfully tilt the axis so that the exchange is not just done by her but through the participation of the group.

During participatory exchange, I am reminded of art historian Grant Kester's writing about participation in public spaces; he loosely defines this idea of the "scripted encounter" as a performance in which participants play an active role but are essentially actors, because the entirety of their actions is based on something provided by the artist.[6] Knight's more recent work involves varying degrees of a scripted encounter. Her earlier performances throughout *Futz* required audience engagement based on spontaneous exchange, which gave the work an unexpected layer that has become a cornerstone of Knight's practice.

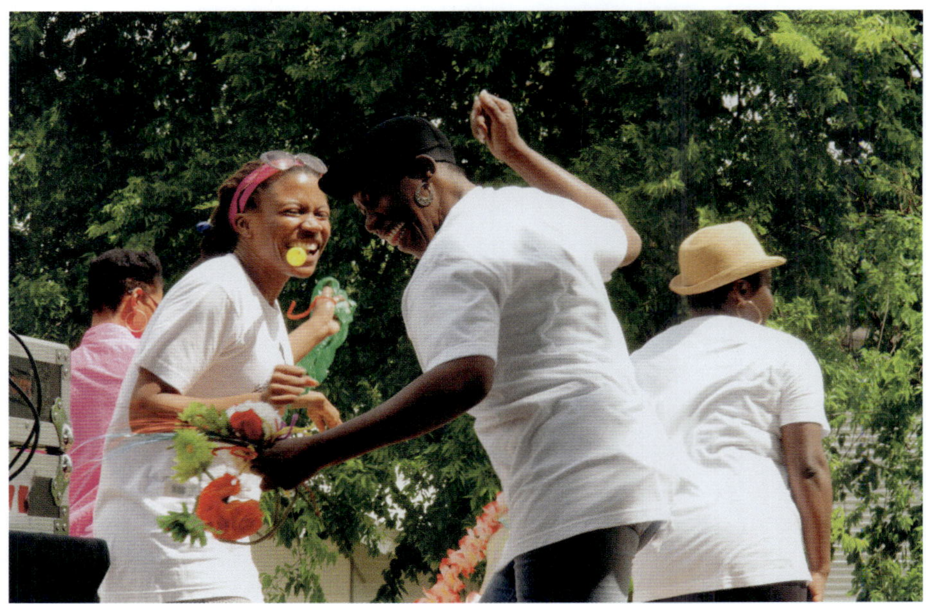

Flower Man Bike Parade, with Autumn Knight, Lisa E. Harris, and M'Kina Tapscott. CounterCurrent, Houston, April 12, 2014

Performance as Social Sculpture

The performances during Knight's installation at PRH were built around experimentation with dancers, musicians, actors, singers, writers, psychologists, and spiritual workers. Another cornerstone of Knight's practice is collaboration, likely because of her background in theatre. The idea of "social sculpture" is an adequate way to describe the portion of Knight's output ultimately steeped in community-building. The term social sculpture was first used in 1979 by artist Joseph Beuys and has been interpreted in many ways, from being extremely conceptual to discussing *the* object and where it is placed in the world to framing the fact that everyone is an artist. The term informed the creation of PRH because social sculpture occurs when one determines to shape the world in accordance with what one would like to see.

In 2010 Knight and artist-collaborator Robert Pruitt formed MF Problem, an art collective established to create collaborative, conceptual, visual, and performative strategies to critique the divisions of race, power, and various inequalities found in social structures. Together Knight and Pruitt organized a gathering meant to call attention to a problem in Houston's Third Ward. A corner store at the intersection of Francis Street and Emancipation Avenue (formerly known as Dowling Street) experienced a sudden increase in prostitution, drug use and exchange, and other illicit activity. Knight put forth a call to action: create work that is meaningful and generative with the hopes of shaping public discourse in a positive way. Together MF Problem and fellow practitioners and collaborators took over the parking lot for a night of music, dancing, playing dominoes, cooking, and general fun. I offer this example to demonstrate both the breadth of Knight's practice and to say specifically how she's used her artistic methodologies to create real change in the world around her. In this scenario, an uncomfortable site was turned into a social sculpture. *Mobile Block Party* decreased the levels of illicit activity in that corner store for some time, and ultimately caused neighborhood residents to see the site in a new way. Its staging allowed for individuals who went to the corner store regularly to remain present but also engage with MF Problem. While participating, they ate, danced, fellowshipped, and reimagined a more positive future for themselves and those around them that seemingly was not present before. While the poetic gesture may have yielded something ephemeral, the "take-over" was an opportunity for individuals to gather and dialogue (and play) over an issue that might have impacted a significant number of people in harmful ways, opting instead for community-building.

A sense of reverence inspired a collaboration among Knight, artist-musician Lisa E. Harris, and artist M'kina Tapscott. In 2014 they created *Flower Man Bike Parade*, a processional performance and public art happening that honored the life, aesthetic, and artistry of Cleveland Turner, a.k.a. Flower Man. Flower Man was a visionary artist and

Dennis

prominent figure in the Third Ward and the Houston community until his death in 2013. He converted houses into large-scale environmental artworks using a cacophony of found objects. He embellished the exterior of his homes (and his bike) with real and artificial flowers. The collaborative parade connected Knight's sense of play to her sense of community. It is part of her practice to honor place even while altering it, and to honor people while engaging with people.

Having the opportunity to observe, critique, and give feedback on Knight's work while she was living in Houston was an honor and of great importance for myself and the Houston arts community. The performances at PRH were critical and engaging—she transformed the art space throughout the viewing period. Collaboration as a cornerstone for performance-making is a unique proposition. Knight found her voice as a performance artist at PRH, forging her own path in the world of contemporary art. She is committed to unmasking and calling into question the assumptions of our reality while using humor and play as a means to break down the barriers between (and within) human beings. When the modern-day political climate is so fraught and heightened with "fake news," bigotry, and overall distrust, Knight's work calls for people to sit with complex issues, question, laugh, cry, and build community to have a better next moment. Through her investigative practice, Knight thinks about visual aesthetics and the history of black narratives. She weaves together experiences that you share and unpack when you are with her while simultaneously setting up opportunities for the documentation of her work to live and be consumed beyond the live performance. The remarkable nature of Knight's practice is connected to the history of black performance art, but also opens up new ways to participate, engage, and critique, thus centering the work on the possibilities of what performance art can be and how it can function in our everyday lives.

1   https://projectrowhouses.org/.

2   Valerie Cassel Oliver, "Putting the Body on the Line: Endurance in Black Performance" in *Radical Presence: Black Performance in Contemporary Art*, ed. Valerie Cassel Oliver (Houston: Contemporary Arts Museum, Houston, 2013), 14.

3   This description comes from the artist and was included on the art cards distributed to the public at Project Row Houses.

4   Naomi Beckwith, "Dark Mirrors: Performance Documents as Bodily Evidence" in Cassel Oliver, *Radical Presence*, 30.

5   See Carrie Schneider, "A Collaborative Review of *Futz*: Autumn Knight's Experimental Research Method and Performance Series" in *Temporary Art Review* (March 21, 2013), http://temporaryartreview.com/a-collaborative-review-of-futz-autumn-knights-experimental-research-method-and-performance-series/.

6   Grant H. Kester, *What We Made: Conversations on Art and Social Cooperation*, ed. Tom Finkelpearl (Durham, NC: Duke University Press, 2013), 4.

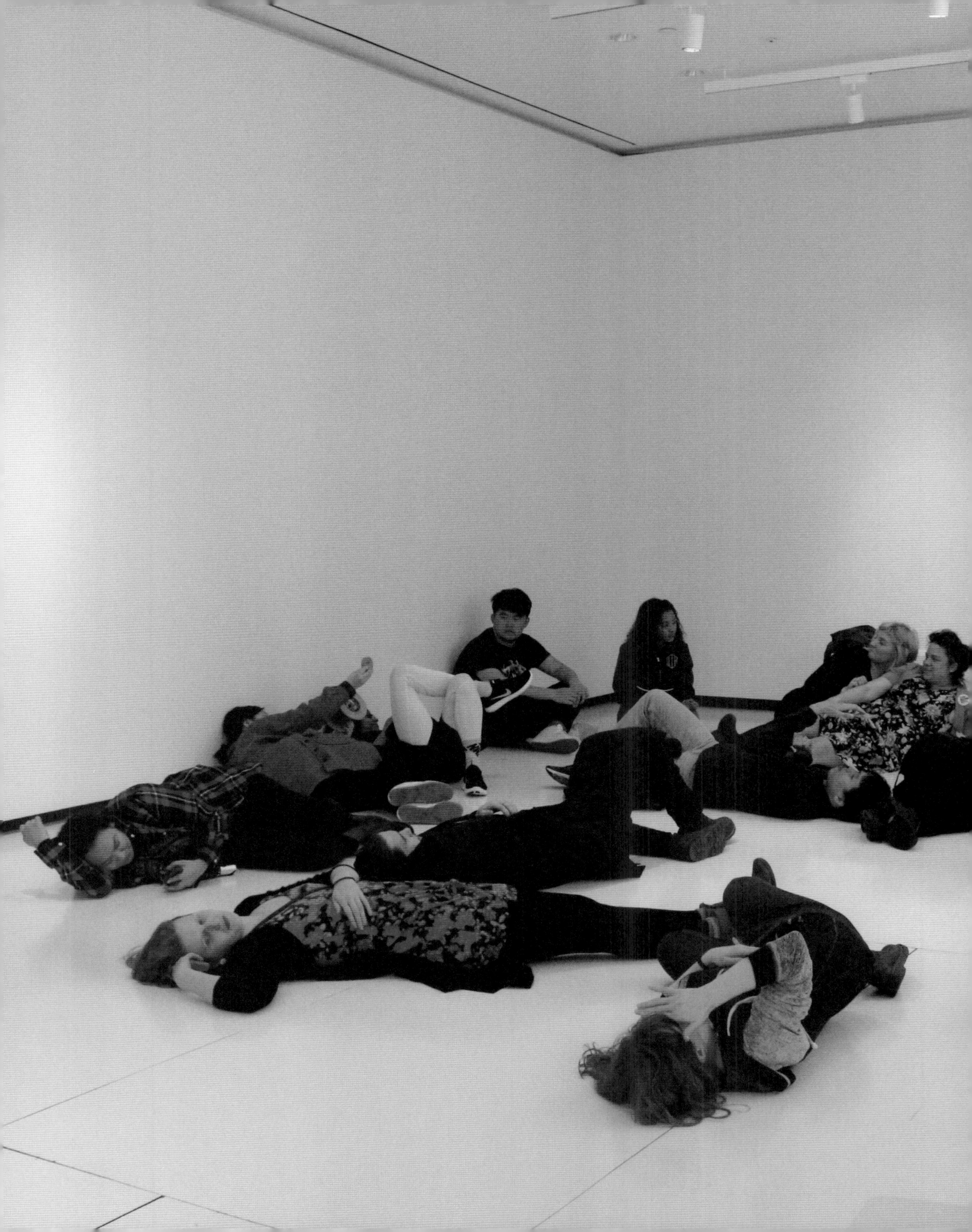

HERE

+

NOW

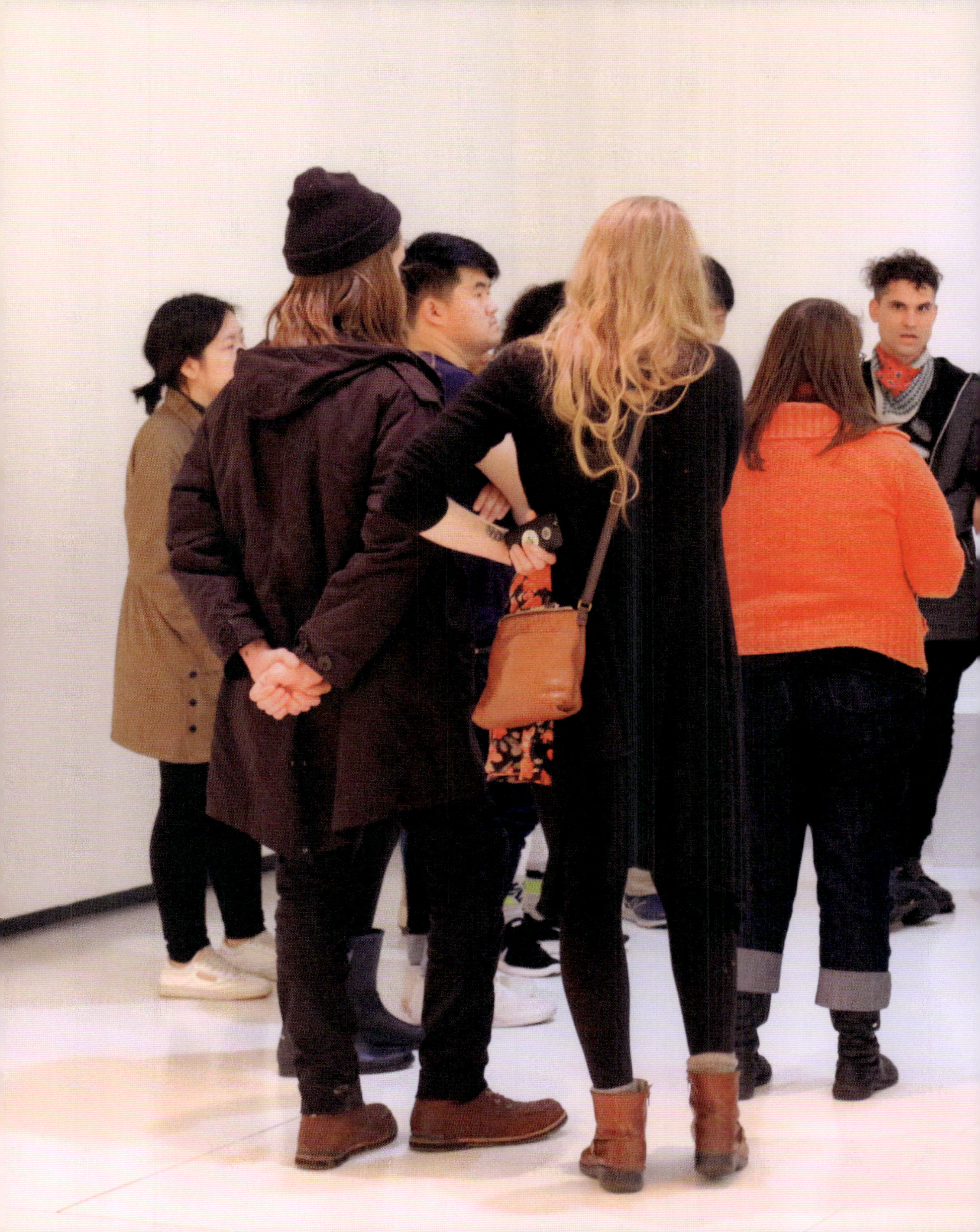

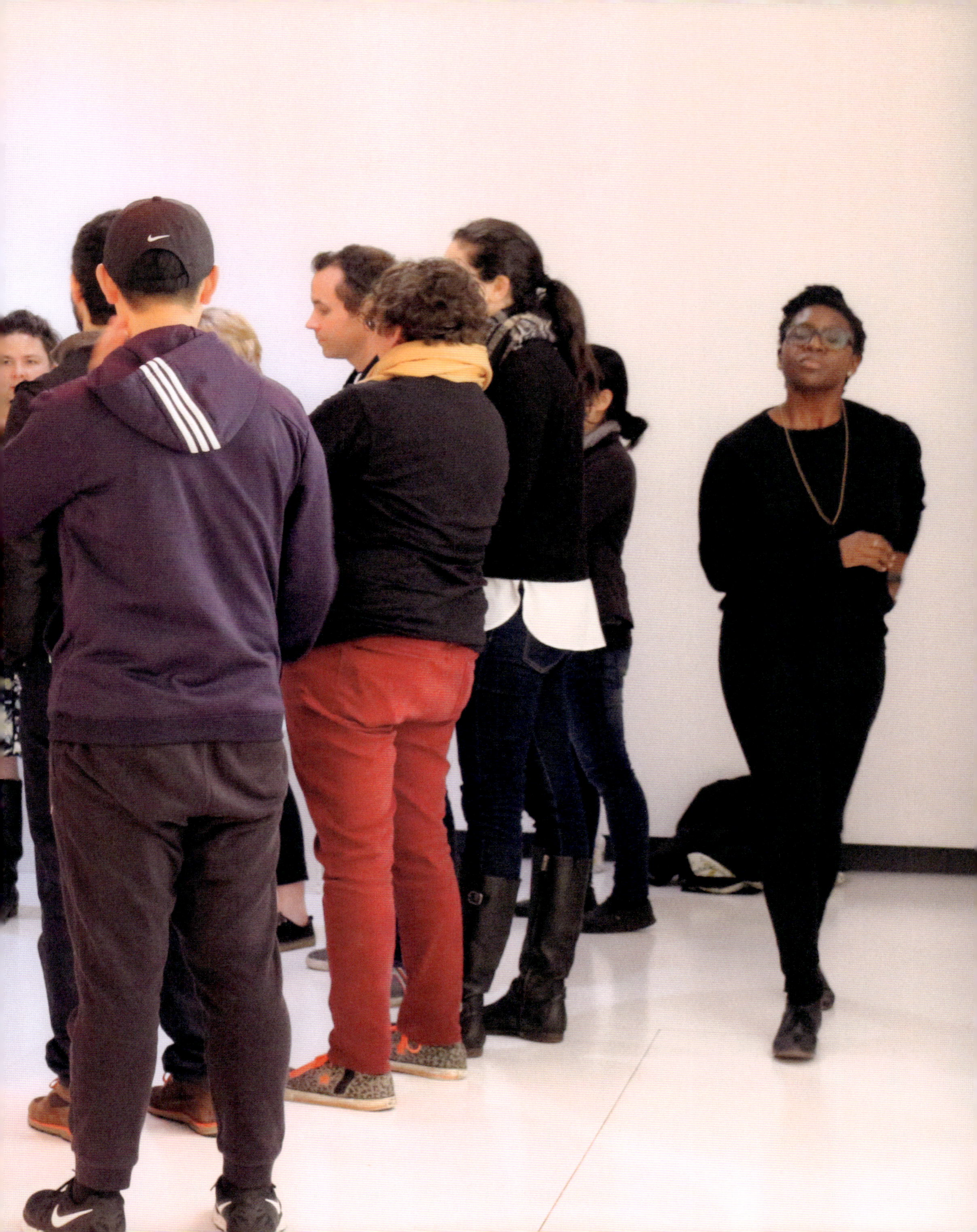

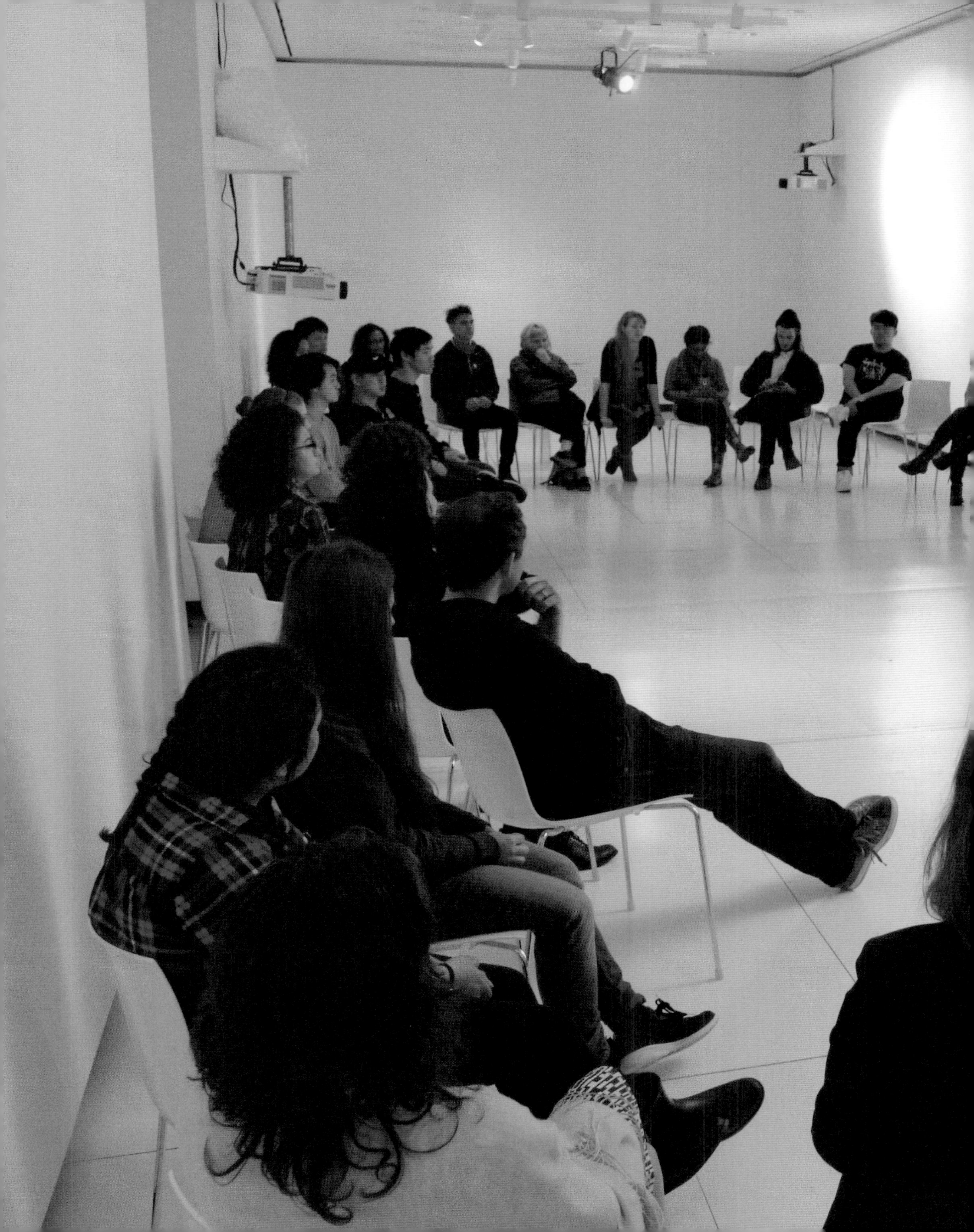

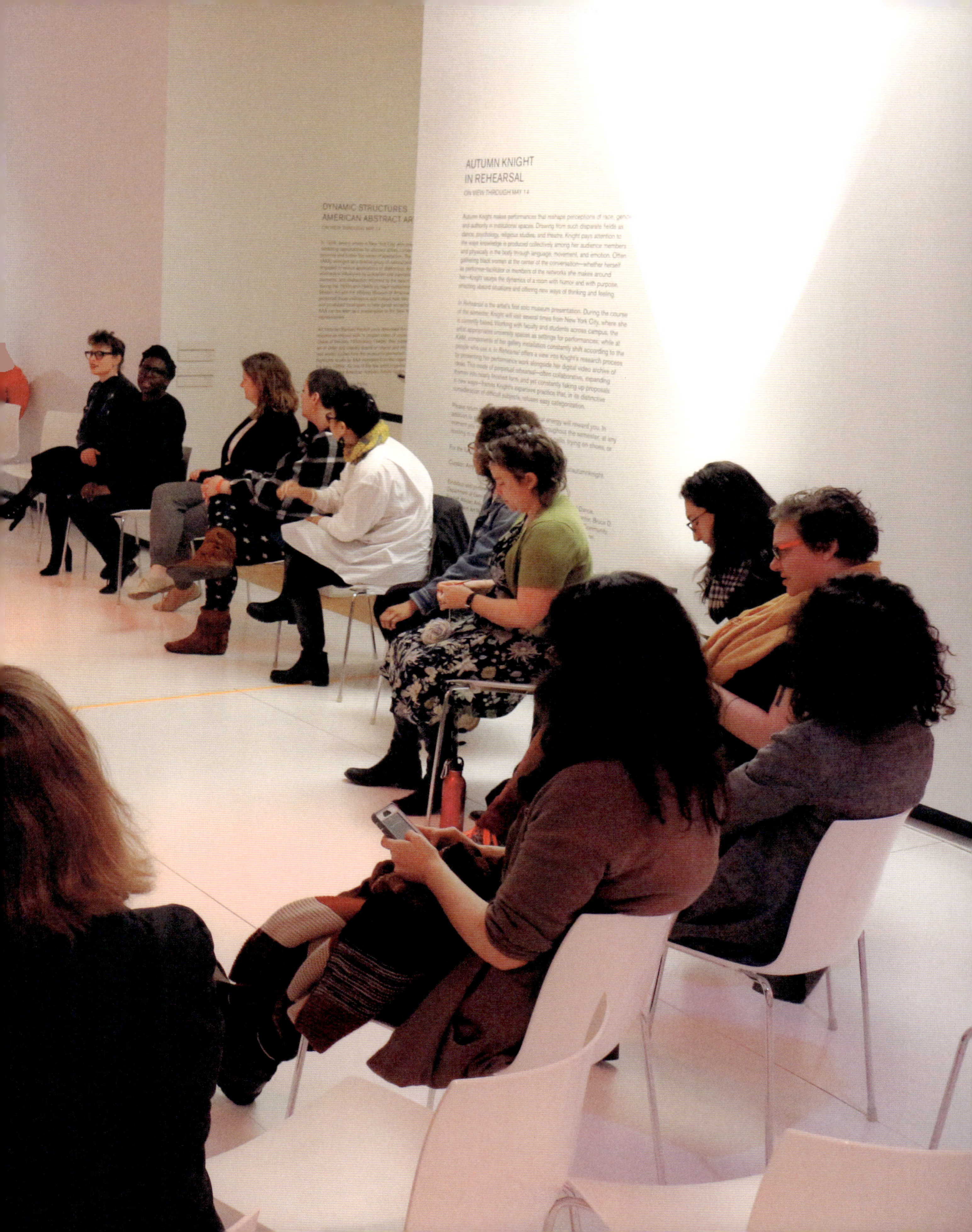

AUTUMN KNIGHT
IN REHEARSAL
ON VIEW THROUGH MAY 14

Here + Now (2013–present) is a constructed
situation exploring group relations as a
means to self-knowledge among participants.
Knight and a consultant collaborator
provide the performance's sole instruction,
to examine oneself in the here and now.

SOUNDTRACK

"Here and Now"
Luther Vandross

Pages 40–47: *Here + Now*, with Autumn Knight and Kelley Hershman.
Krannert Art Museum, Champaign, March 30, 2017

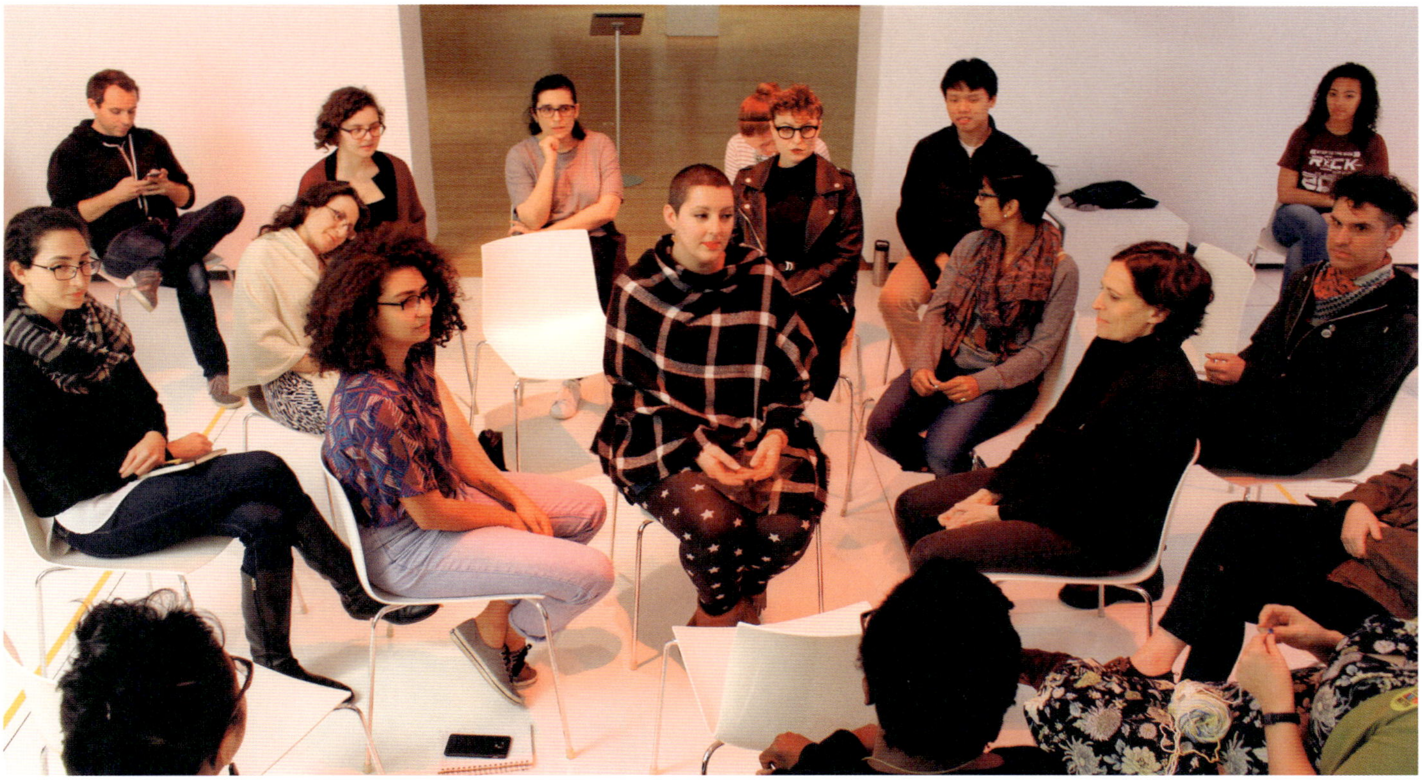

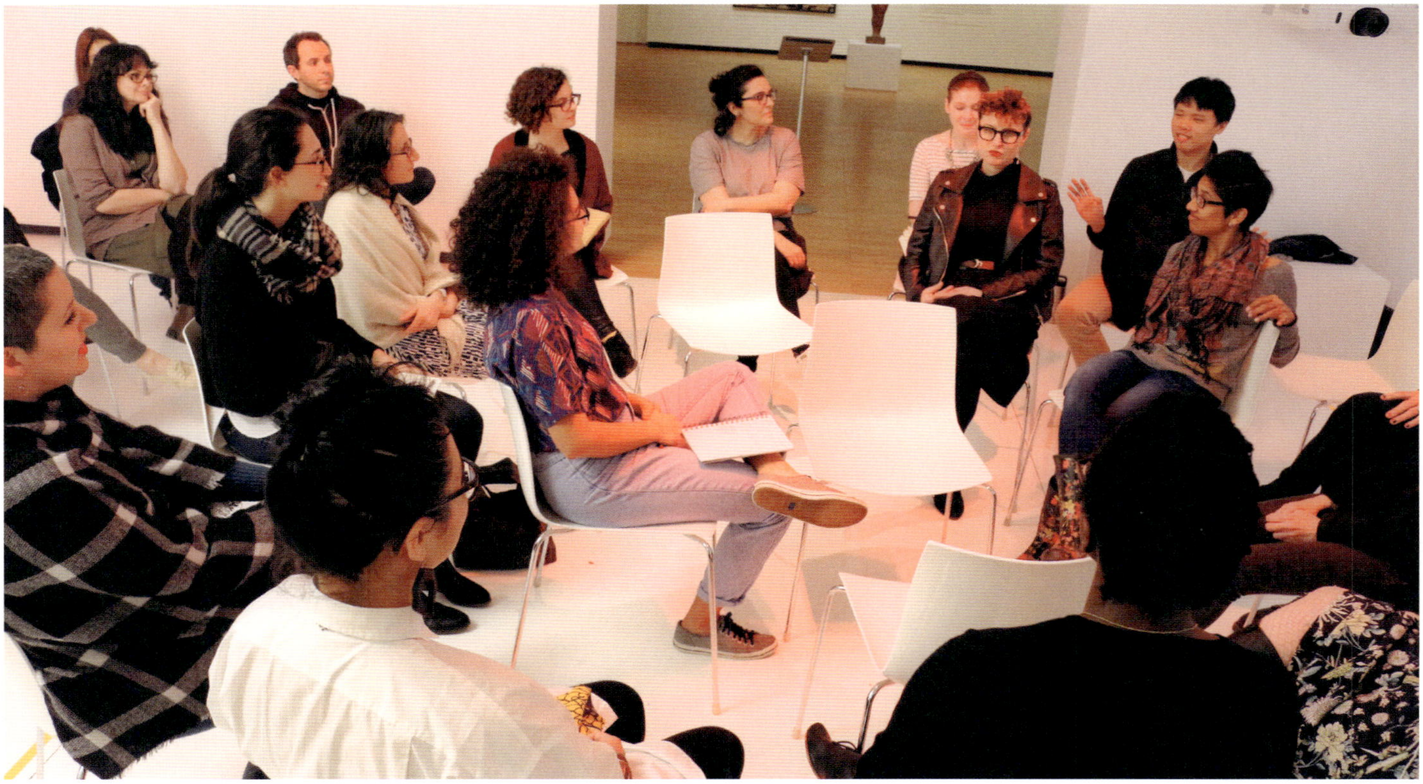

HERE + NOW

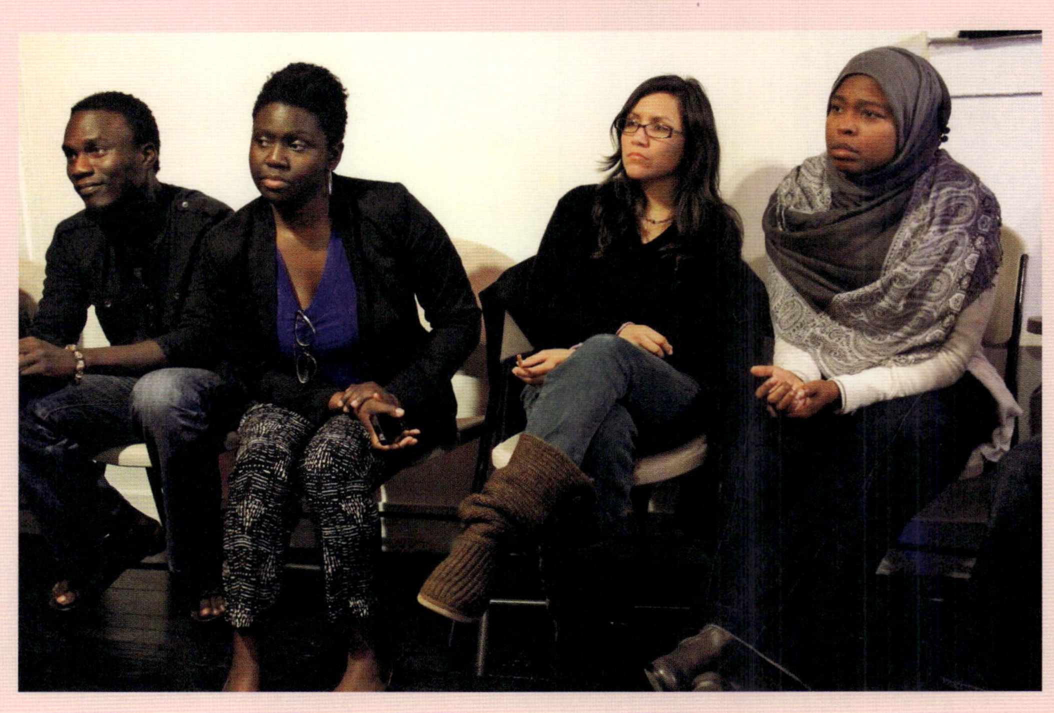

Pages 48–49: *Here + Now*, with Autumn Knight and Kelley Hershman.
Project Row Houses, Houston, January 19, 2013

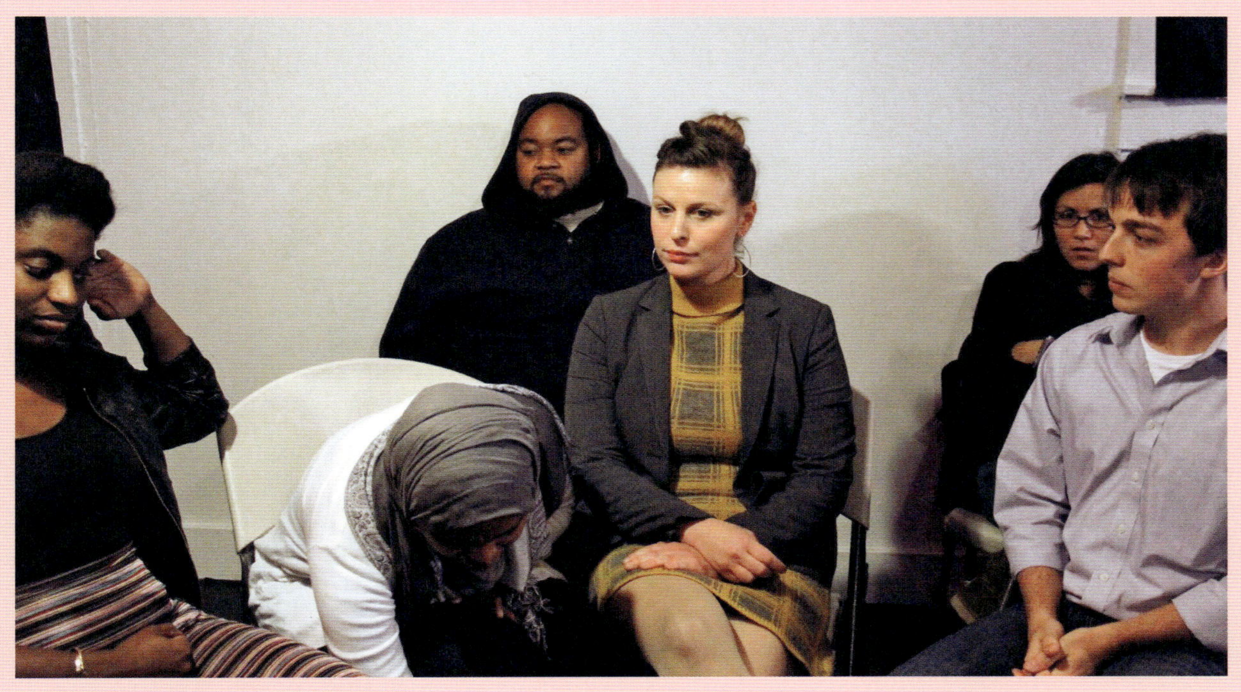

Sandra Ruiz

Crossing the Line:

The Here and Now of Race and Gender

and the Entanglements of Love

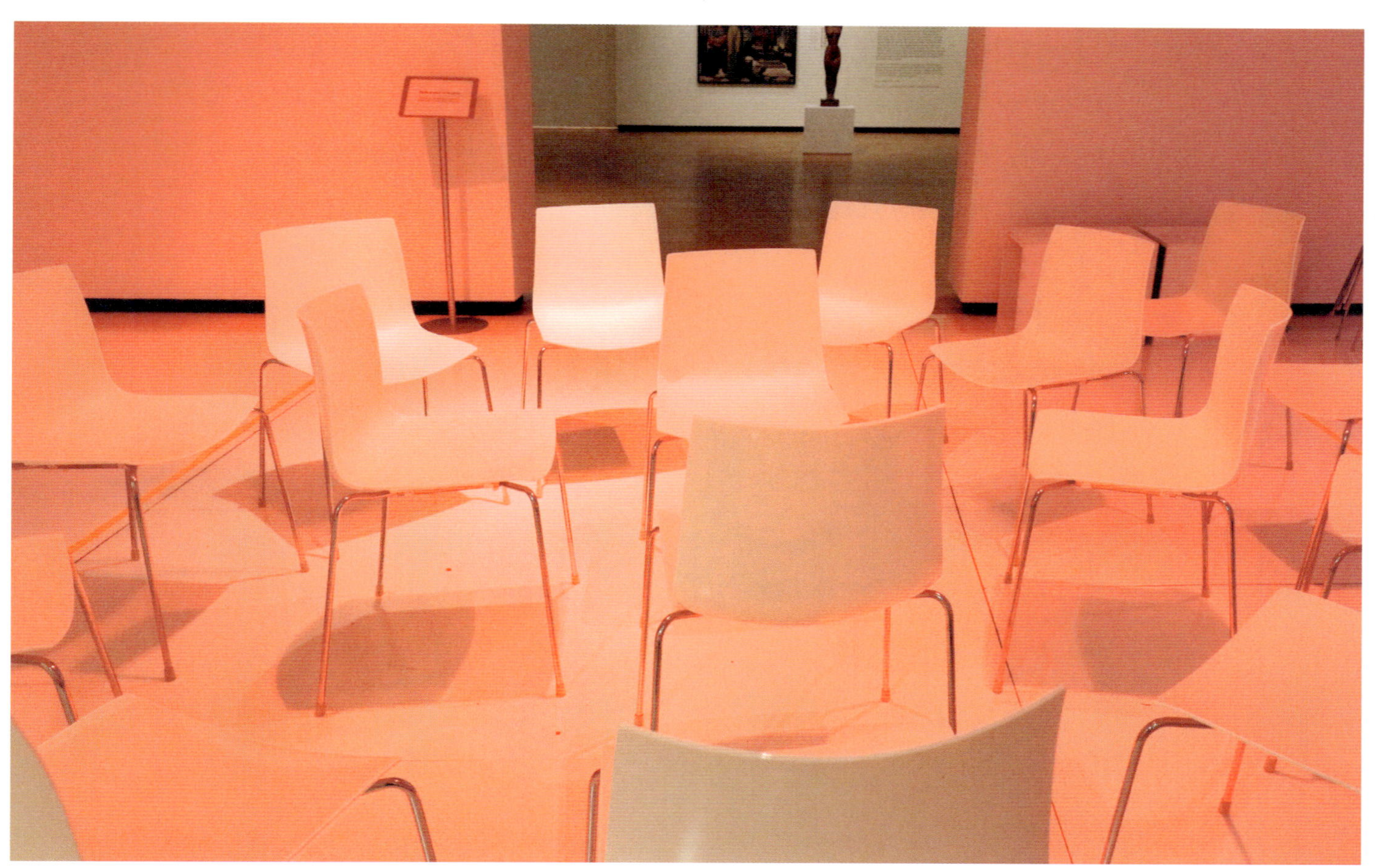

Installation view of *Here + Now*. Krannert Art Museum,
Champaign, March 30, 2017

in
Performance Art
and Pedagogy

How do we account for the unconscious properties of our flesh? That is, how do we negotiate the internal residue of race, gender, sexuality, and those power dynamics that mitigate difference in the space of any institution? What is being thought against our skin that isn't being said? And if the only signifiers that matter are the ones not being directly expressed, who do we become in this space of aesthetics, with and against our own feelings, alienations, and unspoken biases?

These questions sit at the apex of Autumn Knight's piece *Here + Now* (p. 40–49), performed on March 30, 2017 at Krannert Art Museum (KAM), alongside her co-director, New York psychotherapist Kelley Hershman, and under the curatorial guidance of Amy L. Powell. This evocative piece stages a vulnerable, uncomfortable, and even vexing encounter between our hidden feelings and overt behaviors. For Knight, racism, sexism, and xenophobia are as abundant and all-consuming as the white walls of the museum; and the audience, under her careful gaze, is slowly pushed to concede to their unconscious desires, distastes, and cultural aversions.

Pulling from both psychodynamic theory and experimental performance, *Here + Now* is a 150-minute piece divided into three segments: an introduction of the conceptual components of the work, a fishbowl format to study the group dynamic, and a reflective dialogue between the artist and participants. All three installments are temporally and spatially preplanned to mediate the audience's sense of comportment within a group. Following psychoanalyst Wilfred Bion's lead, Knight's social experiment provides insight into the properties of group behavior by delineating our unconscious processes. Like Bion, Knight shows how these processes are always functioning, oftentimes hijacking our sense of self and the social spaces we inhabit and share with others.[1] Firmly convinced that the audience, unknowingly, will take on certain roles within this group setting, Knight situates us in a narrow, elongated, rectangular gallery. This setting, along with the white chairs, walls, and floors, exacerbates the feeling of cultural tightness, or rather feeling emotionally incapable of easily moving in a space that is as long as our unconscious thoughts.

In *Here + Now*, students, activists, professors, art critics, and artists across markers of race, sex, gender, and authority set the scene: sixteen individuals sitting on white chairs, all trying to resolve how to be with one another or how to eventually become the desired group-as-whole. Throughout this performance, Knight and Hershman remind us *to be in the here and now*, to access those vestiges of our historical past which will inform the group and the individual, the singular within the collective. But unable to decode Knight's and Hershman's directions, the audience becomes impatient, frustrated, passive-aggressive with one another, creating a scene of uneasiness across speech and body. Some brave audience members dare to speak, but the gaps in between these moments are met with blaring silences,

Ruiz

reminding us that every word both said and unsaid is the genuine protagonist of this performance. Knight and Hershman sit among us; quietly and deliberately, they watch and wait to jump in, to manage us, like two directors observing their actors onstage from the audience. In this case, however, the audience lives in the space of the performance, creating a delicate distinction between spectator and performer. Every word they utter is planned. Every sentence we extend is reactionary, an unconscious spillage of confusion and anxiety that makes *Here + Now* feel like a drawn-out social experiment turned psychological thriller. Knight's performance exposes the breaks and openings between thinking and doing and knowing and telling, the desire to see and the dread of being unseen, the preoccupations of the participant and the painful casualties of the performance, the burden of race and the imposition of gender play, alongside the fragmentation of language across difference and space.

Knight's work is both performative and pedagogical. There's a lesson to be learned in her calculated instructions, and her practice is best served with a slice of reticent authority performed by this woman of color herself. In readjusting our perceptions of race, gender, and power within institutional sites, she highlights both the psychic and social dynamics that engender relationality and intrasubjective experience. Drawing from dance, psychology, theatre, and performance, with a keen investment in genealogy, Knight underscores how the production of knowledge occurs collectively among her audience members and incites change in their bodies through speech, movement, and unfiltered emotion. Knight uses both place and distinct temporal measures (to force us to be in the moment) to reorient our choreographies of subjectivity in institutions built on hegemonic foundations. Playing with the multiple layers of authority—that is, from gender and race as organizational domains, to the ideological operations of a cultural storehouse (KAM), to the theme of diversity itself as an institution built from intended symbols, myths, and thoughts—Knight discloses how institutions think and how the audience thinks with, alongside, and for them. While it appears that these institutions operate as amorphous entities, Knight in the spirit of Mary Douglas, here, reminds us that individuals conceive, construct, and regulate institutions; in fact, institutions are not forces existing outside of the subject, but rather contrived by them. For her, like Douglas, institutions of all kinds are always already exchanging thoughts and beliefs, informing each other's systems via the human itself.[2]

Particular to Knight's understanding of the human within the institution is the business of Blackness—how it both authorizes and denies her in a site with a long history of showcasing black bodies, not as speaking-knowing subjects, but as objects of display. Knight distorts our sense of "looking at black folk" by coopting the very protocols we follow to erase Blackness. Consequently, Knight refuses to hold our hand through our cultural indecencies. Unlike the Luther Vandross song, where he promises to love us faithfully in the here and now, in Knight's *Here + Now* the only promise she offers is the refusal to harbor our sentiments. Although we imagine it's her responsibility as a black woman to handle and amend our hidden fantasies, Knight rejects the call to any neat and classifiable affection. She is not interested in storing our fetid feelings; instead, she returns them to us, forcing the audience/participant to be accountable to their own unconscious fantasies, regardless of how racist, sexist, and violent they may be.

A Perilous Pedagogy:
The Love Class and Knight

The troubled relationship between modes of difference and the aesthetic domain centers Knight's pedagogical performance. As a performance studies and ethnic studies scholar, this centers my pedagogical-as-ideological positions, too. During Knight's solo exhibition at KAM, I was scheduled to teach an advanced honors seminar for undergraduate English majors. I chose to focus on a version of love, or what I called "A Lover's Discourse: Literature, Theory, and Performance." Following in the footsteps of literary theorist and philosopher Roland Barthes and feminist and queer-of-color and anti-colonial theorists, I promised to tell the truth about love, whether it be unrequited, painfully real, or a symptom of fantasy, and turned to performance art to discuss the politics of intimacy, relying heavily on experimental aesthetics.[3] In order to expose my students to live performance, I joined forces with KAM and Autumn Knight and, in working closely with both, the course set out to answer the following questions: What's required to love another, or "an other," across difference? How do race, gender, sexuality, and authority alter expressions of affection, care, and even love? What happens when these very forms of difference trouble love and engender unconscious entanglements that hurt as much as they heal?

But mostly, how do we work out the unconscious affectations of this elusive term "love," especially as it plays out in the space of aesthetics, both in the classroom and in the museum? And why place Knight's equally challenging and compelling work in direct conversation with love? One would not necessarily call Knight's work, at least not *Here + Now*, an expression of kind affection toward the audience. The performance is emotionally taxing, oftentimes leaving the audience to handle an accumulation of ugly feelings that linger against the collective as well as one's individual skin. *Here + Now* is a heightened whirlwind of emotion that one commits to without knowing entirely the effects of such intensity. But this is Knight's political, pedagogical, and aesthetic plan: to make us liable to our own disaffections in the here and now and again in the then and there.

Playing alongside Knight, but on my own pedagogical stage, I purposely failed to tell my class the truth about love—that is, from the Hollywood version of romantic intimacy to religion's supremely abstract love of a higher power. Instead, we began to repeatedly ask ourselves, What's love really got to do with it? The *it* morphed into all of the messy, prickly, and even violent moments found within art, literature, and performance. In true psychodynamic form, our feelings, uncensored thoughts, and affections entered the spotlight as we engaged with uncomfortable performance art—Knight's work, alongside that of artists Franko B., Ana Mendieta, Ron Athey, Félix González-Torres, Adrian Piper,

and Papo Colo. Aside from viewing difficult performances, the students were asked to use Barthes's book as a guidepost when theorizing alongside thinkers such as Frantz Fanon, Lauren Berlant, Eve Kosofsky Sedgwick, José Esteban Muñoz, Jennifer Doyle, Pedro Pietri, Audre Lorde, and bell hooks. These authors framed our perception of love, making the students ask: "Where's the love in these readings? They are filled with violence, pain, suffering, and negative feelings, but how are these readings about love?"

But this word "love" was just a portal to arrive at something more imperative: those transformative moments that would amend our group dynamic, subsequent social interactions, and understanding of psychic life within our own perilous times. Love was another word for radicalism, race, women of color, protest, queers, the experimental. To arrive at this place, I engaged in several unorthodox measures as a "director" and deliberately crossed the pedagogical line, while also letting them know each time I was doing so. Having only four students in the class—all women—made the following practices easier, but also more emotionally intense, as we began to be both a mirror and mask for each other. What type of institutional redesign was I establishing by telling them that all this

Performance score for *Autumn Knight: In Rehearsal*, with S. Bianca Bailey. Krannert Art Museum, Champaign, February 23, 2017

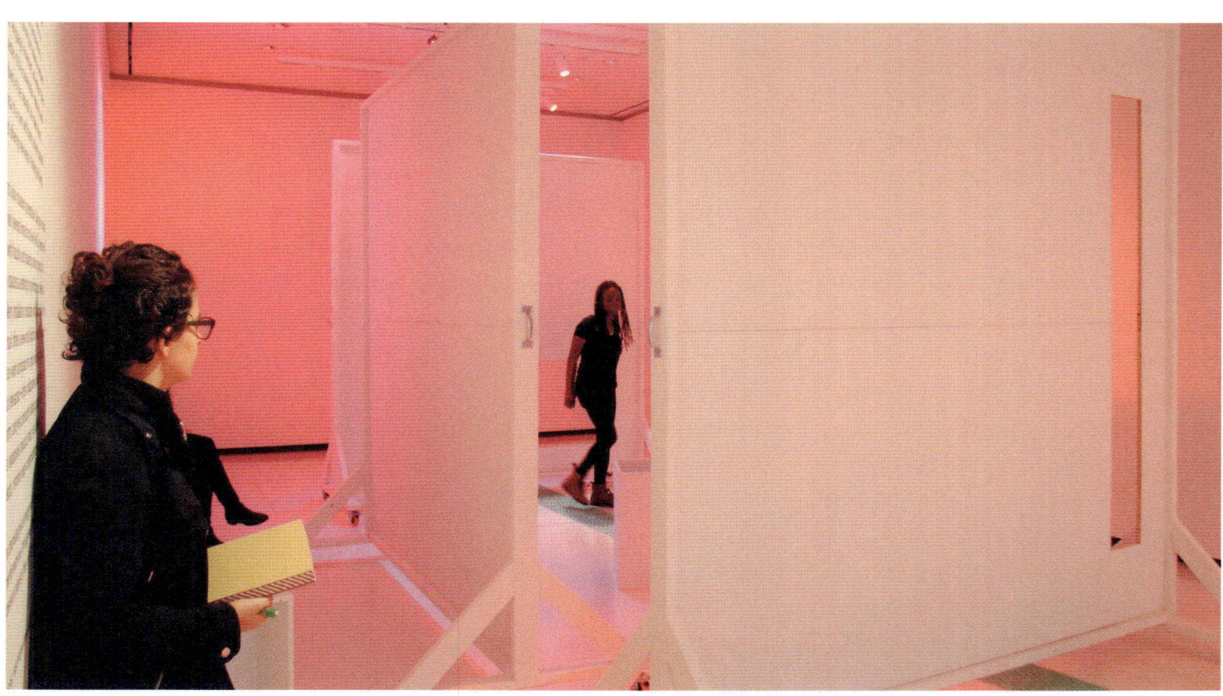

Ruiz

complicated and interlaced thinking and doing was in the name of love?

Like Knight, I crafted my own data analysis. I accelerated intimacy within the group through gift-giving, and I recorded their affective responses to each object. Each student received one present during each class session: each gift corresponded to the course reading, with the personalization of each present increasing throughout the semester. During one week they received monogrammed mugs, shortly after I decided to shorten their first names to just a letter, a designation of intimacy founded on informed consent. They looked forward to receiving a gift each week, often taking photos of each present, logging the progression of objects throughout the semester. Each week I also advanced experiential learning through food and drink: I made tea and coffee, set the table with cookies as if we were in a cafe, used astrological knowledge to create attachment, learned of their popular culture likes and dislikes, and wrote them long, intellectual, and personalized emails and cards. As I watched them "let me" cross the line, I took my own notes on their behavior every class period, watching to see when I could cross it again through a performance object, and when they, too, would start to model my behavior and create their own intimate bonds within the group.

Although created with affection, the course assignments confused them, but helped them build solidarity with one another, and with theory, too. For their midterm assignment they were asked to write a long, performative love letter to one of the performance artists or a character from a piece of literature or a theorist that we covered in class. They were also required to carry around a meditation on love sketchbook/notebook in which they had to diagram, write, or draw out their ideas on topics discussed during class and performances. This was meant to require no premeditation, but to be used at any time and place. For their final exam, instead of writing an essay, students had to verbally show, in a thirty-minute lecture, how the "love notebooks" helped them build a virtual site on the topic of love and theory in performance. The more bewildered they became, the more I distorted their sense of reality, not as an act of disciplinary power, but as an exercise in group-sharing in the space of uncomfortable aesthetics. They relied on one another to get through the moments of spontaneity and improvisation, consequently becoming a unit outside of me: they created a group text message, shared personal emails and notes, shared food and packed lunches for one another, visited the museum and artists' lectures together. Class never ended on time; at times our two-hour class lasted between four and six hours, and not because this extra labor would result in a better grade, for they were all guaranteed a high grade if they merely committed to the course aims. This sense of distortion made them extremely prepared for class; at times they did extra research for a class session. Moreover, it left them open to exploring bold and complicated theory, art, and difference across race, gender, and sexuality.

Yet, this thing called love still internally disorganized them, and so I decided to cross the line further by disrupting their sense of space. Knowing that space carries its own set of social characteristics, I wondered how different sites might alter their own sense of self and make them intimately accountable to the material being learned. I taught a play set in a bathroom, in my departmental bathroom—all five of us locked into the tightest of spaces as we read lines from the text and discussed the most abject of topics: rape, feces, off-color-humor, gender violence, racial poverty. While the bathroom was certainly the most unusual place we held class, I often changed our class space to disorient them in time and authority: my office, a museum hallway, a waiting room, the departmental library, my faculty lounge, and the building's kitchen. This level of spontaneity left them always a bit anxious but, as one student explained, certainly prepared for class, and often excited by thinking itself. There was enough trust between us, and it intensified as the weeks passed: as a group dynamic materialized, powerful feelings were discharged in the space of learning. Enacting a similar aesthetic as Knight, but in the classroom, I created ambitious and difficult acts and scenes in which the intellectualization of feelings, and the emotions of theory and art, enabled a group dynamic equally invested and inclined to be internally transformed. If Knight could turn us into performers and observe our unconscious desires overflow from our very own bodies, I could certainly follow her lead in the classroom by showing how feeling is never divorced from the space of learning, especially when teaching performance art.

Pedagogy's Here and Now: The Entrapment of Feeling

Interested in what the psychotherapeutic scene can tell us about how one learns, I began this group experiment knowing that the classroom is a transformative site, whereby the psychic and social qualities of all subjects are reconstituted intimately. Following in the traditions of psychoanalysis and pedagogy theory, I explore how the unconscious thoughts and behaviors of individuals are internally *moved together*

Crossing the Line

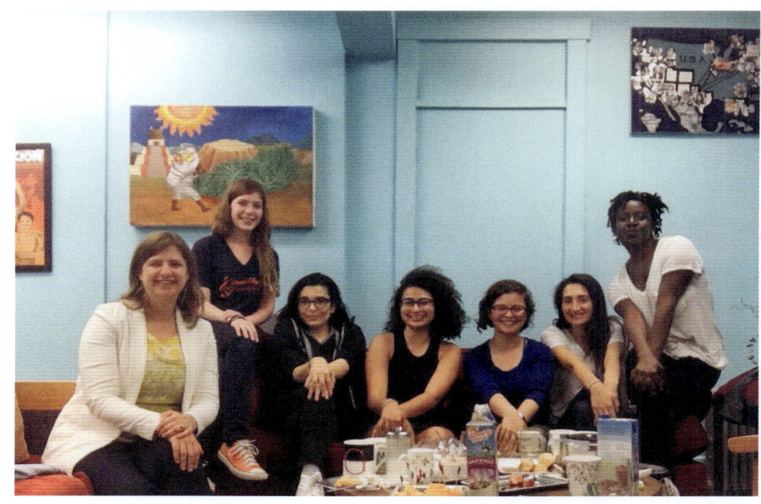

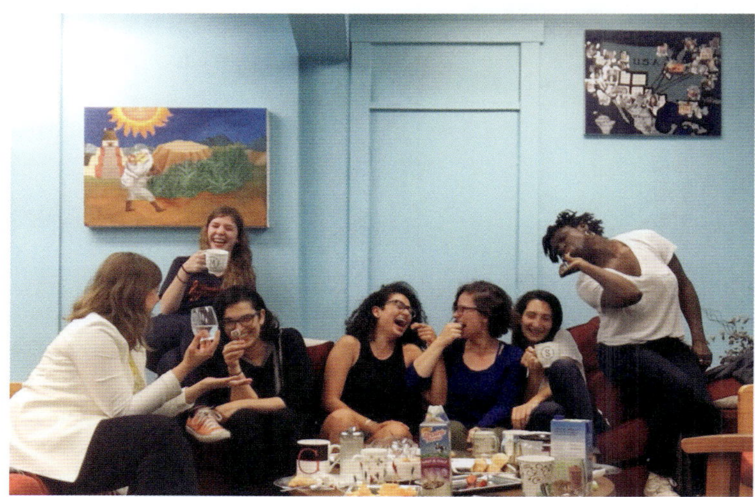

Sandra Ruiz's Spring 2017 class, "A Lover's Discourse: Literature, Theory, and Performance," with Amy L. Powell, M, Sandra Ruiz, G, H, S, and Autumn Knight, University of Illinois Department of Latina/Latino Studies

in the very face of their own discoveries and alienations. The group dynamic of the classroom teaches us about the processes of our unconscious flesh in sites of complication and difference. Pedagogy, here, is not just about teaching, or about the professor who professes, but how one expresses love, desire, compassion into an intimate life of thinking, feeling, learning, and becoming, in a dynamic act of methexis.

Following the insights of feminist, queer-of-color, and therapeutic models for understanding what binds a class, I see performance as central to challenging the construction of the collective. Throughout the semester, moments of transference and countertransference, projection, disidentification, projective identification, and introjection operated as valuable exercises in pedagogy, ultimately amending the properties needed to keep teaching and learning altogether. But to be *moved together* via these intimate psychic states is laborious and emotionally dangerous. It all begins from a performative utterance filled with uneasiness, for teaching is littered with a range of emotions, some never revealed and others committed to print.

José Esteban Muñoz commits to a pedagogical call of his own desires in "Teaching, Minoritarian Knowledge, and Love," whereby he declares in true Austinian form: "I love my students."[4] Following the performative utterance with his own uncomfortable feelings about love and teaching he states: "Now this statement is difficult to enunciate. When I produce such an utterance I feel a force field of

Ruiz

prohibitions flare up...talking about love and teaching should not make me so uneasy. But it does."[5] For Muñoz, love, pedagogy, and a "commitment to teaching theory" is not without its shortcomings. In staging his "theory of minoritarian pedagogy," he "owns failure" as "the process of teaching" that is filled with emotional and discursive misfires. Muñoz sees this, however, in line with performativity's ability to disclose the unconscious fantasies of language. In his formulation of pedagogy, desire sits at the pinnacle of learning, not as a placeholder for transference, but what Muñoz sees as the potential in "the counter-transferential aspects of teaching"—or how "the production of knowledge and, more specifically, the production of desire for knowledge" functions relationally.[6] In translating traditional constructions of transference, he declares his own pedagogical admission: "To perform such an avowal is to show the seams that call attention to one's teaching, to use Lacan's phrasing 'The here and now.'"[7] In trying to distill "pedagogy's here and now" he continues to unveil the conditions of his love—that is, the moments he will undoubtedly fail, feel things "unnatural" to the objective space of teaching, such as fear, abandonment, loss, and his own social and intellectual inadequacies. If love is a radical pedagogical practice, an analytic that works against oppression as a powerful social dynamic advanced through new ways of belonging within and against institutions, then love is often everything we can't yet *say* but *do* anyhow, through failure.

This theory's praxis would be put to the test when Knight's *Here + Now* forced us all to be eternally present. After Knight's performance, the class experienced a transformative moment that altered our group dynamic drastically. Knight, as she endured the audience for almost three hours, knew we'd all eventually unearth our deepest desires and social roles. I made the "mistake" of forcing my students to take their love notebooks and pens to the interactive performance. I, like Muñoz describes, committed a misfire.[8] In the middle of Knight's experiment she powerfully said: "Some people in this audience are violent, they come bearing weapons like pens, they are spies writing down everything, and wanting to be in control." My students' shoulders were hunched over in that affective pose that Sedgwick calls shame, but they still refused to put down their pens. I called out: "It's my fault. I asked them to take notes. Class, please put your pens down now." Another audience member shouted: "Why should they have to?" I replied: "Because it's Knight's performance and she wants them to. Put. Them down. NOW." They put down their pens. Knight then shouted: "Control regained, finally." A sense of shame, guilt, and

humiliation filled the room, mostly on my end, when I realized that I had taken up a tremendous amount of space from the artist, another woman of color.

Later, over drinks, Knight shared that I didn't really make a mistake; my unconscious inclination to be in control as a teacher made the decision. But I had not learned the lesson in the business of Blackness in *our* here and now. I had not learned to subvert the ideological function of the institution; instead I was the institution's other diversity laborer, filling white space in assumed sites and roles of exception. In doing so, I refused Knight's pedagogical lesson in my own act of authority, in an institution that relies on this type of interplay between women of color, that is, to continue being able to see us as visible/invisible objects of display.

My students, however, saw this as an act of love on my part. They felt shamed by Knight, but uplifted by their teacher. Knight's work became the perfect foundation by which to explore the precarious tensions existing between the performer and audience, and teacher and pupil. As one student expressed in our class exit interview: "I expected Autumn Knight to be on my side, you know, from a visible woman of color to another, and she wasn't. Knight let me down. I didn't feel safe." She went on to share: "I expect a certain type of labor from her because she is a black woman. I know this is wrong, but I have higher expectations for women of color as a woman of color; I want them to protect me." This, here, is the sticky residue of Knight's brilliant work alongside Muñoz's understanding of *pedagogy's here and now*. But how do we enact "an ethic of love" that responsibly protects us in the face of oppression and authority?[9] I see this performance of love as an act of radical pedagogy or, as bell hooks sees it, a practice that leads one to the fundamental scene of freedom. In this performative act of loving, its gaps, negations, and entanglements, we find the domain by which to move into an altogether different being simultaneously. Knight's refusal to free my student of her fetid feelings in the moment is central to challenging the emotional labor constantly required of women of color. These scenes of love and disavowal are always interlaced and played off and against one another at all times.

Performing Closure:
The Genealogical Turn
A few weeks after *Here + Now*, Knight and Powell attended our class for four hours, and all four students greeted them with gifts, cards, food, tea, and affection, mirroring my own behavior throughout the semester. Even with these gestures of kindness, we were, however, still harboring complicated

Crossing the Line

feelings about the performance and performer. One student saw this as her opportunity to get "closure" from Knight, to ask Knight what she really wanted from us as audience members. Openly and generously, Knight answered our questions, eventually disclosing the intimate interconnection between pedagogy, performance, politics, and genealogy—a connection that helped me rethink *Here + Now*. Pedagogy, while it is an act of performativity for Knight, is also an enactment of genealogy—one beautifully tied to and complicated by our intellectual-as-familial inheritances. Throughout her visit and even during the dialogue portion of her performance, Knight returned to her memories of being a pupil, or rather the deep bond she still shares with her mentor, Dr. Mary McRae. As she spoke with us, Mary's name often materialized, and unconsciously Knight, too, revealed her own affiliations with learning, mentorship, and love. My students felt intimately included in these moments, I think, as if Knight's feelings were *now* their feelings—or perhaps through time, I, too, could "belong" to them in a similar way. I understood their ambition and longing as a productive moment in the "counter-transferential aspects of teaching" and learning, precisely because I, too, once had my own version of a Mary.

Through theory and aesthetics, these young women began to notice the interwoven thread of mentors and mentees, performance and pedagogy as indistinct acts of affection and thinking. I saw Knight in this thread and wondered if she saw me, too—if we could really see each other against the backdrop of the institution and its call for an authentic act of diversity. Or if I had finally learned the lesson Mary once taught Knight: "Know their shit and know your shit."

But how do we learn to identify the line between shit? If we are called upon to attend to the residue of negation that often accompanies those moments of deep care, how then do we properly enact that love ethic? How do we make the "counter-transferential" a productive act in the domains of performing, teaching, and learning? How do we achieve the performative call to love our students in sites that often break them first? That same student who felt neglected by Knight shared in her exit interview that even though I may have loved her, I, like Knight, failed her.

> I had all of these ugly feelings I was working with throughout your class. I wanted to feel the most special in your class. I wanted to be cared for more than my peers. These feelings would not go away. I did not want to have them, but I did.

> I wanted you and Knight to be gentler with me because I am a woman of color, too. I needed more tenderness.

As the above words express, our unconscious feelings are interwoven into this genealogical thread, whether or not we consciously admit to such binds. At this level of identification, it didn't really matter if Knight and I think we actually failed her; her sense of failure worked in tandem with the complicated tenors of love, deep affection, and care that are always ameliorated by the institution. Importantly, her harbored feelings were now ours, regardless of where we choose to house them, and how we draw the line between different forms of shit. Still, they are singularly her feelings, while also locked into the collective sentiment and labor produced by women of color, always working for and outside the institutional domain. Sometimes their shit becomes ours, and oftentimes ours is never theirs, but in drawing the line, and even crossing it, we uncover how powerful it can be to be moved together in the space of aesthetic production.

Through the complexity of love, we locate the meeting place of a chosen aesthetic practice and pedagogy as a political line of thought—a force that surpasses temporal and spatial protocol by highlighting our very own alienations and biases. I understand that this is a type of perilous pedagogy, but during dangerous times we have to be a bit more promiscuous in our travels. The aesthetic, as Knight shows, is the perfect domain in which to unearth the spillage of unconscious desire, even in the site and citation of our own flesh.

1   Wilfred Bion, *Experiences in Groups and Other Papers* (Routledge: London & New York, 1961).

2   Mary Douglas, *How Institutions Think* (Syracuse: Syracuse University Press, 1986).

3   Roland Barthes, *A Lover's Discourse: Fragments* (New York: Hill and Wang, 2010).

4   José Esteban Muñoz, "Teaching, Minoritarian Knowledge, and Love," *Women and Performance: a journal of feminist theory*, 14:2 (2005): 118. When I use the phrase "in true Austinian form," I am referring to the British philosopher J. L. Austin's book *How To Do Things with Words* (1955, 1975), that Muñoz refers to throughout his essay, specifically in direct use of Shoshana Felman's *The Scandal of the Speaking Body: Don Juan with J. L. Austin, or Seduction in Two Languages* (Redwood City, CA: Stanford University Press, 2002).

5   Muñoz, 118.

6   Muñoz, 119.

7   Ibid.

8   Muñoz, 119–120.

9   By "an ethic of love," I am referring to bell hooks's work in "Love as a Practice of Freedom" in *Outlaw Culture: Resisting Representations* (New York: Routledge, 1994), 289. For hooks, one makes the decision to love and to see that our lives are indeed intimately connected. In this way, love is not merely a feeling, but a way of doing. Awakening to this kind of love, she argues, "can happen only as we let go of our obsession with power and domination." She adds: "We are often seduced, in one way or the other, into continued allegiance to systems of domination—imperialism, sexism, racism, classism." The way out of this for her is through love as a practice of freedom.

                    Crossing the Line

LAMENT

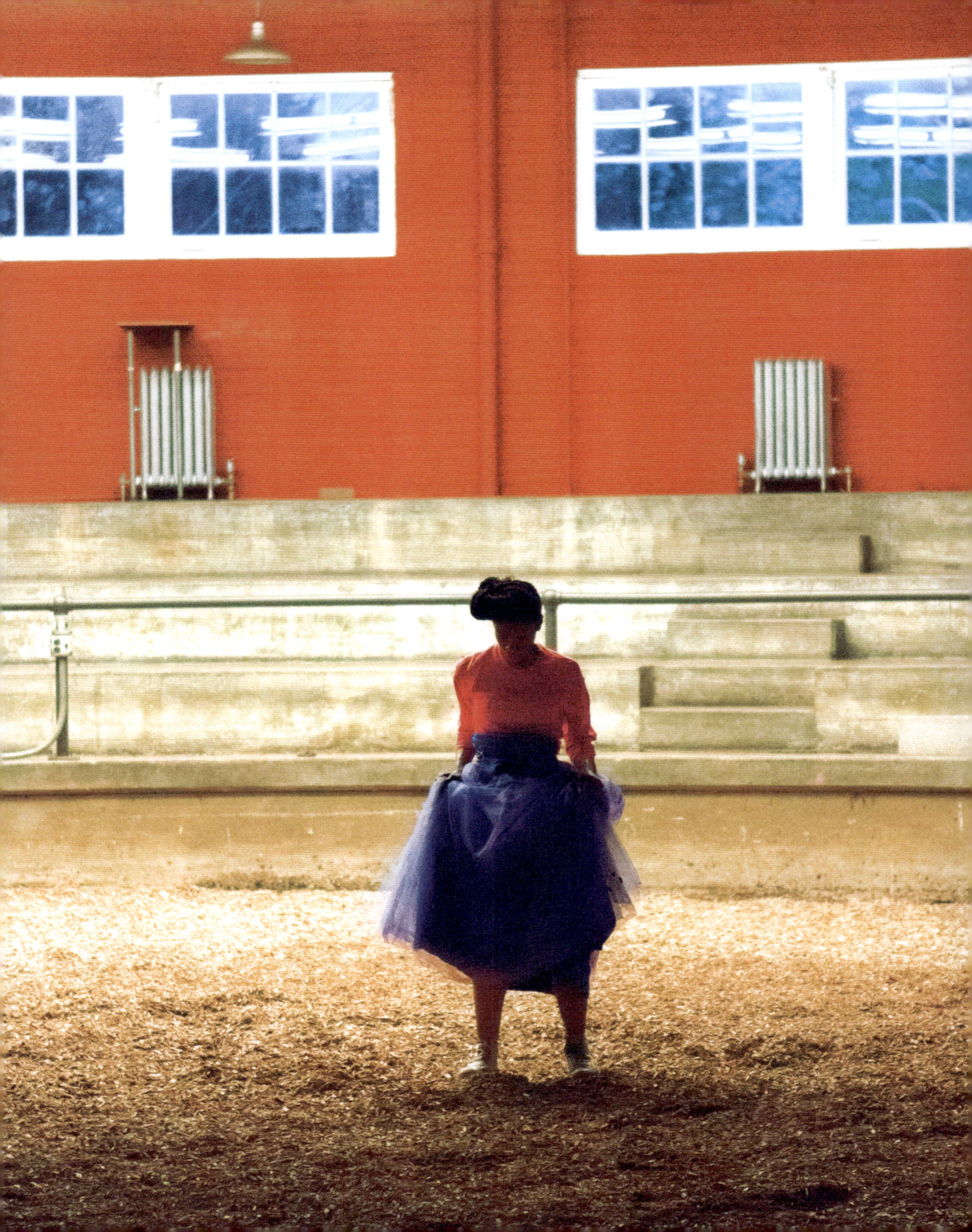

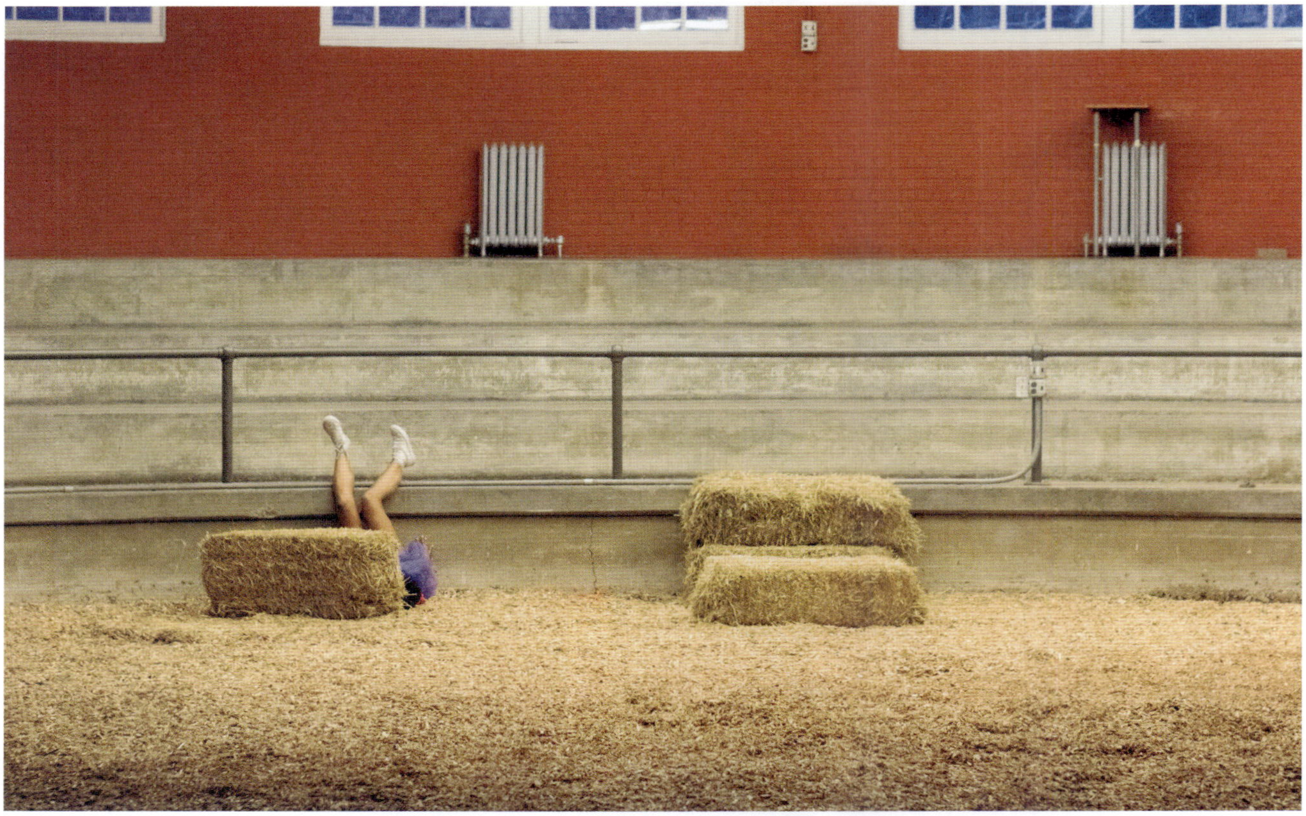

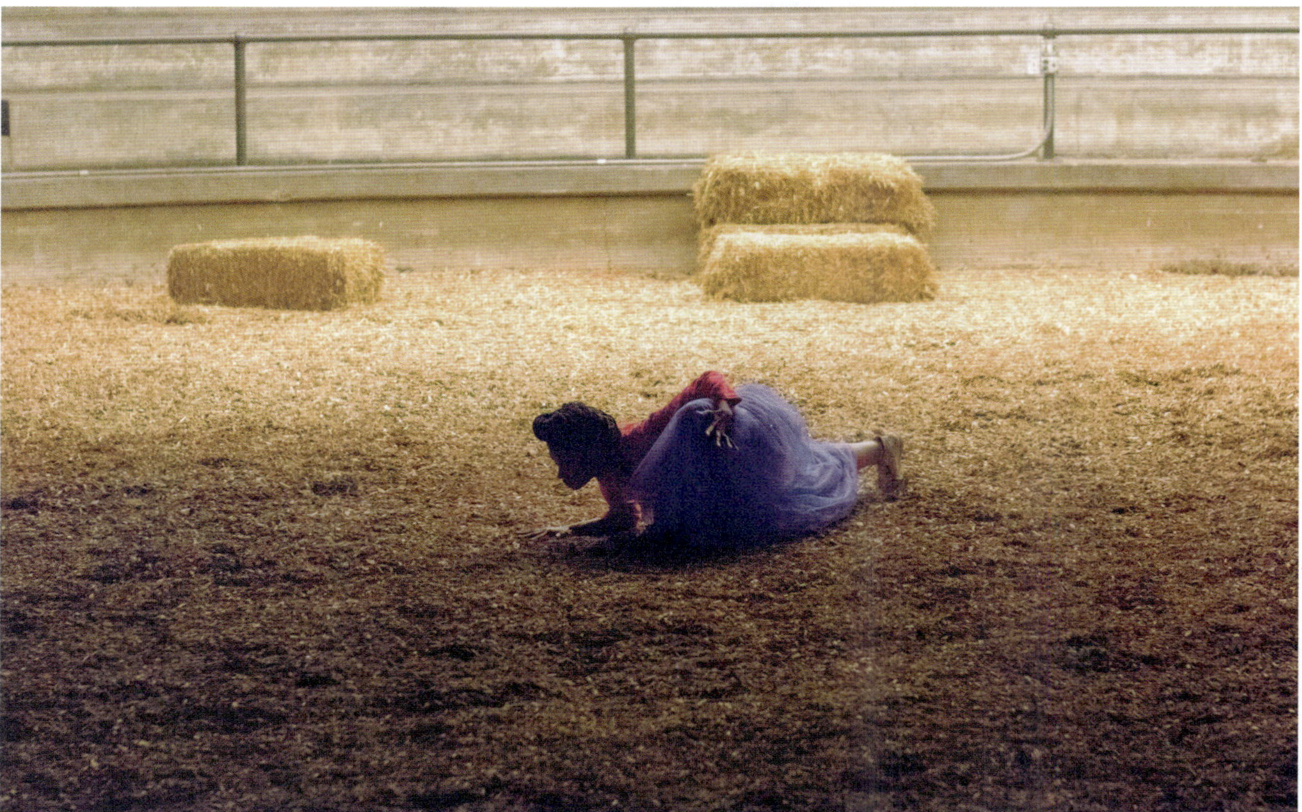

Pages 61–66: *Lament*, with Abijan Johnson. University of Illinois Stock Pavilion, Urbana, April 13, 2017

Lament (2012—present) is a performance for a solo dancer
and choreographed by Knight. The work proposes specific
movements that are coded with addiction, class, and
mental illness while also contemplating various laments
in music and popular culture.

SOUNDTRACK

"Bam Bam"
Sister Nancy

"Targeting Women"
Angela Davis (from *The Prison Industrial Complex*)

Lamentations, 'Black/Folk Song Suite':
III. Calvary Ostinato (quarter note = 80-88)
Performed by Tahirah Whittington
Composed by Coleridge-Taylor Perkinson

"Lament"
Trepverter

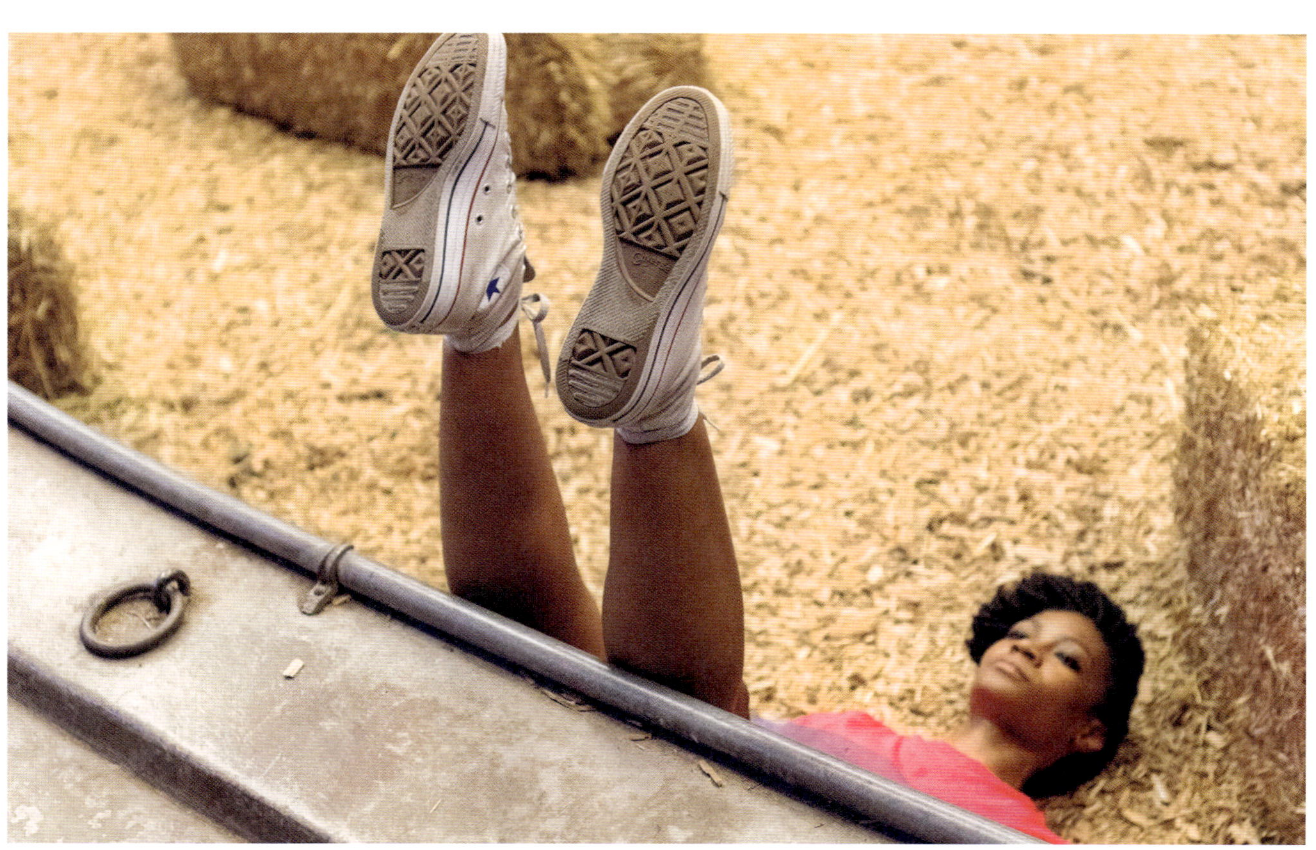

                    LAMENT

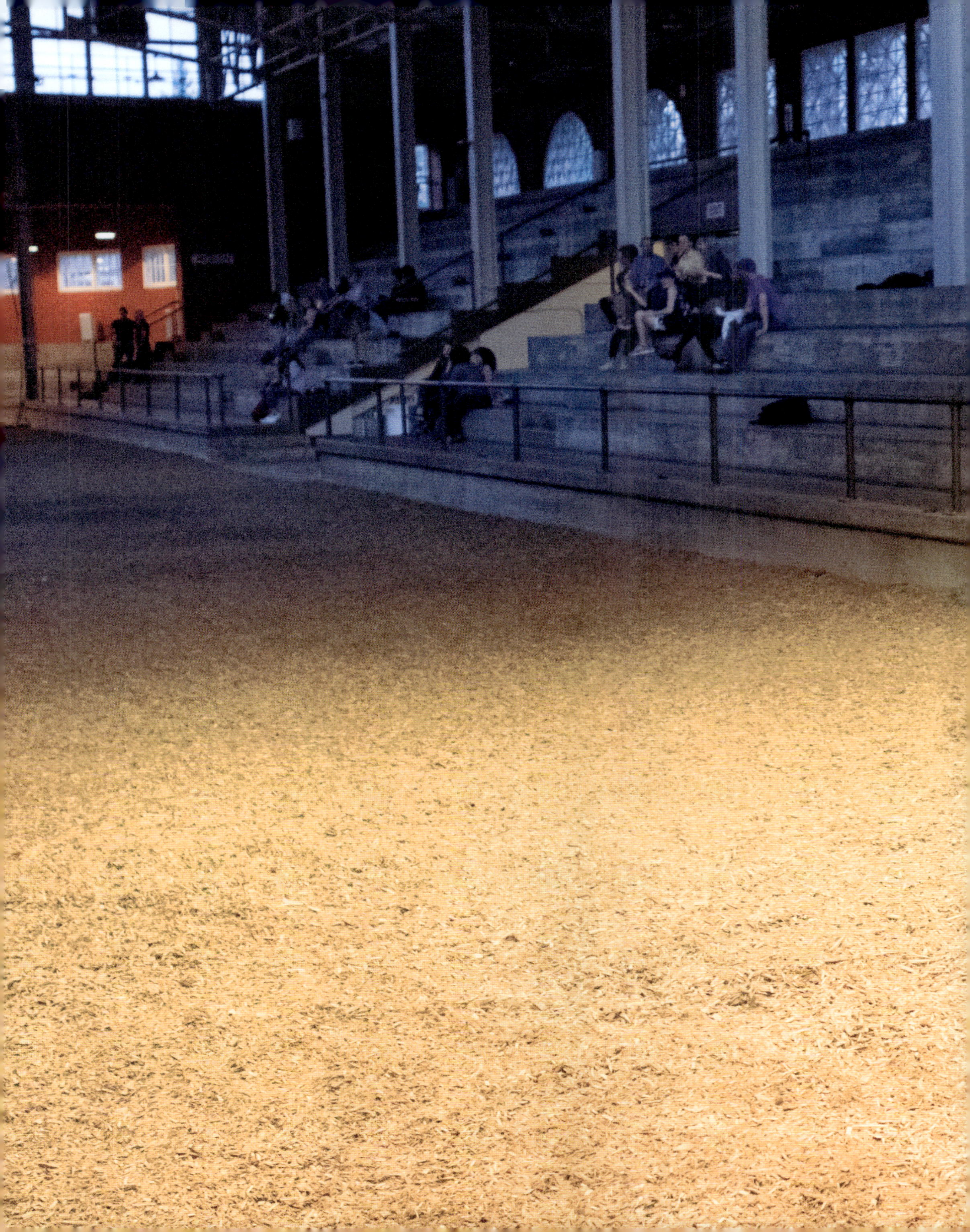

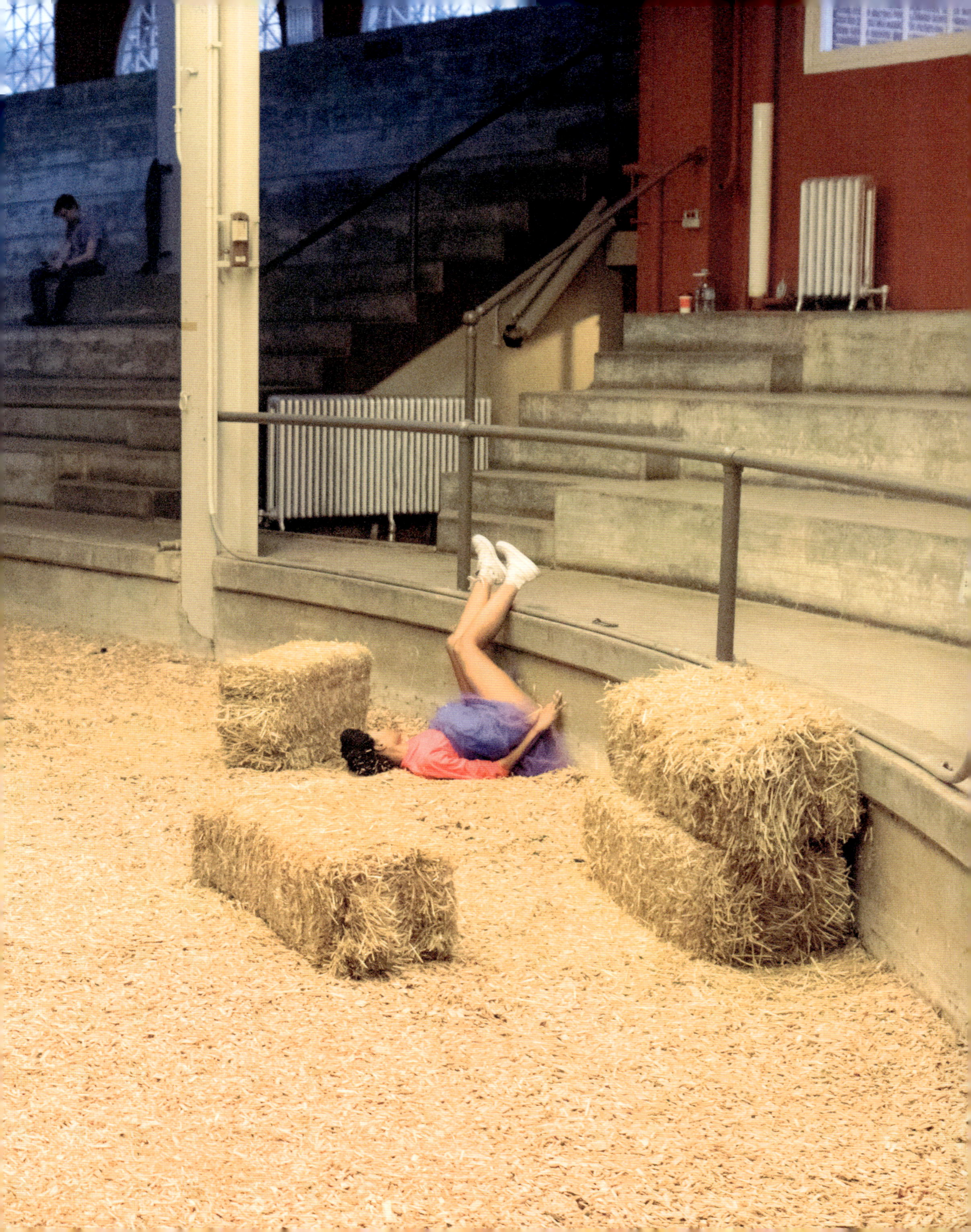

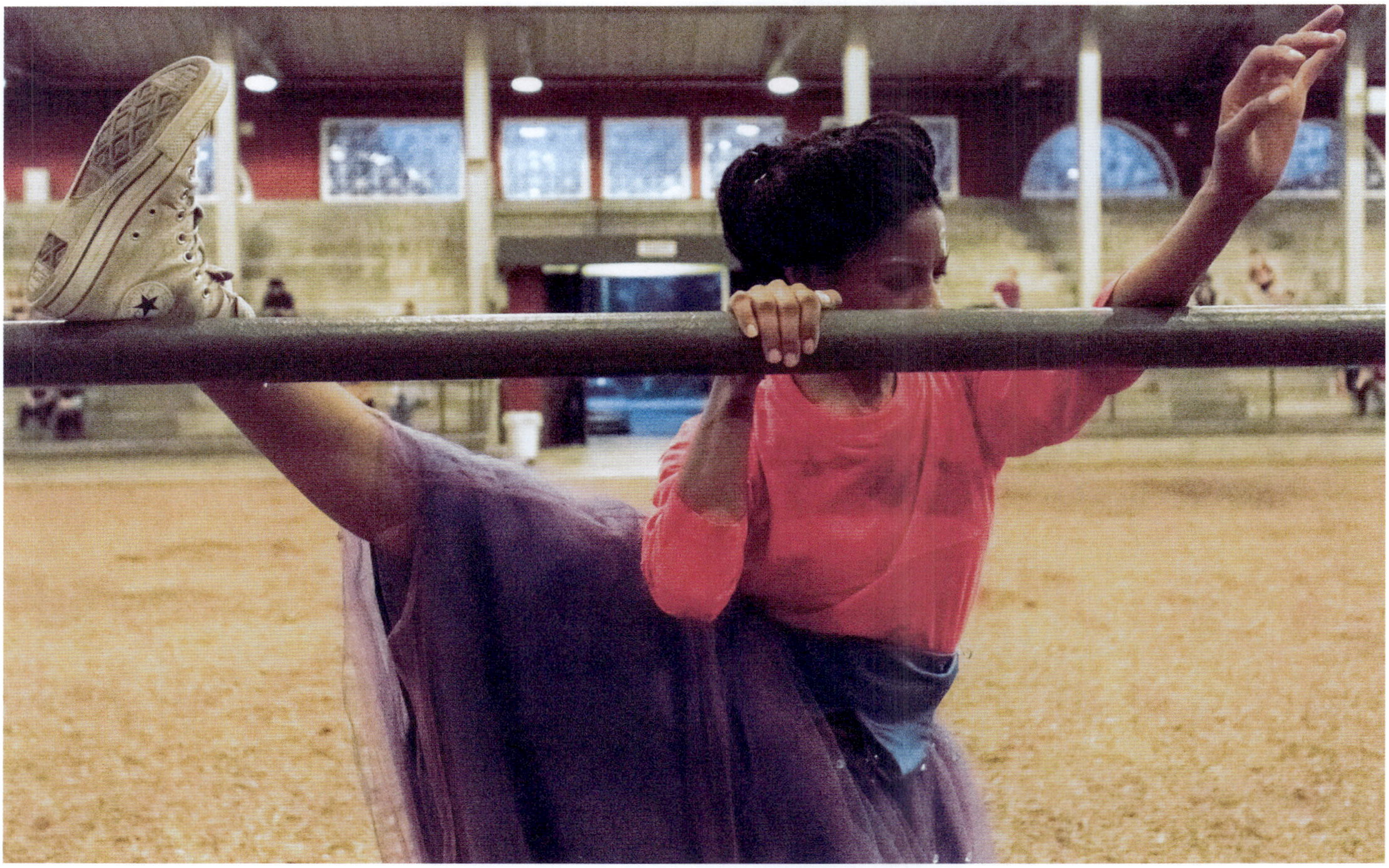

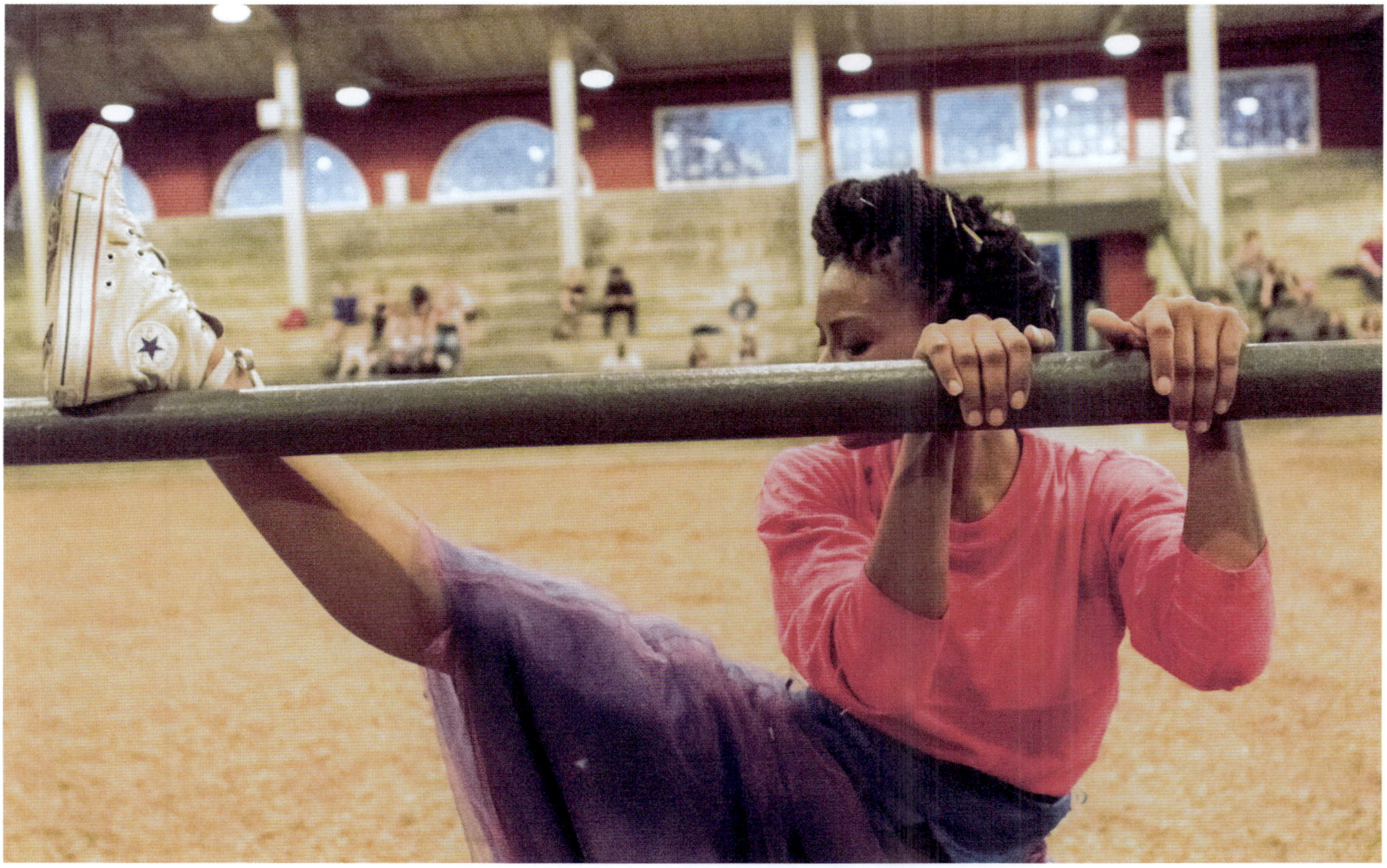

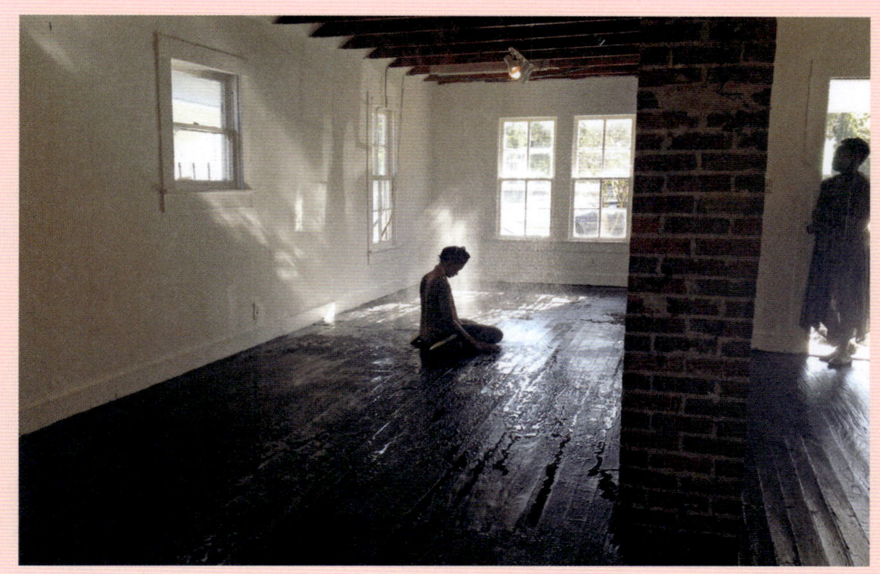

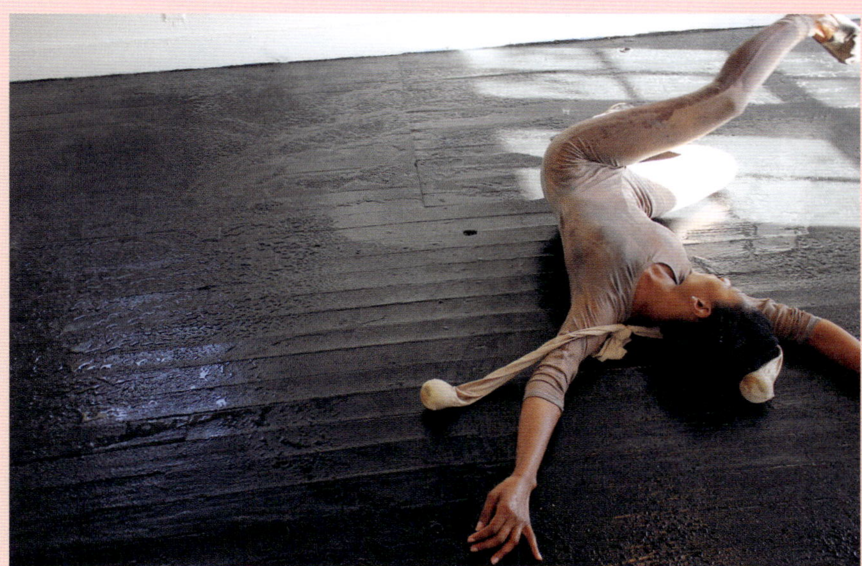

Lament, with Abijan Johnson. Project Row Houses,
Houston, November 4, 2012

Jennifer Doyle

Host
Institution

Video still from *Lament*, with Abijan Johnson, 2017.
Digital video (color, sound), 22 minutes

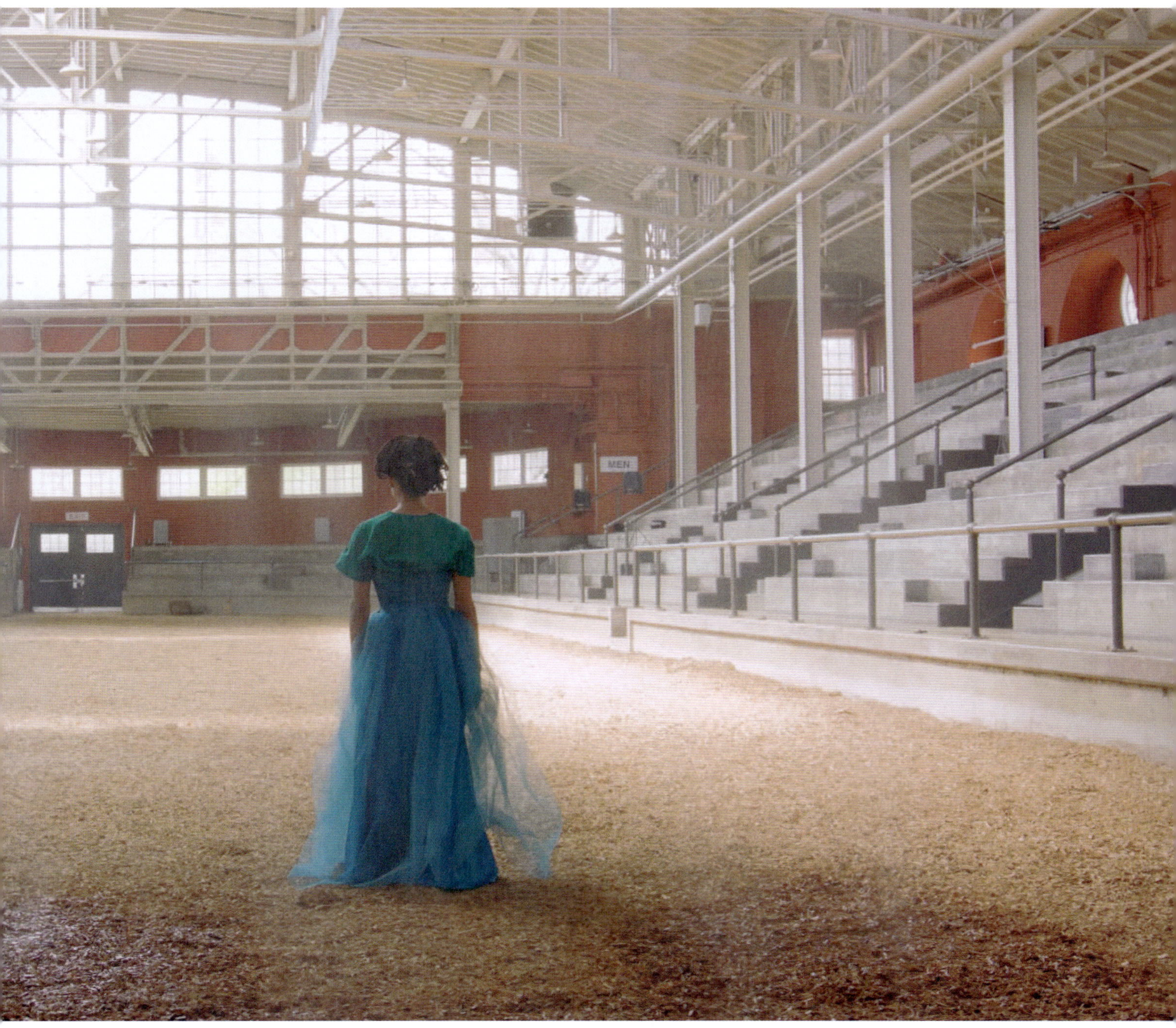

Autumn Knight confronts the institution as a specific kind of material. It is, in her work, a psychic and a physical structure. It is, in her work, exactly what it is in our lives. It is an idea, a set of mythologies, a culture. It has a reproduction system and a life. It is a force which moves through us.

Ambivalent philosophical engagement with institutional structures have a long history in black feminist thought in the United States; the function of the school as an instrument of individual and social transformation is of painful importance in a post-apartheid, post-slavery nation which, for large swaths of time, criminalized black literacy. In the wake of histories of enslavement and segregation, the specific forms of sexual/symbolic abjection foisted on black women have left black women in the here and now with overdetermined forms of obligation—the obligation, in particular, to instruct. Knight's work confronts this scenario. Rather than take as her subject, as what her work is about, the implicit assumption that women of color will operate as some kind of ideological nurse for the world—she takes it as her material. Before turning to *Lament* (p. 60–67), Knight's performance that is the focus of this essay, let us consider the symbolic load carried by the encounter between black teachers and students within the space of a school formed with the explicit aim of drawing black life into institutional economies.

When the reader first meets Helga Crane, the melancholic heroine of Nella Larsen's 1928 novel *Quicksand*, Helga is mustering up the energy to quit her job. She is teaching at Naxos, a southern school for black children (loosely modeled after the Tuskegee Institute). She had developed a "deep hatred for the trivial hypocrisies and careless cruelties which were, unintentionally, perhaps, a part of the Naxos policy of uplift."[1] She bristled at her role within the institution, a school that transferred anti-black values onto black children in the name of improvement. She felt, furthermore, that the students themselves sensed this fundamental problem—the institution's hostility to their very being.

Instinctively Helga was aware that their smiling submissiveness covered many poignant heartaches and perhaps much secret contempt for their instructors. But she was powerless. In Naxos between teacher and student, between condescending authority and smoldering resentment, the gulf was too great, and too few had tried to cross it. It couldn't be spanned by one sympathetic teacher. It was useless to offer her atom of friendship, which under the existing conditions was neither wanted nor understood.[2]

Larsen here is describing the distance between an institution's promise and its reality—the operation of the school as an instrument of discipline and discrimination, and the deep forms of betrayal that unfold around the staging of that practice in the name of social justice. As Sarah Ahmed writes, "using the language [of diversity] does not translate into creating diverse or equal environments. This 'not translation' is something we experience: it is a gap between a symbolic commitment and a lived reality." The language of a commitment to diversity can be used within an institution as a "mask [...] to create the appearance of being transformed,"[3] it can disguise the institution's role—or, rather, our participation within the institution (as teachers, students, and staff)—in reproducing raced and

Doyle

sexed forms of violence. The scandal of Larsen's novel is Helga's own internalization of anti-black feeling—she is deeply attracted to and repulsed by the forms of black life which escape institutional capture. This difficult novel tracks her restless movement through the world; Helga, the orphaned child of a white mother and a black father, experienced herself as "an obscene sore" for the white family which, out of duty rather than love, saw to her education. Her ambivalence nearly breaks the story apart. By the novel's end Helga has impulsively rejected cosmopolitan social forms of the Harlem Renaissance and disappeared in her role as the preacher's wife in a small Southern town. She has become a baby-making machine, incapacitated by the physical toll of bearing five children and by a depression so profound she can hardly speak.

The boundaries of the institutions in which we work and that organize our lives are raced and sexed. The institution knows itself through this sense of what it is not and whom it cannot accommodate. That said, institutions do not think and feel in and of themselves—the thoughts and feelings of an institution move through us. They collect in our bodies, as fuel and as toxins. We construct and enforce their narrative traditions, mythologies, and folklore. We live with those stories—the institution's givens, its scandals, its rumors, its forms of common sense. We encounter these narratives from our positions inside, outside, and on the edges of the institution—supervisor, supervisee, student, staff, teacher. Hired or fired. Accepted and rejected. Administrator and worker. The teachable and unteachable. We encounter the institution differently, and we encounter each other through these forms of differentiation. That is what Larsen describes—a teacher's sense of the gulf which divides her from her students, from students she cares about and understands. She identifies with her students, and she does not.

The institutions that govern our lives exert a force on us. Our relationships to them are the site of much psychic drama, much psychic pain. Our relationships to them have histories—histories that precede and exceed us. Our relationships to them are primal.

The institution is, in the words of Melanie Klein, the Good and the Bad Breast.[3] It socializes and subjects. It is Father. It punishes and rewards. It has rules. It has the power to create and annihilate. It is Mother. In this sense, the Institution—especially the institution whose structure is hierarchal (like a school)—solicits from us a paranoid form of relation; it can encourage what psychoanalyst Michael Balint theorized as a "malignant" dynamic—dynamics that triangulate and are "inseparable from conflict;" dynamics that take the form of "a constant threat of an unending spiral of demands or needs" and which culminate in "addiction-like states."[5]

Knight's is a challenging institutional practice. Within the world of contemporary art, we are more familiar with "institutional critique," a set of artist practices which, normally, reveal the institution's hidden power structures. The works most identified with institutional critique center on an unveiling—the spotlighting of the politics of the members of a museum's board of trustees (Hans Haacke's *Poll*, 1970, and *Manet-Projekt '74*, 1974), or the mapping of the structural racism of a museum's collecting and exhibition practice (Fred Wilson's *Mining the Museum*, 1992; James Luna's *The Artifact Piece*, 1986). The institution solicits, accommodates, and absorbs this practice. If a work was once an intervention in the institution's present politics, it becomes, itself, an institutional artifact. The value of institutional critique, traditionally, is generated by a revelation of the institution's secrets; the artist, much of the time, appears to sit just outside of its structures. The artist's intervention appears as a correction; for the artist of color, their simple presence can become an intervention (thus Native American artist Luna displayed himself). In making that intervention, the artist may become a figure not entirely unlike Helga Crane—an ambivalent, melancholic instructor.

The suite of works that make up *In Rehearsal* confront this paradoxical situation directly. Knight confronts the contradictions that shape the experience of raced and sexed subjects within the institution, as well as the work of anti-racist but privileged subjects. This material is much closer to what, within the institution, is called "diversity work"—the very particular work assigned to the symbolic *other*. Knight works with diversity work, with its affective forms of labor, while also *in herself* representing and effecting diversity work. Her practice maps the distance that Ahmed describes, and it conjures that distance as a group problem—a problem of the group and defining the group. I experience her work as addressing subjects like Helga and her students—the minoritarian group that forms around shared experiences of alienation, difference, and grief.

The performance video *Lament* drops the viewer inside the University of Illinois's Stock Pavilion—a 1913 arena for showcasing and judging livestock (and used, now, for a range of events, including performance). We see a woman's legs in the air; she is positioned behind a bale of hay and against the stockyard's ring wall. Sonically, we are also dropped into the middle of a 1997 speech by Angela Davis

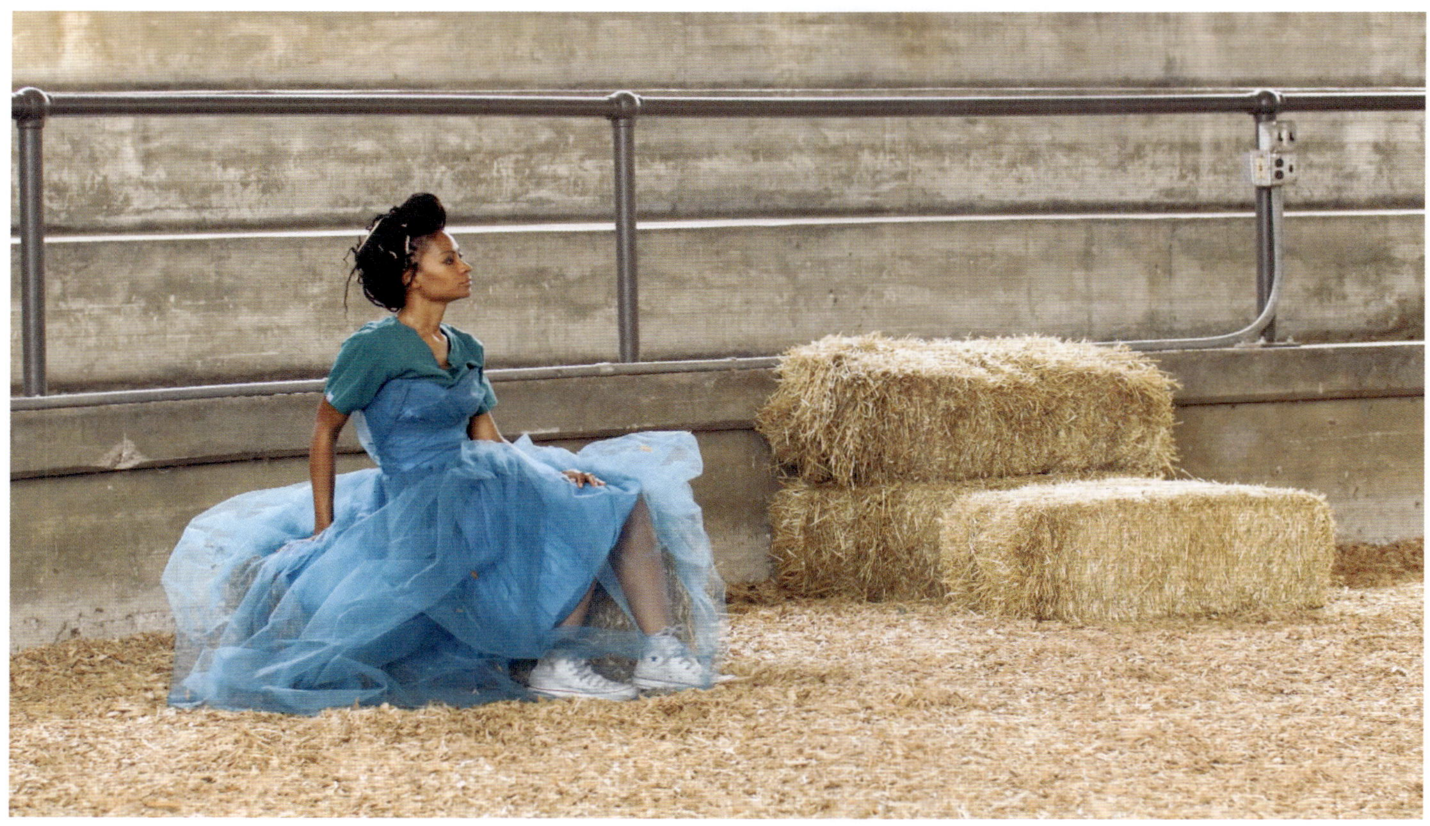

Pages 72–73: Video still from *Lament*, with Abijan
Johnson, 2017. University of Illinois Stock Pavilion,
Urbana, 2017. Digital video (color, sound), 22 minutes

on the prison industrial complex, a speech first delivered at Colorado College. We hear a quick intake of breath, and the sharp, crystal ring of Davis's voice—a voice which grounds its listener so that she can take in Davis's sweeping review of the situation of black women in the United States.

> And now that the welfare system has been disestablished and there are no jobs for the women [who rely on welfare] who are told that if they don't work, that's just too bad.

These women, she explains, "haven't had the opportunity to go to an institution like this."

There is a cut, and we are now much closer to the woman on the screen. Her legs fall forward, towards us, and she rolls up and over the hay bale, tumbling into a seated position. She crosses her legs.

> What's going to happen to so many of these women?

Davis's voice carries a sense of truth and also disbelief.

> Where are they going to find a job? How will they pay for child care in order to guarantee the conditions that will allow them to work? What's going to happen with so many of these women? Many will have to look for alternative modes of survival since they can no longer depend on welfare. They are going to be lured into the drug economy, the economy of sexual services. Two of the major alternative economies available to people not allowed to participate in the mainstream economy. That's going send them straight into the prison industrial economy.

By this point, dancer Abijan Johnson is sitting, ladylike. She is wearing what looks like a hospital dress

Doyle

underneath a tulle-heavy gown. Her braids are gathered up in a crown—she is regal. Davis's words conclude:

> If things do not change, we will see ever larger numbers of women going into the prison system.

This, in other words, is what is going to happen. That is, in fact, what has happened. Between 1980 and 2005, for example, there was an eightfold increase in the number of women in prison. Black women are incarcerated at four times the rate of white women.[6] The women serving sentences in state and federal prisons have shared experiences of poverty, drug use, intimate partner violence—experiences that prisons cement and consolidate. Most have not had the opportunity of an "institution like this"—the world of possibility organized into a university.

The soundtrack paces us with a good beat of silence before we hear the soft, round, plucked notes of Coleridge Taylor-Perkinson's short composition for solo cello, *Lamentations: 'Black Folk Song Suite': III. Calvary Ostinato (quarter note=80–88)*. Here, Knight invites us into a world of citation. Calvary is believed to be the location of the crucifixion of Jesus, a hill just outside Jerusalem's wall. Taylor-Perkinson was named after Samuel Coleridge Taylor (1875–1912), a black British composer who was himself named after Samuel Taylor Coleridge (1772–1834), the famous English poet-critic. The sound of *Lamentations* folds together the structure and tones of classical music, popular song, and spirituals. "Calvary Ostinato" hovers in the sonic space between cello and banjo, between high and folk culture. It does not sound like a solo at all; this work contains a multitude.

Davis's words and Taylor-Perkinson's music become devices for a walking meditation—Johnson staggers, saunters, crawls, sprints, and lays down on the ground of the pavilion as these words and notes resound in our brains. I watched this performance video twice before I fully recognized that most of this work is danced in silence. Johnson's movements are not scored by these aural references; her movements absorb them. In the artist's words, Johnson's movements (choreographed here in collaboration with University of Illinois Dance lecturer Rebecca A. Ferrell) are "coded with different languages of class, addiction and mental/physical abilities"—they are citations from below, meant to conjure the figure and fate of the women Davis asks us to hold in mind.[7] The people who made this work and the people who see it are less the women of whom Davis speaks than they are the women that Davis speaks *to*. They are women who have access to the opportunities the institution affords.

Lament maps the distance between the women of whom Angela Davis speaks and the women who make and see this work. Women of color, working from within the institution, may signal that institution's commitment to diversity even as they are subjected to its racism. One's mere presence is a sign of some kind of progress. Minoritarian subjects within institutions that reproduce structures of knowledge, power, and authority are constantly oriented, positioned, situated in relationship to those people who "haven't had the opportunity to attend an institution like

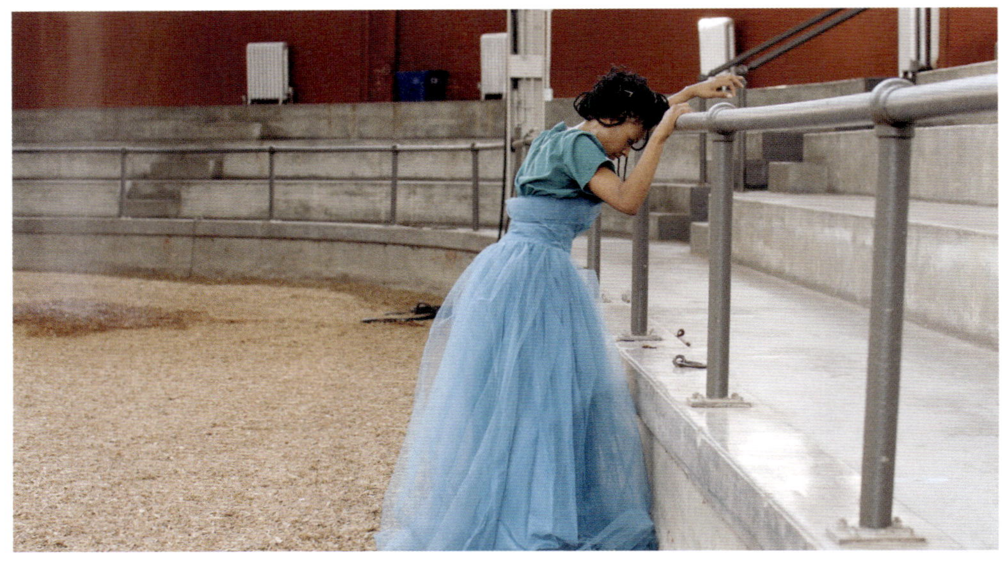

Host Institution

this." The institution understands itself as "opportunity" for this subject, even as that subject (presumed incompetent) embodies the ones who do not belong.[8]

One is both there, and not.

Johnson, on screen and in the ring, is alone and she is not. She is the hole around which the institution swirls. She is a bur, a shard, a piece of shrapnel working its way through the institution's flesh.

Jasbir Puar's recent articulation of the "mutually reinforcing constellation" of "capacity, debility and disability" helps us to grasp and work through *Lament*'s place within Knight's institution-work. "While some bodies may not be recognized as or identify as disabled," Puar writes, "they may well be debilitated, in part by being foreclosed access to legibility and resources" available to those whom the institution recognizes as disabled.[9] These terms, understood in relation to each other, help us to articulate the impact of the systems that limit the life possibilities for individual women and the difficulty of recovering those forms of debilitation into a form of institutional accommodation. Understanding capability, debility, and disability in mutual relation to each other may help us to understand the momentum that makes it feel as if we cannot stop the marking of specific bodies as destined for institutionalization and incarceration. *Lament* is a meditation on the distances between capability, debility, and disability as produced by and through interlocking systems that absorb and expel bodies—healthcare, education, social work, incarceration. Systems within which black women have a particular signifying power (as an embodiment of systemic potential and failure). Here, the hybridity of the setting for this performance—an arena for showcasing livestock, a working animal science classroom—lends peculiar notes to this performance. Johnson, situated in a chattel-space, is too close to an obscene reference.

Knight's lament is both noun and verb—the performer grieves and is the living embodiment of loss. She conjures the woman who is not there, within the space of the university. She is the woman that many of us who are a part of the university and the contemporary art world know well. She embodies the women we left behind when we went to school, the friends and neighbors who didn't make it through, the women on the street we don't or can't recognize.

What kind of space does this woman need in order to be held? In what kind of structure does she need to be cared for? Who are her people? *Lament* unfolds around these questions—the inquiries of the black subject positioned within institutions that organize themselves against minority life.

The philosopher and clinician Félix Guattari thought deeply about our relationships with institutions. For him, the internalization of a sense of the institution's power structures should be understood as a failure, as a refusal of the institution's potential, as a blockage of the group's possibilities:

> A fixed transference, a rigid mechanism, like the relationship of nurses and patients with the doctor, an obligatory, predetermined, 'territorialised' transference onto a particular role or stereotype, is worse than a resistance to analysis: it is a way of interiorizing bourgeois repression by the repetitive, archaic, and artificial re-emergence of the phenomena of caste, with all the spellbinding and reactionary group phantasies they bring in their train.[10]

Those of us caught in struggle within the organizations within which we work, those of us driven to despair over the abuse of power and authority within the institution, those of us who find ourselves riveted to the crisis of institutionalized forms of violence try the patience of our friends—who sometimes misdiagnose us as suffering from the above-described "fixed transference," as suffering from an *overidentification with the institution*. Why, we are asked, can't we just detach?

Lament answers that question. We cannot because it is the institution which has attached itself to us. The institution knows itself through us. It has latched onto us. We are the breast that feeds it. (Knight takes up the figuration of the maternal body within institutional structures in *An experimental freezing of a room through metaphorical means*, p. 76–87.) Our outrage, our complaints and grievances, place us in a metonymic relationship to the university. We *are* its trouble. The institution bodies forth its contradictions in us. We are the bodies which reveal the institution's truth: the institution is nothing without us. The institution's material existence begins and ends in our bodies.

Knight's work reveals that many of us do not inhabit institutions so much as find ourselves used in a conjuring of the institution. It is Helga's awareness of this that propels her out of the school where she works: she does not know how not to be the instrument of her students' subjection. She does not know how not to dissolve into the school, how not to be dissolved by it. I return to Guattari: "For whom do I speak? Am I really only one of those pathetic agents

Doyle

of the academic ideology, the bourgeois ideology, who try to build a bridge between the classes and so contributing to integrating the working class into the bourgeois order?"[11]

These issues—the problem of the individual in relation to the institution—were conjured very differently in Knight's *Here + Now* (p. 40–49). This participatory work puts the audience through exercises that invite them to cohere as a group, culminating in the staging of a kind of encounter session. All but two of the more than fifteen participants (including me) self-identified as women. The group's conversation with itself—its greatest sense of cohesion—formed around collective worry about the absence of men from the group, white men in particular. White men were a minority for this event's audience; why was that, we asked. When Knight and her co-facilitator pointed this out, we were confronted by the ease with which we, as a group, had internalized a sense of ourselves as lacking, as missing something. We, as a quasi-institution, had reproduced the sense of white masculinity as the thing that we needed to realize our potential and possibility. We had, as a quasi-institution, turned our gaze away from the subject of *Lament* and invested our sense of authority and power in a symbolic patriarchal figure—in the man who could not care less about us.

Lament asks that we tend to our sense of the institution and its authority, that we see the woman who is *here* and *now*. That we be present to the world of grief generated in the wake of the foundational exclusions that yield a sense of a group's identity and value. That we consider what it means to inhabit "an institution like this" with intention, with love.

1   Nella Larsen, *Quicksand and Passing*, ed. Deborah McDowell (New Brunswick: Rutgers University Press, 1986): 5.

2   Ibid.

3   Sarah Ahmed, *Living a Feminist Life* (Durham: Duke University Press, 2017): 90.

4   Melanie Klein, *The Psychoanalysis of Children* (London: The Hogarth Press, 1932).

5   Michael Balint, *The Basic Fault: Therapeutic Aspects of Regression* (London: Tavistock Publications, 1968): 15, 146.

6   Regarding statistics for women of color and rates of incarceration, see: "Women of Color & Prisons," INCITE!, http://www.incite -national.org/page/violence-against -women-color.

7   Autumn Knight, artist statement regarding *Lament*, http://autumnjoiknight .com/lament/.

8   See Gabriella Gutiérrez y Muhs, Yolanda Flores Niemann, Carmen G. González and Angela P. Harris, eds., *Presumed Incompetent: The Intersections of Race and Class for Women in Academia* (Logan, Utah: Utah State University Press, 2012).

9   Jasbir Puar, *The Right to Maim: Debility, Capacity, Disability* (Durham: Duke University Press, 2017): xv.

10   Félix Guattari, *Molecular Revolution: Psychiatry and Politics*, trans. Rosemary Sheed (New York: Penguin, 1984): 17.

11   Guattari, *Molecular Revolution*, 210.

AN EXPERIMENTAL MENTAL FREEZING OF A ROOM

THROUGH METAPHORICAL MEANS

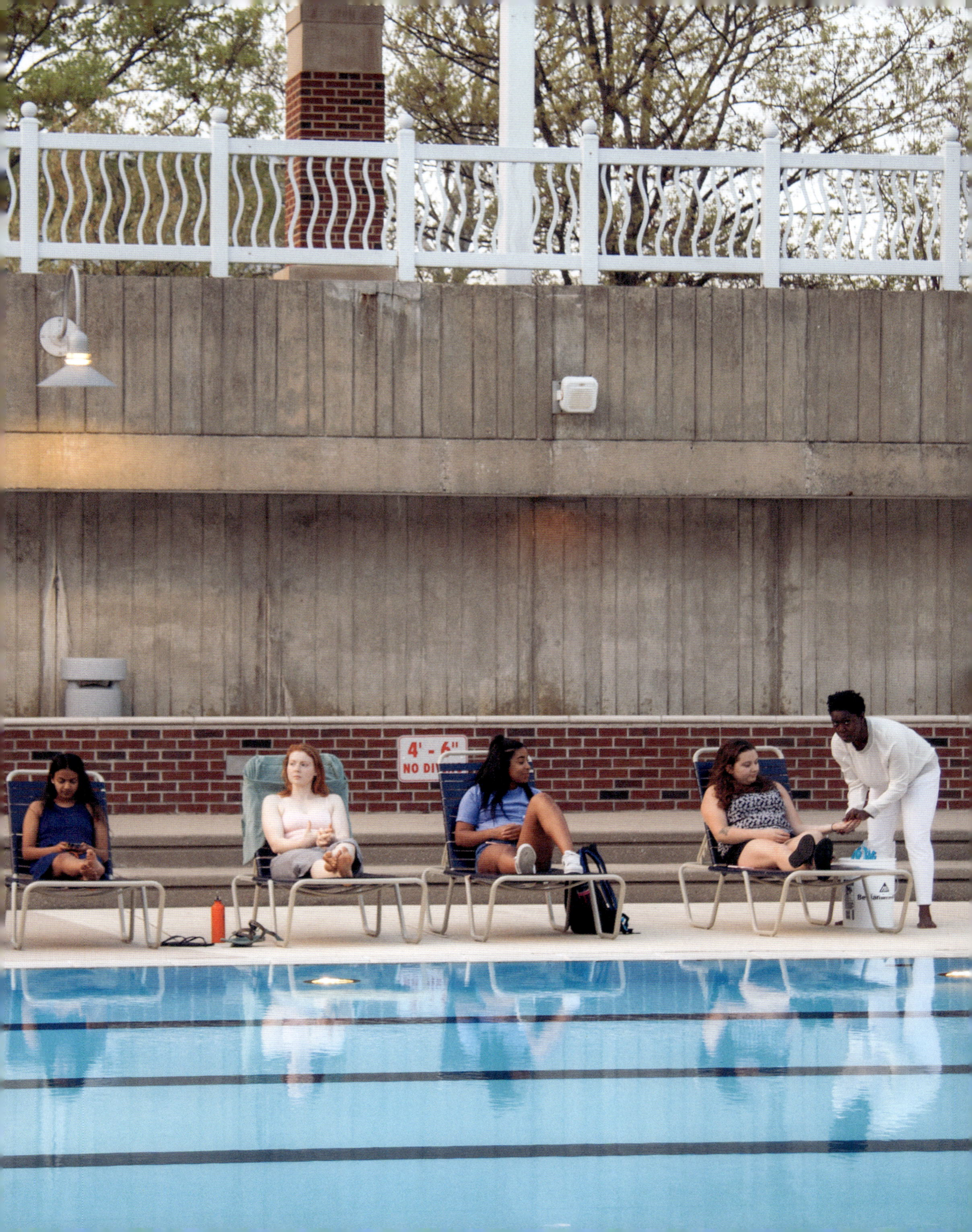

*An experimental freezing of a room through metaphor-
ical means* (2013–2017) interprets two scores of
artists' instructions from the longstanding exhibition *do it*: Iñake Bonillas's *Cold Storage Room* from
2001 ("Keep the temperature of a room at –18°C")
and Shilpa Gupta's untitled score from 2012 ("LOOK
STRAIGHT / DON'T SEE"). Knight appears as a maternal
figure cradling a bag of ice while articulating her
body around the performance space. She moves with
the soundtrack of various courtroom scenes convey-
ing legally sanctioned violence against black
people, beginning with George Zimmerman's acquittal
of the murder of Trayvon Martin in Sanford, Florida,
in 2013.

AUDIO SOUNDTRACK EXCERPTS

"Raw video: George Zimmerman's not guilty verdict
      read in court," WESH 2 News, news broadcast,
      July 13, 2013, https://www.youtube.com/watch?
      v=nI6ymXpIxZw
A six-woman jury found George Zimmerman not guilty
of second-degree murder and manslaughter on
Saturday, July 13, 2013. He is now a free man.

"Sandra Bland's Mother Speaks with Rev. Al Sharpton,"
      MSNBC Exclusive Interview, news broadcast,
      July 24, 2015, https://www.youtube.com/watch?
      v=hJ4sYjjZ2Ks&t=66s
As the investigation into Sandra Bland's death continues, Rev. Sharpton talks exclusively to Bland's
mother. Hear what she had to say about the case and
the fight to get justice for her daughter.

"Courtroom drama in death of 2-year-old" [voice of
      Kenneth French, whose daughter was killed in
      shooting in Detroit], WXYZ-TV Detroit, news
      broadcast, July 16, 2014, https://www.youtube.com
      /watch?v=ujC6KHIFvQc&t=57s
A fiery exchange punctuated a hearing in the murder
of a 2-year-old in Inkster.

"Transgender Cleveland woman disappeared day before
    her body was discovered," cleveland.com, news
    broadcast, August 2, 2016, https://www.youtube
    .com/watch?v=fn9TXIcb03Y
Skye Mockabee, the 26-year-old transgender Cleveland
woman whose body was found in a parking lot on July
30, always sought to please those around her, which
makes her death even more confusing to her live-in
boyfriend, William Philpott.

"Oklahoma City Cop [Daniel Holtzclaw] Cries In Court
    After Being Found Guilty, Attrack, entertainment
    channel, December 11, 2015, https://www.youtube
    .com/watch?v=SEqPkvqhils
A rapist cop will be making friends in jail for a
long time.

Pages 77–85: *An experimental freezing of a room through metaphorical means*, with Autumn Knight. University of Illinois Activities and Recreation Center, Champaign, April 19, 2017

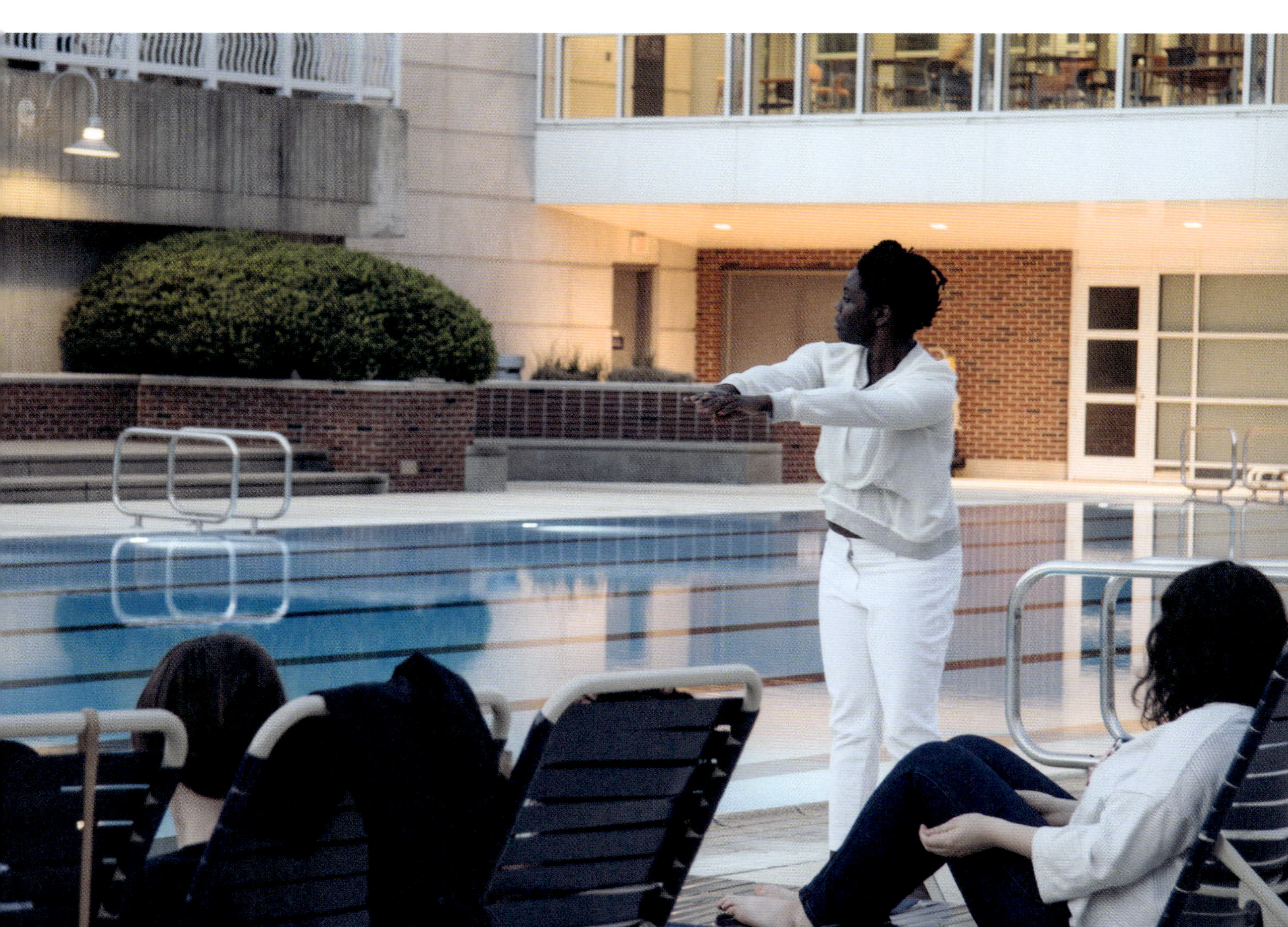

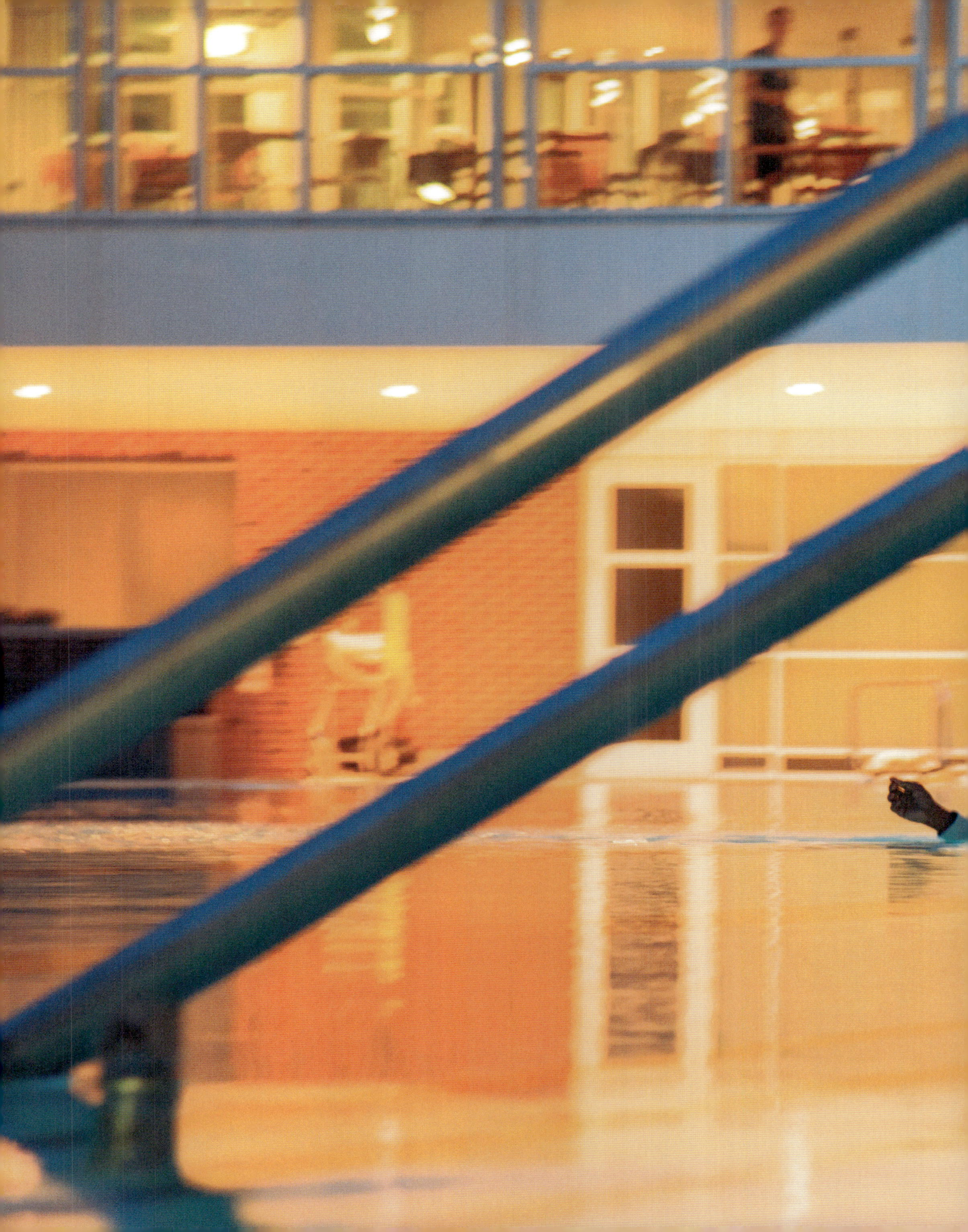

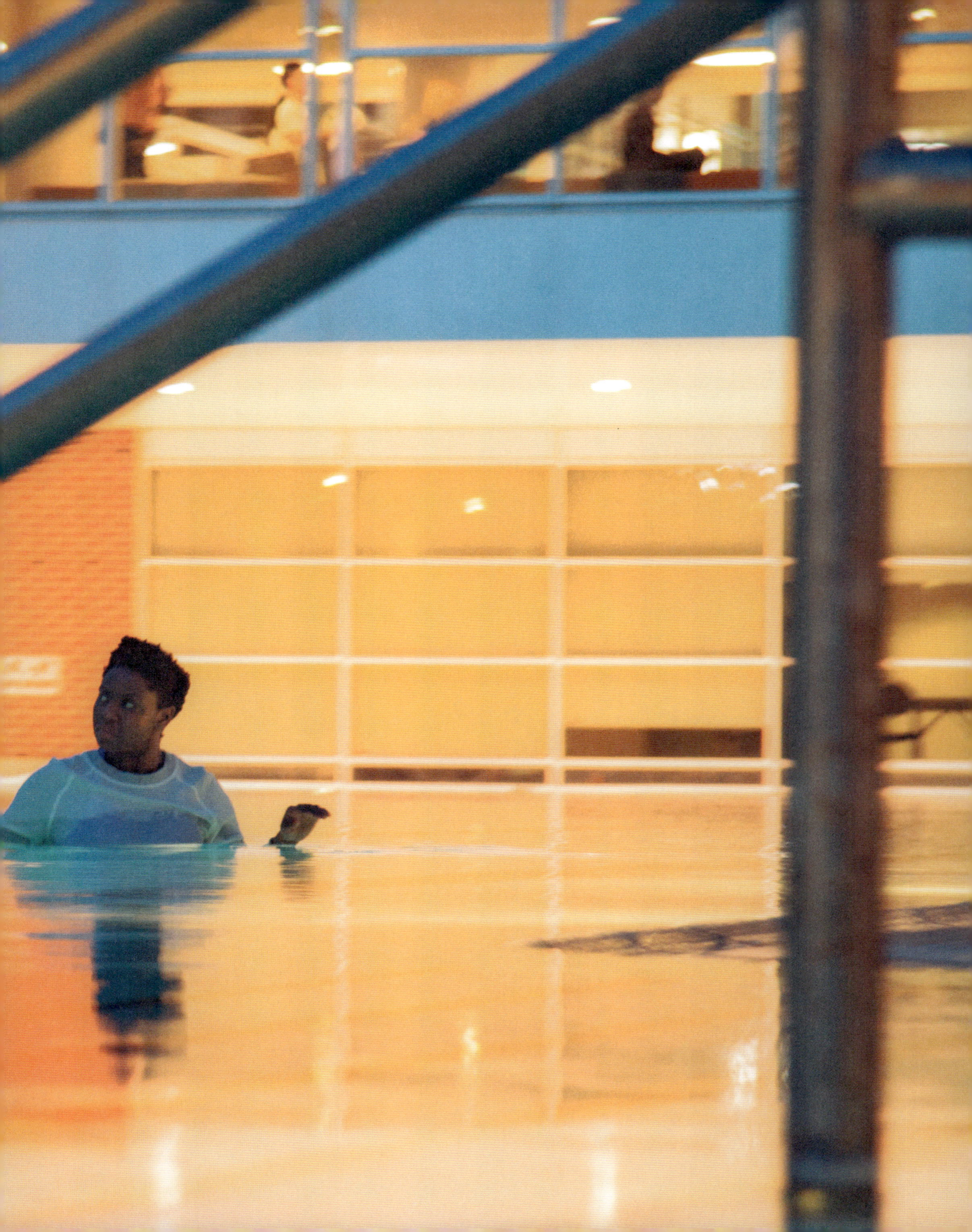

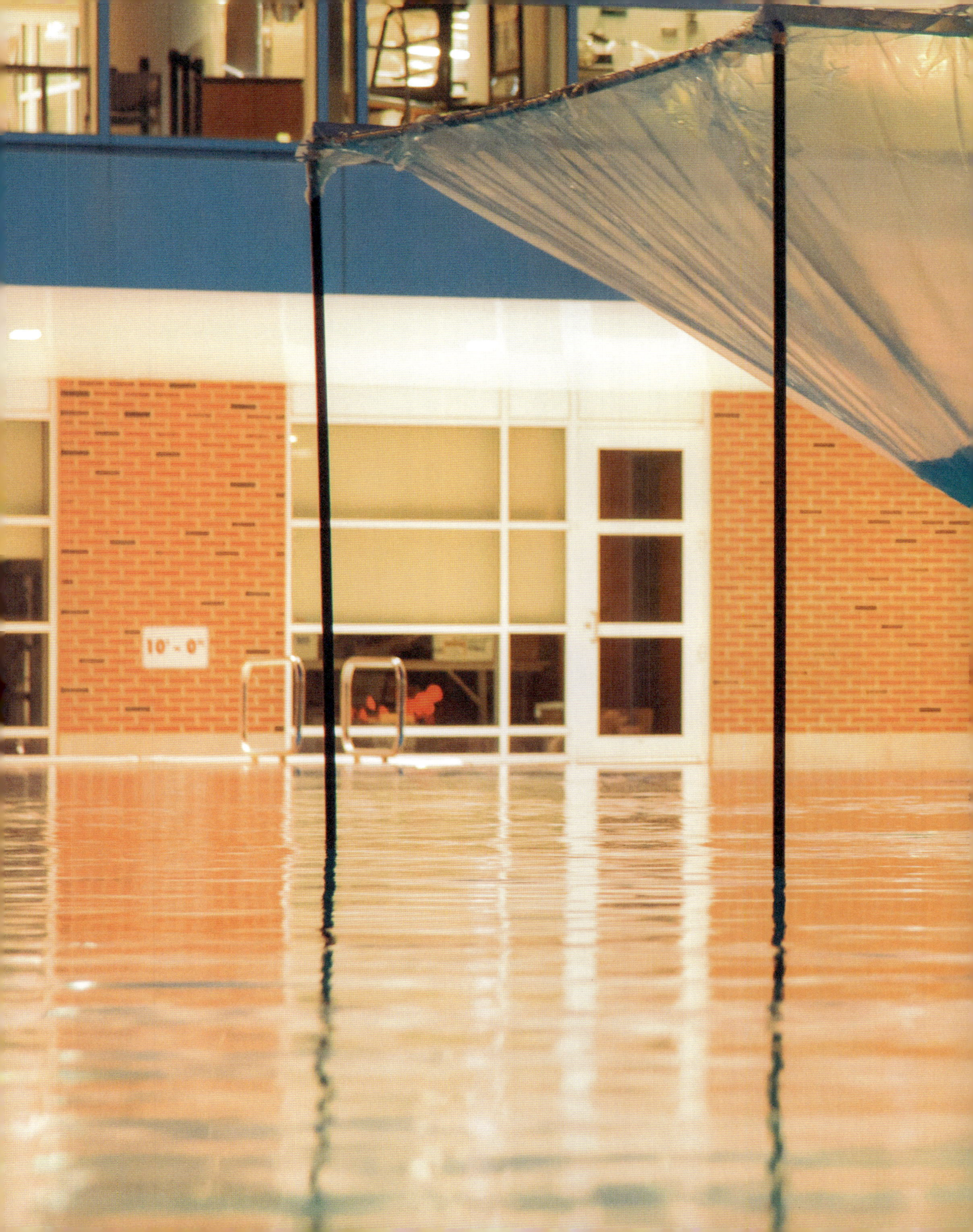

10' - 0"

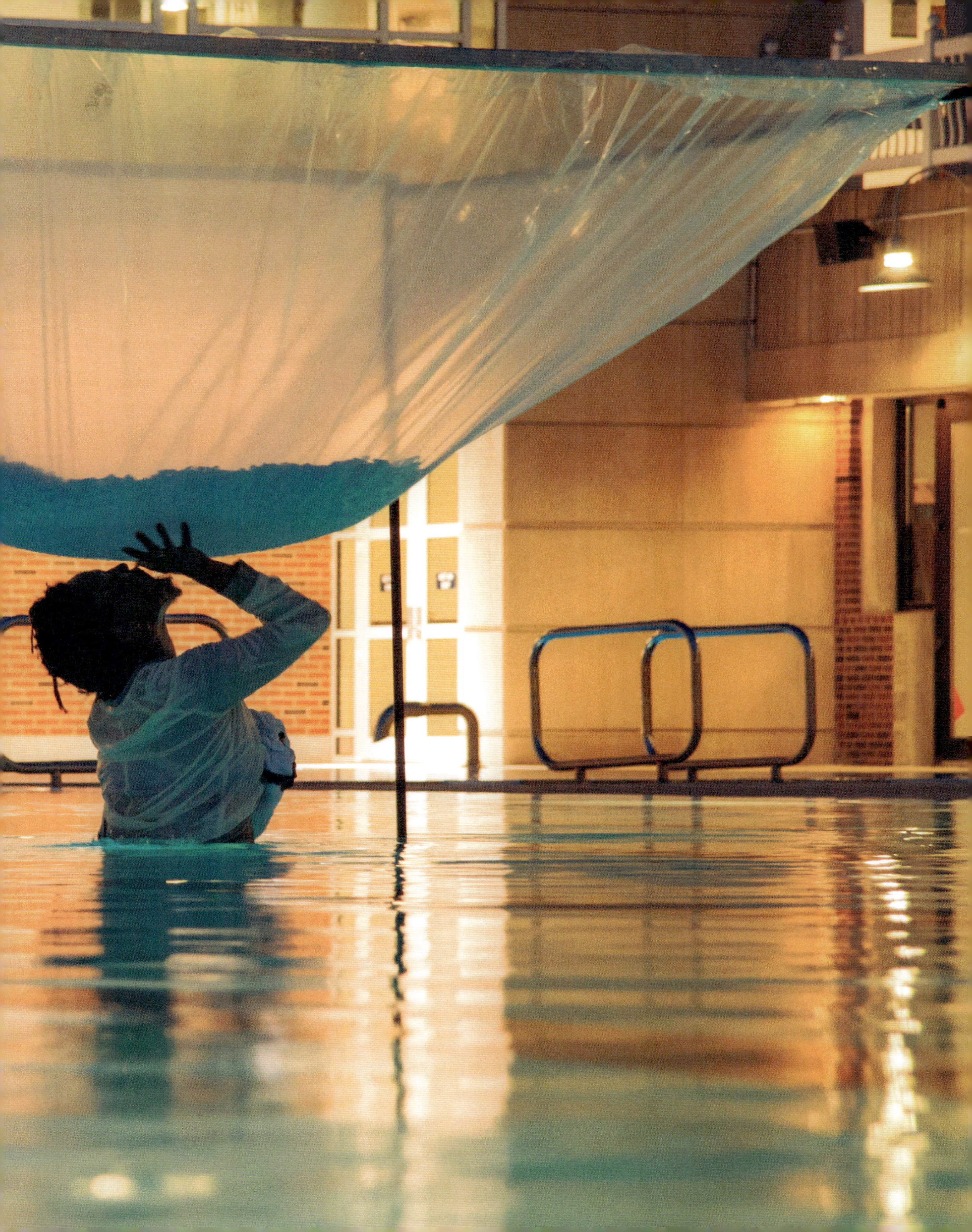

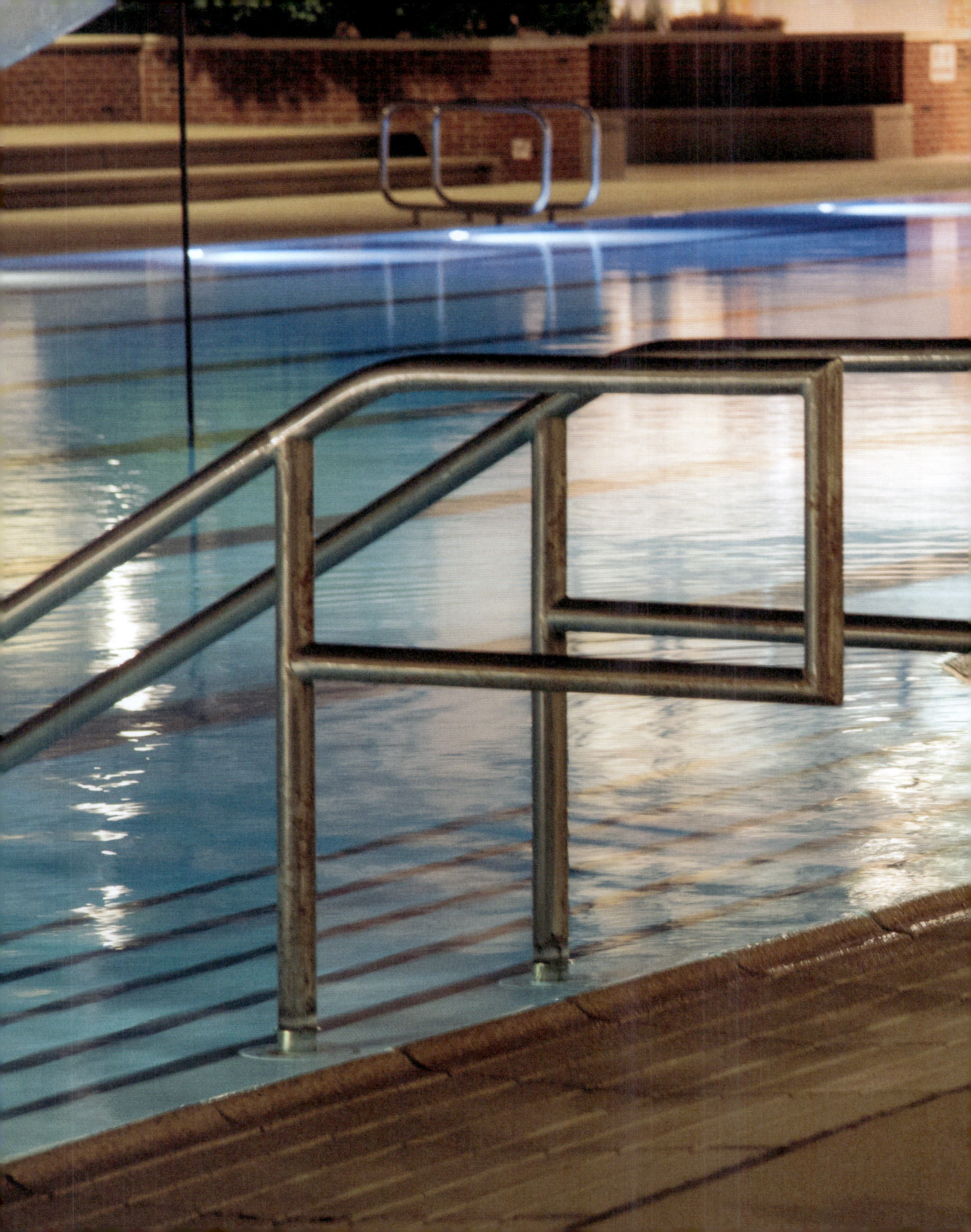

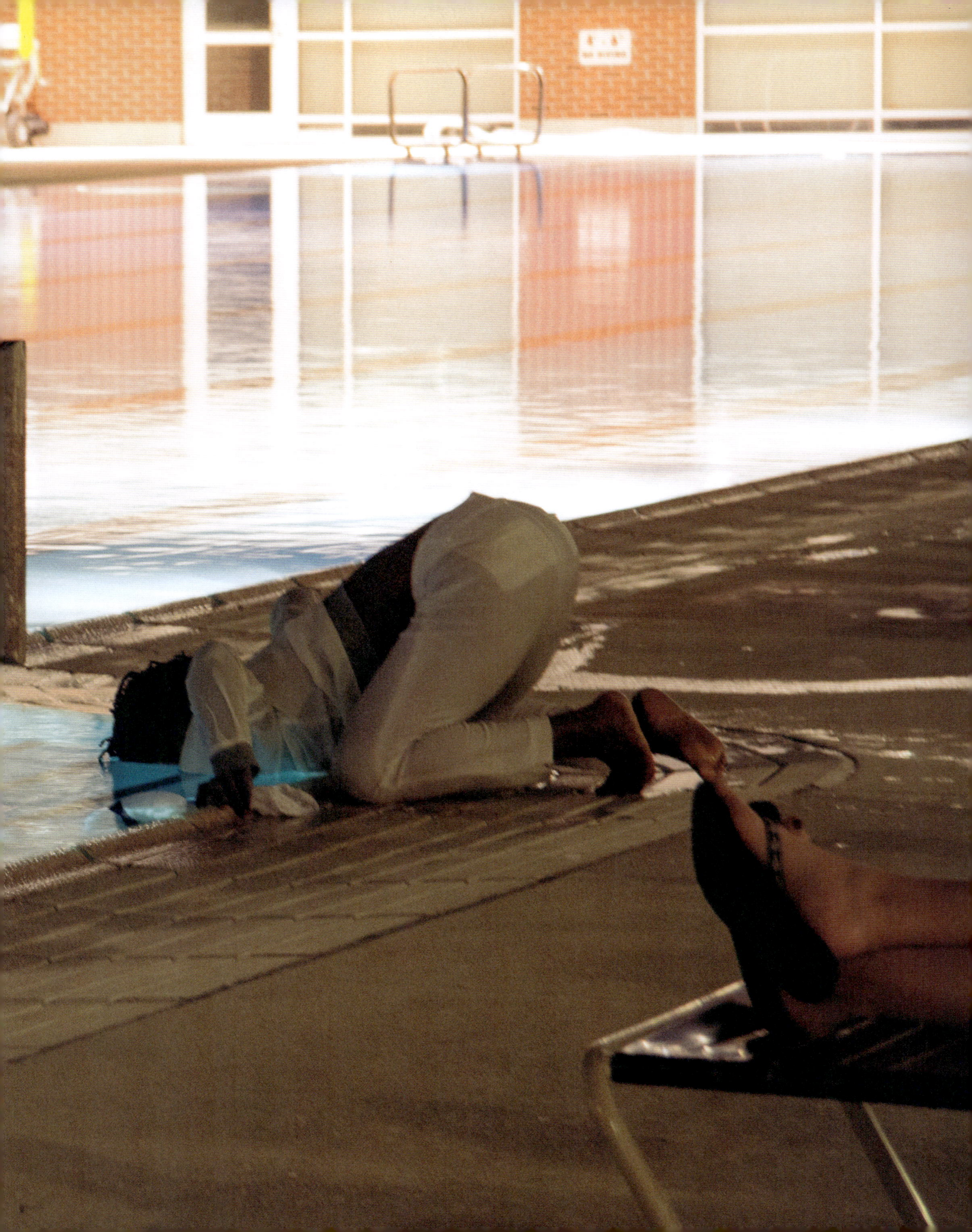

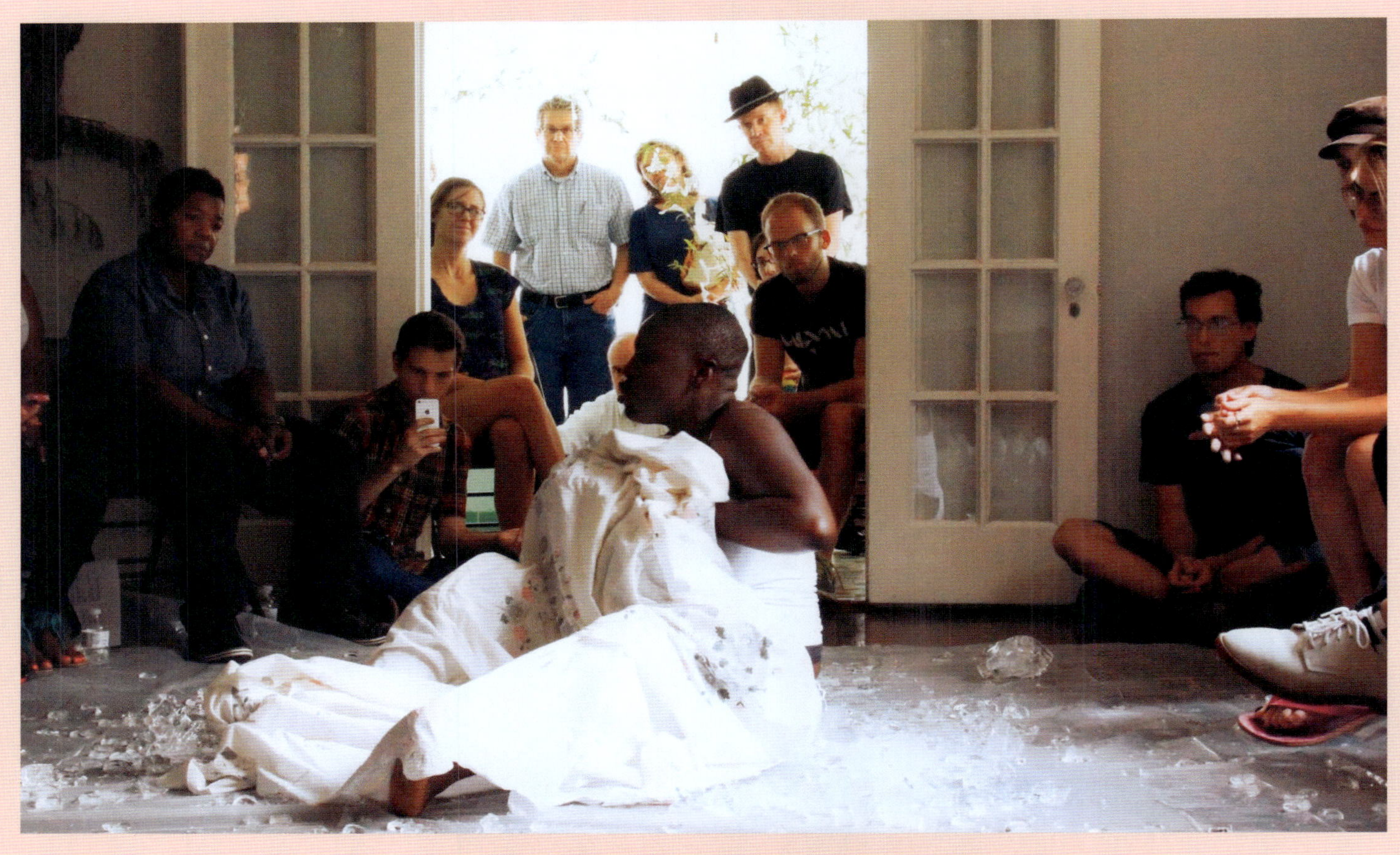

Pages 86–87: *An experimental freezing of a room through metaphorical means,* with Autumn Knight. Alabama Song, Houston, July 27, 2013

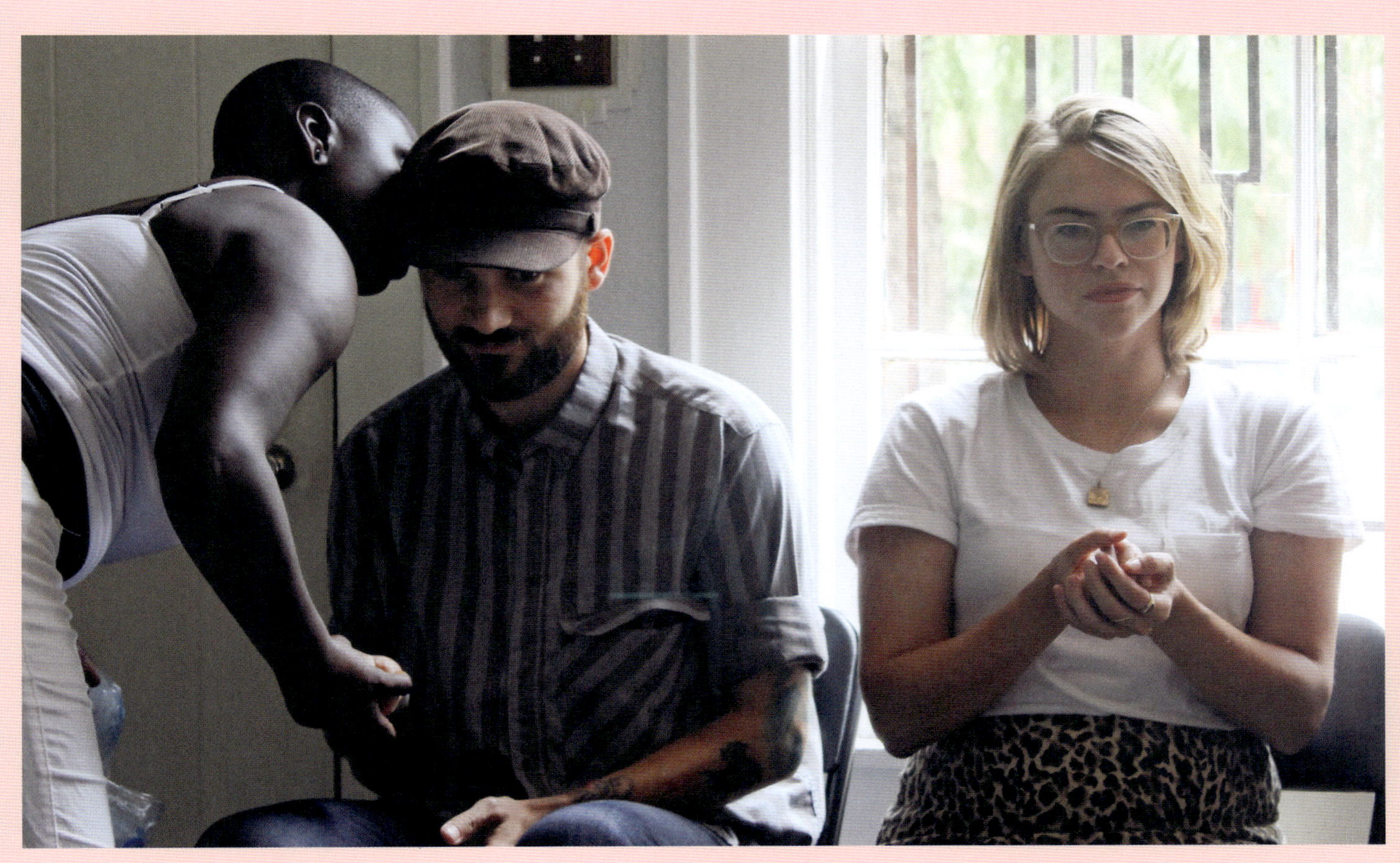

AN EXPERIMENTAL FREEZING OF A ROOM

In Conversation

Autumn Knight with Cynthia Oliver

This conversation was conducted on Skype on January 10, 2018.

Autumn Knight **What is your life right now?**

Cynthia Oliver Years ago, as an independent artist in New York, I wrote something called "Am I a Circus Act? Or an Artist Living in New York?" for an online magazine. I still feel that way, that I am always spinning multiple plates. I am working with my team on *Virago-Man Dem*, which we're getting ready to take on tour. I am gearing up to teach Technique this coming semester. I was teaching a grad theory course last semester. So I gotta get my head and body in gear for this. And then, I was crazy enough to accept a position as the Associate Vice Chancellor for Research in the Humanities, Arts, and Related Fields at the University of Illinois. I started that in the fall (2017). It's a steep learning curve so I'm still learning the position. The thing I love about it is working with my colleagues on their projects. And I have a 13-year-old.

That ripe age.

And [I have] an artist-husband and a mom in a nursing home and family in the Caribbean that've been affected by the hurricane. So I'm a circus act. That's my life right now.

Why a circus? Because when people think of a circus they think out-of-control. I'm thinking about those performers who stand on one leg and all of their other limbs are up in the air balancing plates.

I'm not thinking out of control. Everything has to be in a very careful balance. And, you know, it's like anything. When something needs more attention, you give that thing more attention and the other things get perhaps a little less attention, and then it shifts. And it can shift daily. What is your life like right now?

Well, I have an artist home. I mean, artist-husband.

He is your home, right?

He is my home. Actually, I just said yesterday that he is my home because I've been traveling and I thought coming back to our apartment in New York would be home, but he's here with me on this trip in Marfa. I'm still home because we're here together.

My family will meet me in Philadelphia soon. It's always special when they meet me on the road. And my son—it amazes me how this has been part of his life, meeting mom on the road or being with mom on the road as I make something. It's really special this year because the Painted Bride Art Center in Philadelphia is where Jason [Finkelman] and I met, and they are about to sell the building to create a new model in terms of how they present and support art. It's the end of one phase of the life of that building, and we'll be there together.

That's lovely. You often collaborate with your husband. Is Jason also going to collaborate on *Virago-Man Dem* in Philadelphia?

Yes, he's already done his work for that piece. He made the music, so he'll get to hear and see the work in a different space.

What is it like to collaborate with your partner? I'm thinking of specifics because I collaborate with my partner too, and we cross disciplines a little bit.

What does your partner do?

He's a visual artist. When we do collaborate, he provides some visual or audio component or he gives his conceptual opinion about what I'm working on. Another pair of eyes. How does your partner function? Obviously he does music and you do movement. That seems like a natural pairing. But what else does he provide?

Our collaboration manifests in a bunch of different ways. He and I are in conversation from the time I first start conceptualizing a project. We'll start talking about the ideas before we even think about our respective contributions, before I start thinking about what the movement is going to be like or before he starts thinking about what the music is going to be like. Just batting ideas back-and-forth. What I'm going to read. Where I need to go. And then I think about who I want to embody it. He'll have ideas about the people we know who would be good cast members for the work, and then once I get into the nitty-gritty of it, he'll come into the studio. He's so attuned that he doesn't generally say very much in that space. He just watches and takes notes. And then we have lots of conversations while he's cooking dinner. He's the family chef. I sit at the counter and he's doing his masterful cooking and we brainstorm in those sessions. And then once we're in the studio together...well, we've gone through a number of different ways of working together. He's watched me making a piece and then made stuff to

what I made. And then there was a period where I would make everything in silence or with other recorded music and he would watch the tape. For *Virago-Man Dem* the work was more modular. I made a bunch of chunks and rotated the order of them around, which made him kind of crazy because transition from one section to another is key for both of us. I kept having to change the transitions, and he kept having to change the transitions. And it pissed him off. What is next, damn it? Why did you move that? And so we got into fights in the studio and the performers were not sure how to respond or deal with us in those moments, but you know, that's what we do. It's our relationship. Actually, we are celebrating our twenty-first wedding anniversary tomorrow.

Congratulations!

Thank you. It's hardy enough that it can stand a good fight. That's what we do and we always come out of it really loving the work. He asks me the hard questions. I give him my honest answers. I love what he makes because it's so different for every work and it's exactly right for the piece. But there are those moments in getting to the "exactly right" when there are things that are not right and I don't like it and I don't want it and I want something else. And there are times when I want something and he's like, "That's not right for it. I'm not doing that." For *Virago-Man Dem*, before I even stepped in the studio there was a musical texture that I wanted to be in the work and I had been asking Jason for it. He had made it for someone else years ago and I loved it and I wanted it in this piece and he refused to let me have it.

Why?

He said, "It's not right for this piece." So, anyway, our working relationship is complex.

Right. But did you get it?

No!

No?

No. Damn it.

Do you have a process in place to get past that moment? Is there a thing that you're like, "Ok, when we get to this moment, this is what we're going to do?"

No. We are improvisers. We improvise every time. Okay?

Okay. Keeps it interesting!

It does. It really does.

It's interesting you talk about that process, because I was reading an article in *The New York Times* that reviewed your piece and I noticed that you worked with Stacey Robinson.

Yes, and John Jennings.

I love that their team is called Black Kirby. All of the images in your work are so vivid; they look like photographs. How did you come to this iteration of collaborating with John and Stacey?

It was long in the making. In 2010, John and I were collaborating here at the University of Illinois on a piece for students called *Closure for Blood Gutters for Veins*. I often experiment with ideas on students and we present the work here before I tweak it for the professional arena. All my stuff starts out with lots of silly, fun conversations, usually over food. John is a buddy of Jason's and he would come over to the house and we would be talking about imagery around superheroes and power and race and gender. And so we decided to work on this project together, and while we were in process—John did the drawings; Jason did the music; I worked with the dancers—I get a diagnosis of breast cancer and I have to drop everything and fight for my life. And I had a beautiful dance graduate student who was in the cast, Nibia Pastrana Santiago, who became my interlocutor. She conducted the rehearsal for me, came to my house, showed me video, got an assignment to go back to the studio with, and we'd kind of go back and forth. So we were trying to still make the piece happen even though I was in treatment. One day I asked John if he would go in the studio and work with the dancers in a particular way. That was the beginning of making a dance with John doing the visuals. And we made it happen. It didn't come to

the full fruition of my vision because of what I was dealing with at the time. So we made a promise that we would work together again because it was so dope. We had such a great time even though I was struggling. And so, when *Virago-Man Dem* started to make itself known in my world, in my spirit, in my head, and in everything I would think about, I started talking to John again and we were right on the same page. He initially came to one of my first residencies in Florida at the Maggie Allesee Center National Center for Choreography (we call it MANCC), and started just doing these free drawings while we rehearsed. And then we had intense conversations with each other and with the dancers afterward. John was moving around. He had gotten married. He was in Buffalo and then he was recruited to UC-Riverside and he was working at the Nas hiphop center [Hiphop Archive & Research Institute at the Hutchins Center, Harvard University]. I mean, he was ridiculous. And so we were like, "Okay, how do we make this manageable for all of us?" And he said "Well, you know, my drawing partner in Black Kirby is coming to Illinois and you need to meet him anyway, so why don't we hook that up and then see if maybe this is a project for Black Kirby?" And so I met Stacey during a residency where John Boesche, who does the projection in the work, was experimenting with some stuff. We only had one dancer here, Duane Cyrus. Susan Becker, who was doing costumes, was there. Stacey came into the theater and we were all playing around. He was like, this is where I need to be. And so we all hit it off. We would have these conversations (again, more conversations), and I would say these are the images that I think need to happen in this place. We kept generating material. Long story, but that's how that [collaboration] came about. It started with John and then grew to embrace Stacey as well. I understand from John that Jack Kirby is an iconic graphic artist, and so they took a twist on that and made their collaborative team Black Kirby to insert blackness in the graphic arena.

That's great. That's really wonderful.

Tell me about your process with your partner.

Right now I'm creating a performance called *Grand Opening / Grand Closing* for the closure of Marfa Contemporary in West Texas. I charged Robert [Pruitt] with

making a short video to project during the performance. We're trying to put together imagery that really deals with Marfa and what the Latino presence means in Marfa. We decided to make a video of a wall of people with their backs turned. And that was Robert's idea: to think about the ways that it [art] does and does not serve certain people and if the people here even need it to serve them. The great thing about collaborating with a partner who has seen your work is that he says, "This reminds me of your piece, *Wall*." He suggested it should be women so that it mirrors the *Wall* piece I did before with black women.

I love that partners can reflect your history and concerns, that you may have even forgotten, back to you.

Absolutely. I feel like I often have to create from scratch every time we get an opportunity, and I generally have stopped doing that. Robert's suggestions helped me with that with this work. This performance in Marfa is a special commission because I was invited to create a separate ritual for the closure of the space. Robert does large-scale drawings of women and figures. So the way he's able to think about the body and color and a background or space is part of our language.

Tell me more about this image of backs turned. Are you incorporating that into your performance work? Are you thinking about that as a motif in what you're doing?

I'm thinking about disregard metaphorically. The core performers are instructed to disregard the audience. For example, there's a party happening in another part of Marfa Contemporary to celebrate the closing right after the performance; I'll have the catering staff walk through and disrupt the performance.

How unfortunate.

There's a sense of trying to create resolution when there is none. You know, my mother passed away very recently.

Oh, no. I'm sorry.

So I am definitely thinking about non-resolution. Things having to end whether you're ready for them to or not. They do not have closure. You have to manage the closure on your own with your own sort of ideas or strategies. There may be a choreographed moment where the performers

who won't be in the video will come together and recreate that in some way. We're also having live mariachi performers. It's a circus, if you will. See? I love the word "circus." I definitely feel it's circus imagery.

The multiplicity of things happening simultaneously. What I like about your work—and I haven't seen enough, so I will forever be a fan and be following you now—I love that play of what is supposedly appropriate and inappropriate, that distance that you span and then interrupt. I feel like that's one thing we have in common. I have been looking at certain kinds of slippages in behaviors in a variety of spaces, and your work does that really skillfully and surprisingly. It erupts in a variety of places and really takes your audience off guard, catches us, and makes us realize what conventions we've been adopting maybe without question, or maybe we just haven't been brave enough to interrupt or upend them. You know?

I agree. You mentioned slippages of behaviors in a variety of spaces. How do you feel like that shows up in your work? Because it made me think about another question I had for you, about using text in the middle of movement. Not stopping for it, but just using text while movement is happening.

I feel like the mute dancer is this convention that's like, "Why?" When did that happen? Who said that we have to shut our mouths to move our bodies? Most of the time we don't do that anyway. One of my colleagues here, actually the woman who's responsible for me being at the University of Illinois, was my undergraduate teacher and she reminds me from time to time that when I was an undergrad I used to make work with language in it, which I don't remember now. It's again this return to multiple things happening simultaneously. While your body is saying one kind of story—vocally, emotionally, mentally—there could be other things happening. It could be in sync sometimes but other times it's completely disjointed. Or it could be oppositional, and I'm interested in all of that. I'm interested in what we move through our days performing while there might be a whole other mental narrative—emotional, psychological narrative—happening while this thing is happening. I'm interested in the same thing that I maybe just projected onto your work.

I'm fine with that.

Well it's always about you! Just that appropriate and inappropriate behavior. The things that we say and think that might be completely different. And so I love that, but I also love the cultural anchors. I feel like one of my missions in my work has also been about recognition. That coming up in a predominantly black culture, this North American culture, gets so little acknowledgement in terms of its value, that my mission has been to point out to each other, to ourselves (not even to the outside eye...), the immense genius in our culture, and that happens on a daily basis. And so a lot of that is vocal.

Yes.

I remember as a young person my mother told me about The Dozens [an African American custom in which two competitors, usually males, go head-to-head in a competition of comedic trash talk]. She is from Harlem and my father is from the Virgin Islands. There's this word-smithing that is practiced and of value that I heard on both sides of my family from the time I was very young. And so I feel like my work is simply a reflection of all of that and recognizing that value.

When your family told you about The Dozens, was it a warning or a celebration? Or was it teaching you how to do it, and how not to do it?

My mom was always, as she would jokingly say, "edumacatin" me. So, she would... If I came home and I was bent out of shape because somebody pinned a nickname on me, she was like, "Girl, you better sharpen your skills. And don't be getting all down, sourpuss about it. How are you gonna come back to that?" Part of it was educational and part of it was her saying, "Get with it. Embrace it." She would tell me about her experiences and she would make me laugh. I mean, my father does the same thing now and he's about to be 90. I was just having a conversation with him the other day, and I don't know how we got on this, but he was telling me about a friend of his and the man's nickname. I was guffawing because one of the things that we do is nickname people. We nickname people to the point where you might not ever know their given legal name until they're dead. You know? You find out at the funeral

when you read the booklet. It's like, "Oh, man! That's what his name was? We always called him 'Scrunchy,' you know, because he's such and such." And so it was always educational. And I think my parents' attitude was—yes, your feelings were hurt. I'm sorry. They would acknowledge whatever was happening. But this is what tradition this comes from and you gotta pony up. Let's do this. And then it would become fun and it would connect us to our history. When I'd go out in the street and hear folks really hitting each other hard with it, I might have a different attitude about it. I might be able to laugh it off. You know? I feel like they both gave me tools. What was your experience with The Dozens?

I definitely encountered it as a child. I remember how elaborate the insults were. When I was in middle school these two young boys used to meet me in theater class. "You so black your mama put you in the oven and forgot to take you out!" "No, you so black!" Just back and forth. I feel like I wasn't raised to hurt people in that immediate way. Or I think I was just so stunned. But I think I did learn how to do it. I just couldn't do it in that moment when it was happening to me. I think it's also about the circumstance under which you encounter it because a lot of white kids were around, too.

Very different.

A different audience. Which I think makes a difference and maybe it's not The Dozens anymore, depending on the makeup of the group.

I would agree with that. It's also interesting if you throw in sexuality. I'm thinking about my gay brother who had to defend himself in a certain kind of way. He would hear me and say, "Girl, you better learn to slice and dice." I felt like I had a posse that was training me. But what's interesting to me now is to see my son who is encountering this stuff through YouTube videos. Because of the culture he's growing up in, the kids don't necessarily do that to each other, but they do it in this performative form on YouTube. It's one part of the cultural practice that attuned my ears to this dexterity that we have about language that becomes a part of a certain kind of performance. I saw this in your work *El Diablo y Cristo Negro* at Krannert Art Museum, when you directed the students where they were performing as gods.

It's funny that you say dexterity around that age because I was thinking about improvisation. That The Dozens lends itself to improvisation and really paying attention to what's in the room. Because in some ways that's what The Dozens is, taking in the details of a person's behavior, their aesthetic, and amplifying it. And you better be quick.

You gotta be quick. So much about improvisation is about paying attention to what people are doing so I can comment on it really quick and create a juxtaposition. Creating something absurd or trying to tap into a thing that we're all thinking but can't say. And commenting on why we can't say that. So it's that roundabout thinking, like...

What could you choose to say instead?

Right. The way we tend to dress up our thoughts.

In some ways I feel like you do a kind of outing of a certain kind of behavior.

An outing of...a type of pretentiousness or of performativity that we have learned. Like you're recognizing these are things we have learned. I know that we are integrated individuals, but how much of this is actually practiced and rehearsed and we're afraid we're going to get our parts wrong from day to day, moment to moment? And then asking the question in your process, is this really useful.

Right.

Or what happens when we do go off script? Because there is the opportunity to discover something new, if we can allow the mistake. If we can make room for the moment of embarrassment or shame or doubt or confusion. If you just make a little room for it and you won't be a boulder and roll down the hill and crush us all. That can be a good place to live in, you know? And some lucrative and generative things come out of that space. But I think it's like another place where you and I are both going for an acknowledgement of our in-common humanity. And a little forgiveness.

A lot of forgiveness. I think having a place to project onto, presenting myself and my idea as a place to project onto. I'm creating this moment. I'm okay with experiencing those things. To be the mirror or to show you what that can look like.

We are both interested in discomfort as a potential, as a moment of possibility. As an infinity of possibilities. But, you know, I used a lot of improvisation in my last piece [*Virago-Man Dem*], but I usually work in a very calibrated way determining exactly what we're doing and when. There are variations that happen, of course, and I embrace those, but choreographically it generally has been quite precise except for this piece. You work in this improvisational area and have to do that Dozens-like quickness all the time. How do you manage that? How does that become a collaborative partner for you?

I think your description is accurate, of leaning into that place of discomfort as the place of possibility. I talked with my therapist once about this fear I have that I'm always improvising. It always feels like I'm doing things last minute and on the go. I feel like a magician and I'm pulling rabbits out of my hat. And she said, "What if there is no bottom to that hat?" I was like, "Ooh, that's a good one." That's why you pay therapists the big bucks! But yeah, what if there is no bottom to that? And so I feel like relying on improvisation is a place I can always go to. When you place your work on other bodies, how much space do you allow for precision and improvisation?

It's funny because as I was saying that there's that strictly calibrated and very specific element, there's part of me saying there's always space for variation. That other thing that happens is always of interest to me. When I make something on somebody else, I never expect them to look like me. That's the first thing. I am interested in them because of who they are and what they look and move like. And so I'm always fascinated by how the movement gets translated in their bodies. We'll work on refining it rhythmically or in terms of shape, but how it gets performed is really particular to that individual. I want them to own it to the extent that they feel like they can amplify it and honor it in a way that feels right to them and the character and the work. So there is an amount of freedom, I hope, that they would feel. It's about casting too. Who you cast, their level of maturity, and their life experience. Their willingness to be vulnerable and make mistakes. All of that becomes a part of the alchemy. Right?

That's one of my favorite parts of the process, the casting. I feel like that's an art unto itself.

It can be torture or it can be bliss. And sometimes all at once.

It's really interesting that on your website you have a section for having been in works by others. I don't know if that's common in the dance world, but I found it really lovely.

Dancers often start out working with other people and then maybe some of us will move on to doing our own work. I initially did not want to. I had no interest in choreography. I wanted to be the instrument. It wasn't until much later in my career that I was encouraged to do my own work and then kind of fell in love with it. As much as I'm tormented by it, I love it. I still take those moments to learn and be fed by others, take time out and work with other people, be in another person's process. You know? Take the responsibility off my own shoulders for the entire work. And just delve into a part. I love that. What about you?

It made me think about the artists' work that I've been in in the last few years. Normally it's video work here or there or I read something. I think I want to do it more.

I think this might be a prime opportunity for us to discuss the possibility of one day making something together.

That would be a dream come true.

We should talk about it.

We really should. I can come through. I can deliver.

Me too! I can put another plate on!

Knight Oliver

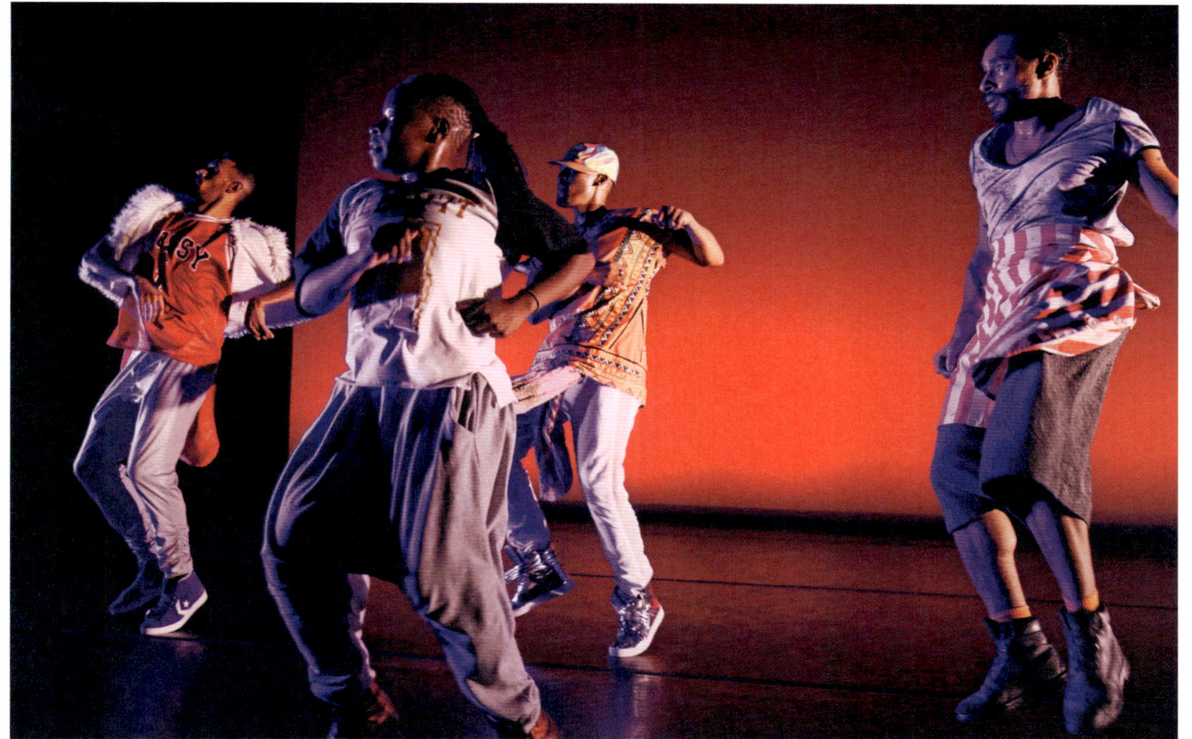

Cynthia Oliver, *Virago-Man Dem*, with Jonathan Gonzalez, Ni'Ja Whitson, Duane Cyrus, and Niall Noel Jones. BAM (Brooklyn Academy of Music), Brooklyn, October 25, 2017

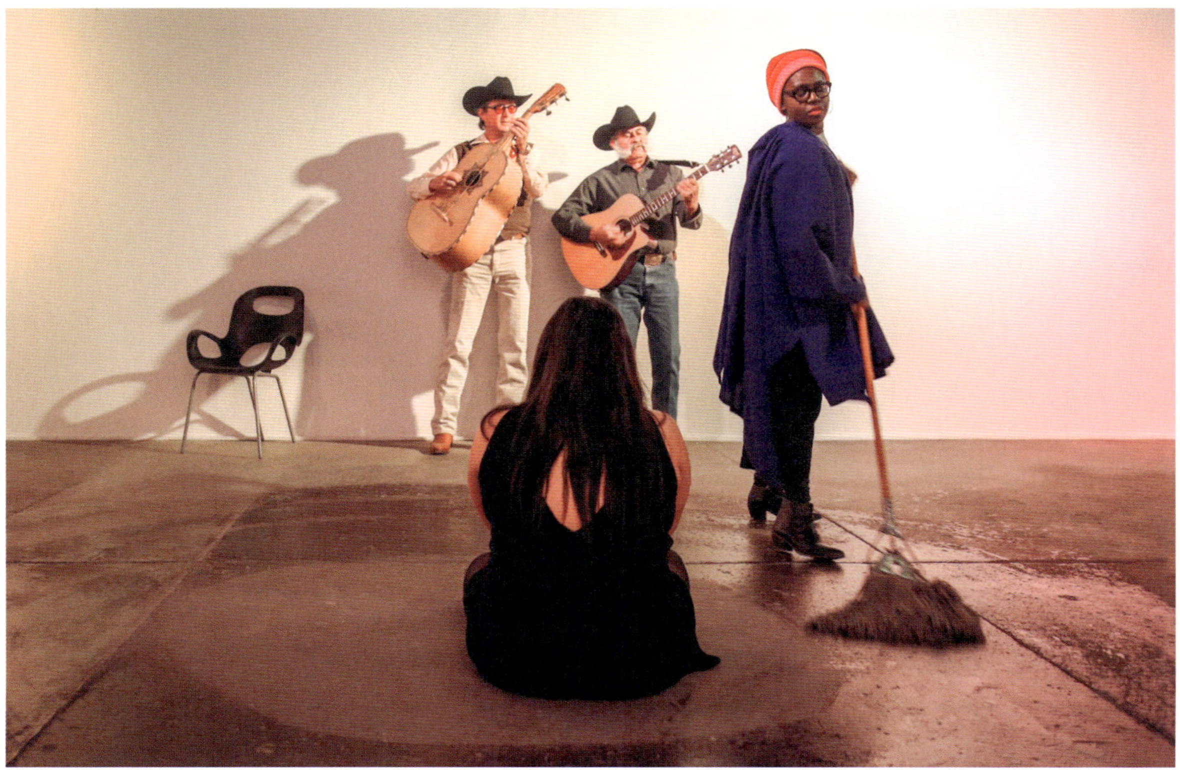

Grand Opening/Grand Closing, with Autumn Knight. Marfa Contemporary, Marfa, TX, January 13, 2018

     In Conversation

PERFOR-MANCE

SCORES

Knight composed performance scores for S. Bianca Bailey, a University of Illinois graduate student, who performed solo for one hour each week over the course of nine weeks in the exhibition.

Week 1: Work with the Space
Explore the sculptural elements of the installation—moving walls.

Week 2: Books + Read
Read a book through the holes in the walls. You can do this in whatever way you see fit. The book should be a book by and/or about black women. Every 7–10 minutes or so, read a paragraph aloud.

Week 3: Shoes
Sit between two walls, one on either side of you. The wall with the biggest hole (at the bottom) should be on one side; the wall with the vertical cutout should be on the other. Bring a bag of shoes to the gallery space. Put the shoes on and take them off. Repeat this for the entirety of the hour. When you're done with a pair, discard them through the holes in the walls. When you finish the bag, gather the shoes and start again. I want you to tell a story, or a series of stories, from your life. To no one in particular. You can mutter under your breath as you tell the story. Don't look people in the eye on this one. This is an internalized performance.

Week 4: Wells
Talk about your well project in Kenya. Move walls, without using your hands, into different geometric shapes.

Week 5: Classify + Catalogue
The task is to organize everything in the entire gallery (walls, blocks, and whatever crap you've dragged into the space) neatly, to perfection. Once you've done the first round of organizing objects into a linear, grid-like pattern or structure, go back and reorganize by color, texture, similarity, shape, etc. Clear your mind while doing it. When people enter the gallery space, offer to organize their things. Ask: "Can I empty out the contents of your bag and arrange them, organize, and group them? Please." Recategorize and reorganize until you can't anymore. Do it (mostly) silently.
A meditation.
A slow crazy going.
A spiritual undertaking.
A mind-clearing.
An obsessive action.
A thing that looks nice.

Week 6: Reading a Play
Read *In the Blood* by Suzan Lori Parks.

Week 7: File
File your nails onto black clothing (covering your lap, sleeves, shoes). This is an endurance piece. This means that you'll have to pace yourself over the course of an

hour. The piece is about the human body
wearing away through acts of maintenance.
It is also a demonstration of the strive
towards physical perfection that can possi-
bly be achieved through "time." The white
nail powder on black clothes is the evidence both of this process and of doing
tasks in the light that we normally do in
the dark. If possible, I'd like you to only
speak with your eyes. Speak meaningfully,
but communicate only with your eyes. Make
eye contact and go back to filing. This is a
public/personal moment. This should be
done in the ghost light. It is a meditation—
to remember, to forget, to think through,
to be mindless, to think joyous thoughts—
while creating perfect nails.

Week 8: Who You on the Phone With?
Call someone and talk to them for an hour.
We don't need to hear the other person's
part of the conversation—only yours. If
you are listening, then let the audience
be exposed to that. This is another explo-
ration of the public/private + internal/
external space. Think about who you can
talk to for one hour. Who can give you this
gift of time? Who would you like to talk
to for an hour? We rarely make time for
a full phone conversation. Usually if it
happens, it's an accident. Indulge.
Reconnect. Be mundane. The hope/purpose
is to slow down time.

Week 9: Stay Here a Bit Longer
Than You Should
Intermittently throughout the hour,
in-between, during, and on top of the
other tasks, ask visitors to "stay here a
bit longer than you should." Do whatever
you have to do. Tell them this is your
last performance. Tell them you feel sad
when they walk away. Tell them you
appreciate their presence. Tell them you
need them to stay just a bit longer. Ask
them to watch you do one more thing. Use
eye contact. Smile. Implore them to stay,
just for a bit.

Part 1: Speak the Speech, I Pray You
(15 minutes or so)
Speak one sentence or a few words in
each language that you speak.
Communicate across these barriers.
Speak with your mouth. Start with
these languages. Then move to inde-
cipherable languages.

Part 2: Get the FUCK Down.
(An Endurance Performance)
Bring headphones and music into the
space. Dance continuously. This will
probably require a playlist. Ideally
you could create or access a playlist
that has a range of emotions associated with it. Your favorite songs.
Filling you over and over with memories, with gladness, with lust, with
motion. Dance all over the space.

Part 3: Leave Something Behind
Leave one thing in the space you
honestly do not need. Ask others to
do the same. (This can be a physical
object or a mental or spiritual one.)

Pages 99–101: Performance score for *Autumn Knight:
In Rehearsal*, with S. Bianca Bailey. Krannert Art Museum,
Champaign, February 2, 2017

PERFORMANCE SCORES

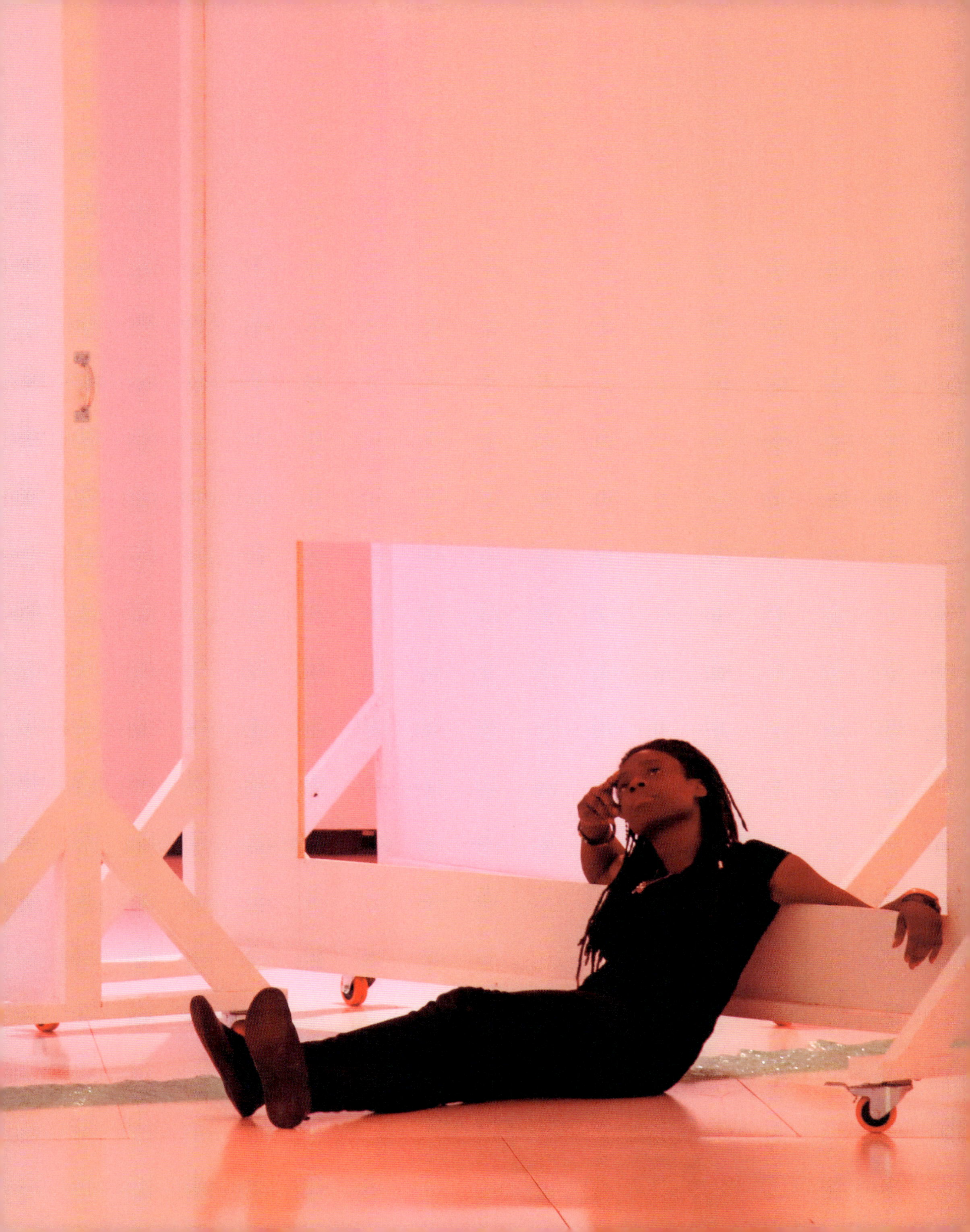

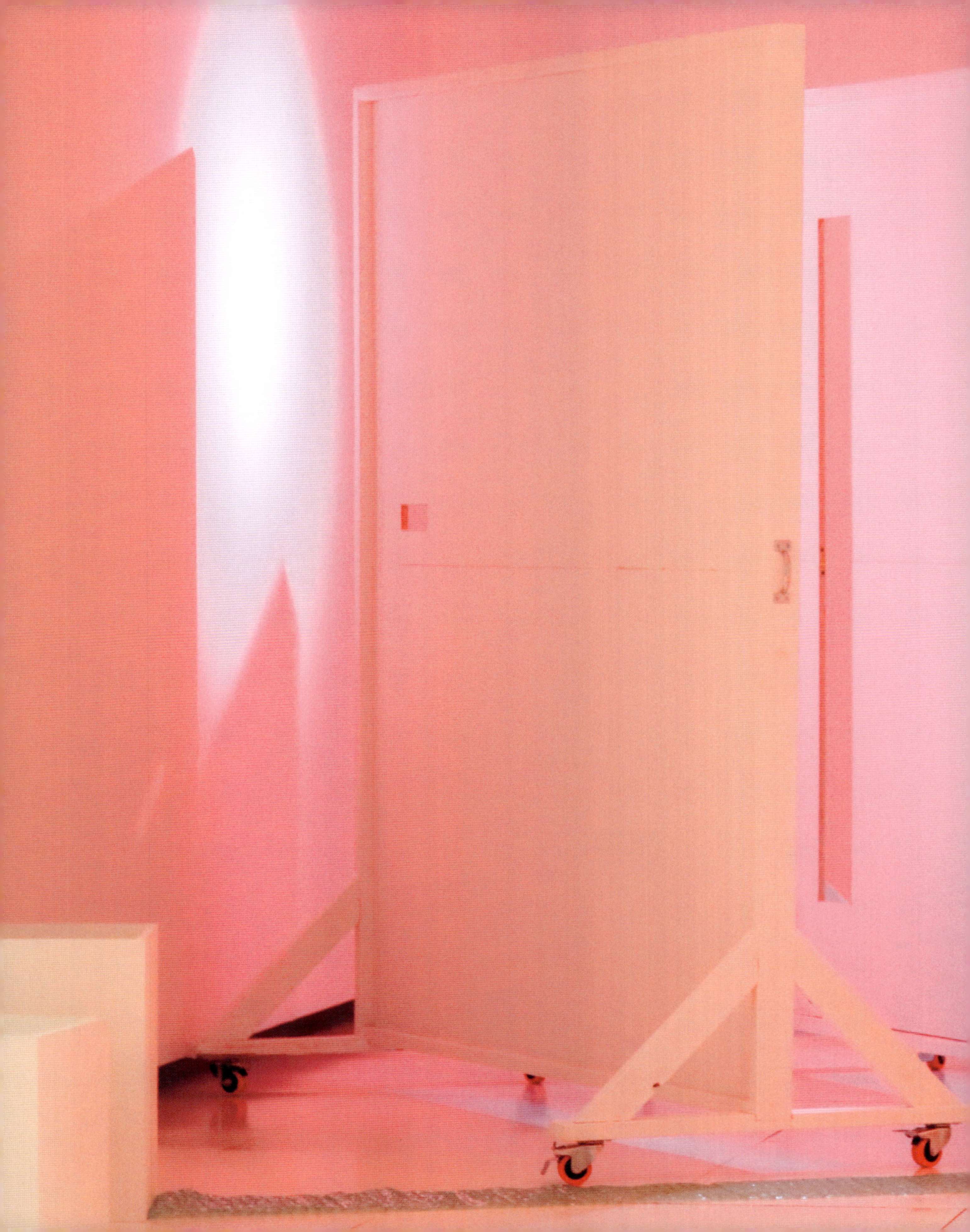

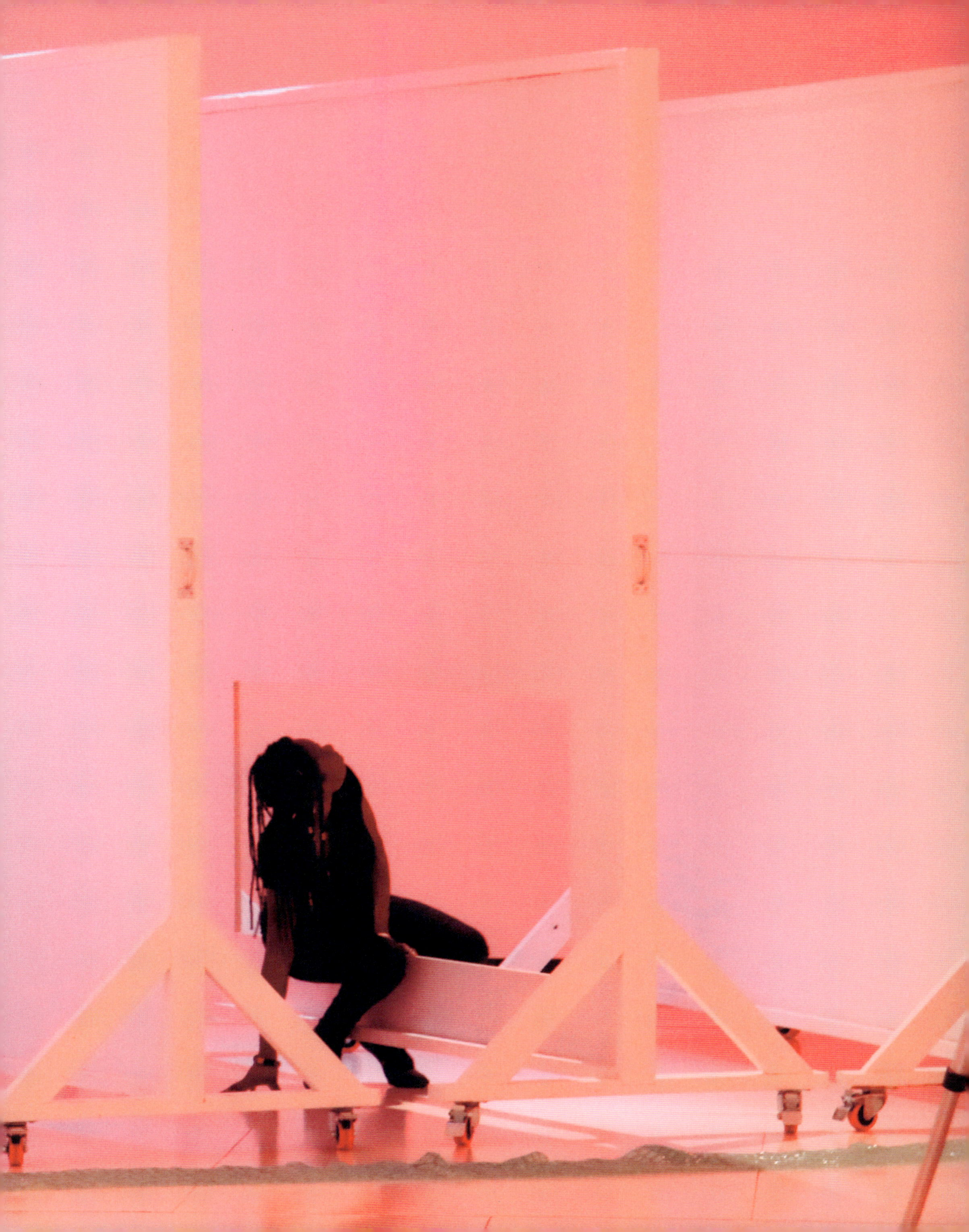

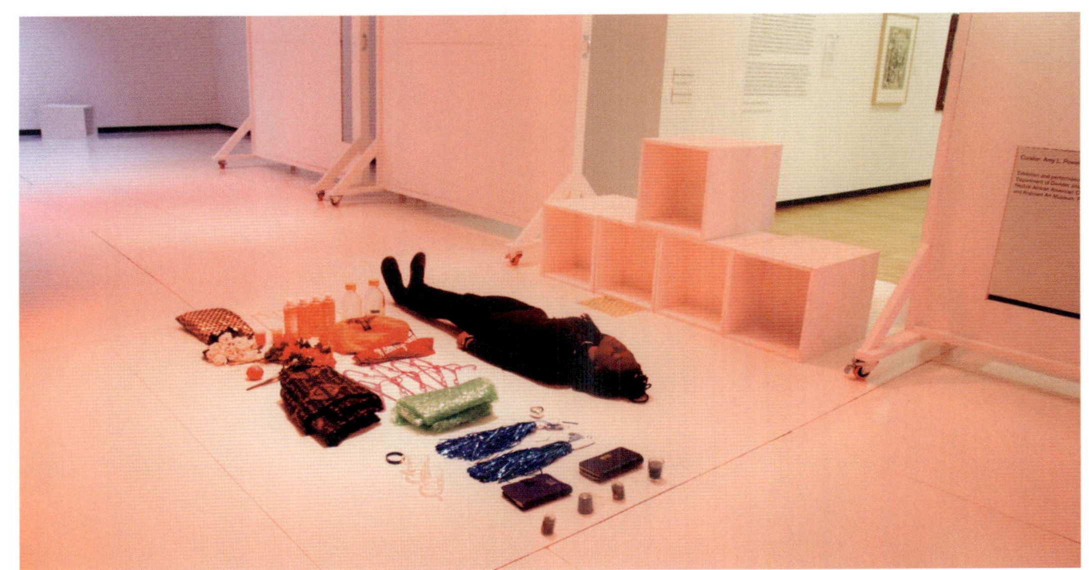

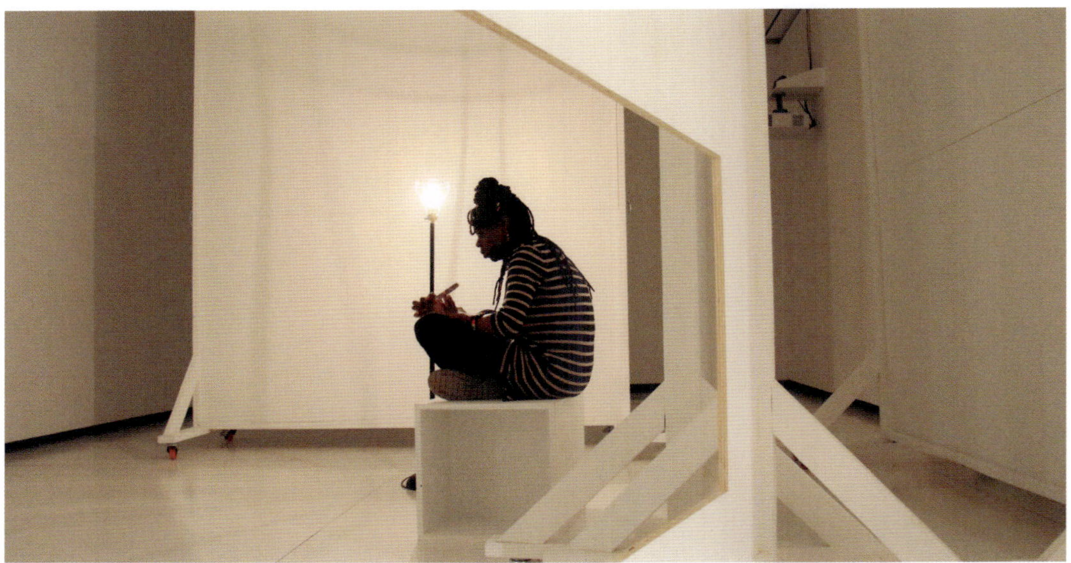

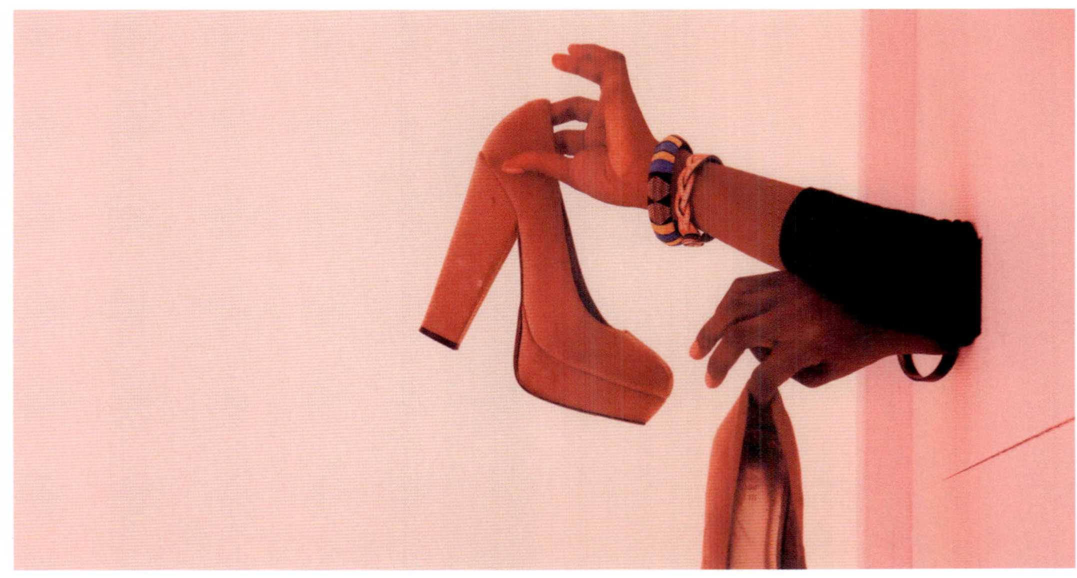

Pages 102–103: Performance scores for *Autumn Knight: In Rehearsal*, with S. Bianca Bailey. Krannert Art Museum, Champaign, March 2, 2017 (top of both pages); March 17, 2017 (middle of both pages); February 16, 2017 (bottom-left); February 23, 2017 (bottom-right)

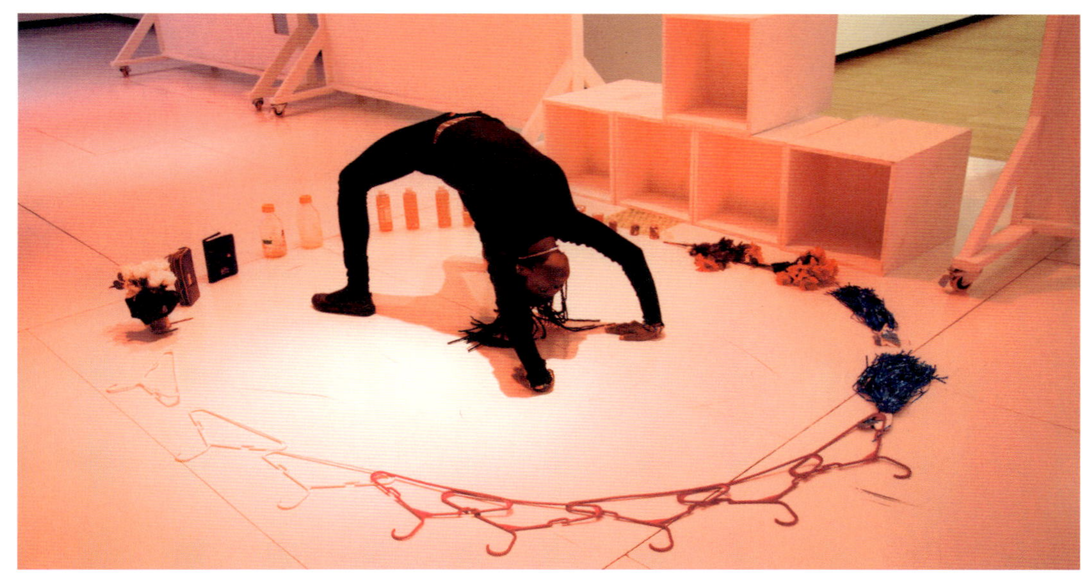

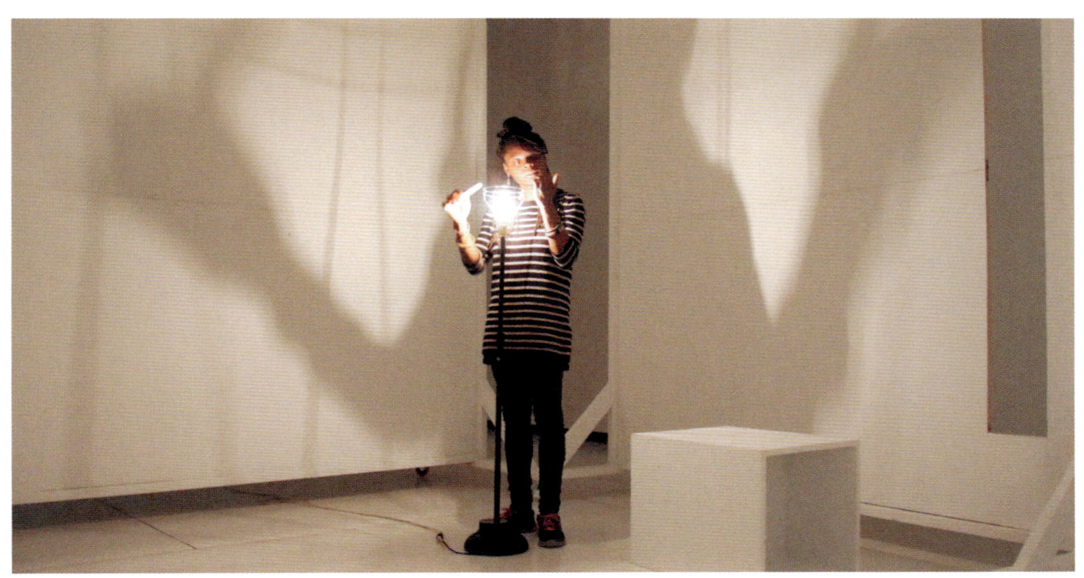

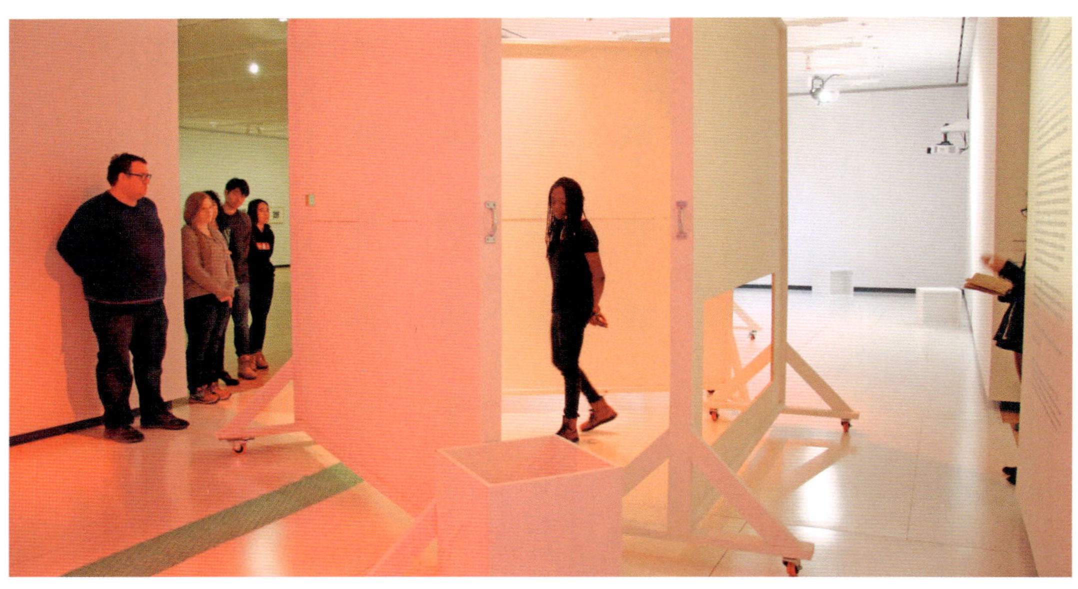

Knight composed performance scores for Holly Garrett, a University of Illinois graduate student, who performed on cello for one hour during two weeks of the exhibition. These scores were written as companion pieces to *Lament* (p. 60–67).

Part 1: April 5, 2017

The meditation: Would I rather be feared or loved? Easy. Both. I want people to be afraid of how much they love me. (Some Shakespeare, Lear?) (Michael Scott?)

The LOOKS: Hair: Pulled back. Whatever will allow you to lay flat on the floor. You will have balloons tied to your head. They will float several feet above your head. Tie the balloon strings around your head like a headband. Black clothing. A combination of textures would be nice. Bare feet.

Part 1: Pizzicato Perkinson (5 min)
Perform first lying on the ground in the blue part of the gallery in the center of the room with your head facing the center of the gallery space. Lay at an angle if you can.

Part 2: Perkinson (10 min)
Play in the corner of the gallery facing the wall in that same general space. In the way that we rehearsed.

Part 3: Crumb (10 min)
Play seated in middle of the gallery space, in the doorway. Give face. Communicate a range of facial expressions to the audience. Do it anyway, even if no one is there.

The Middle: Pizzicato (5 min)
Pluck. Pluck. Whatever you like. Ideally there would be some dissonance here, some haunting, some excitement, some joy, some lament. There can be longer moments of silence here. There can be improvisation.

Part 4: Bloch (10 min)
Play behind the wall with the lower part cut out. This wall should be in the pink area of the space.

Part 5: Pizzicato Perkinson (5 min)
Here you are lying on the floor, half in the gallery and half out. Your head should be in the gallery closest to the front entrance of the museum. At the end, slowly pull the balloons down. One by one, stab the balloons. Exit.

Part 2: April 26, 2017

The meditation: You are the sky, everything else is weather.

The LOOKS: Hair: Pulled back. Wear all white if you have it. Or a white top and black pants, if you don't have all white. Hair wrapped in aluminum foil. You may be able to get some foil from the café in the building. An insane amount of foil. Maybe you can make a ponytail with the foil? Bare feet.

Part 0: Stand staring for 3 minutes while holding your instrument. Look forward. Stand somewhere in the gallery away from the light so the audience has to look for you.

Part 1: Pizzicato Perkinson (5 min)
Perform first lying on ground with half your body lying outside of the gallery—on the side with the sculptures and abstract work.

Part 2: Crumb (7 min)
Play your cello in the center of the gallery. Shake your head from side to side. Give face. Communicate a range of facial expressions to the audience. Do it anyway, even if no one is there.

Part 3: Bloch (7 min)
In the corner. Play facing the corner. Any corner you choose. A different corner than last time.

The Middle: Pizzicato (5 min)
Perform behind the wall with the large part cut out. Pluck. Pluck. Whatever you like. Ideally there would be some dissonance here, some haunting, some excitement, some joy, some lament. There can be longer moments of silence here. There can be improvisation.

Part 4: Perkinson (10 min)
Play behind the wall with the long vertical slit. Be visible in the slit.

Part 5: Pizzicato Perkinson (5 min)
Here you are lying on the floor again. This time with your feet on the wall if possible.

Part 6: Place your instrument beside you. Lay there facing up for 3 minutes.

The end.

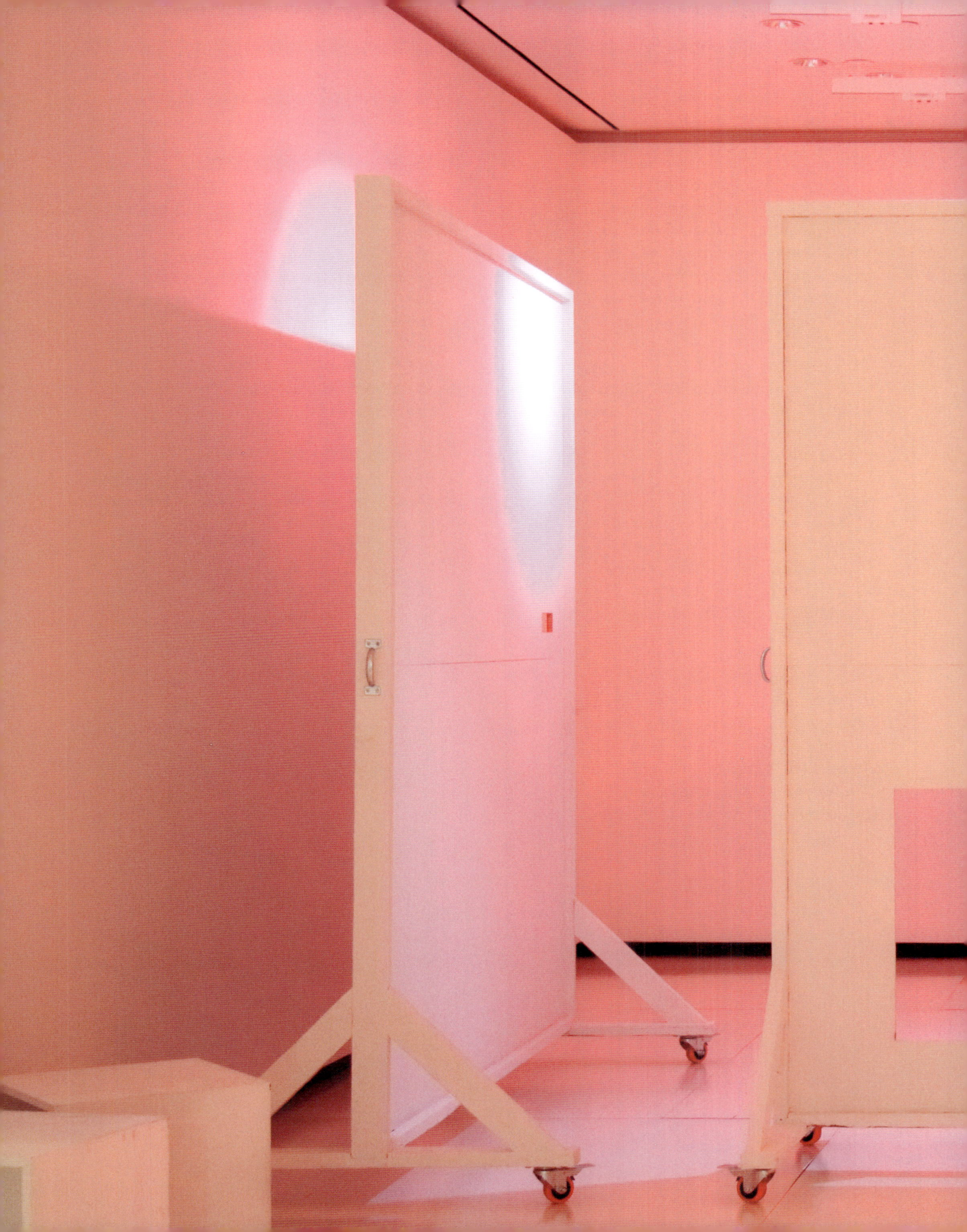

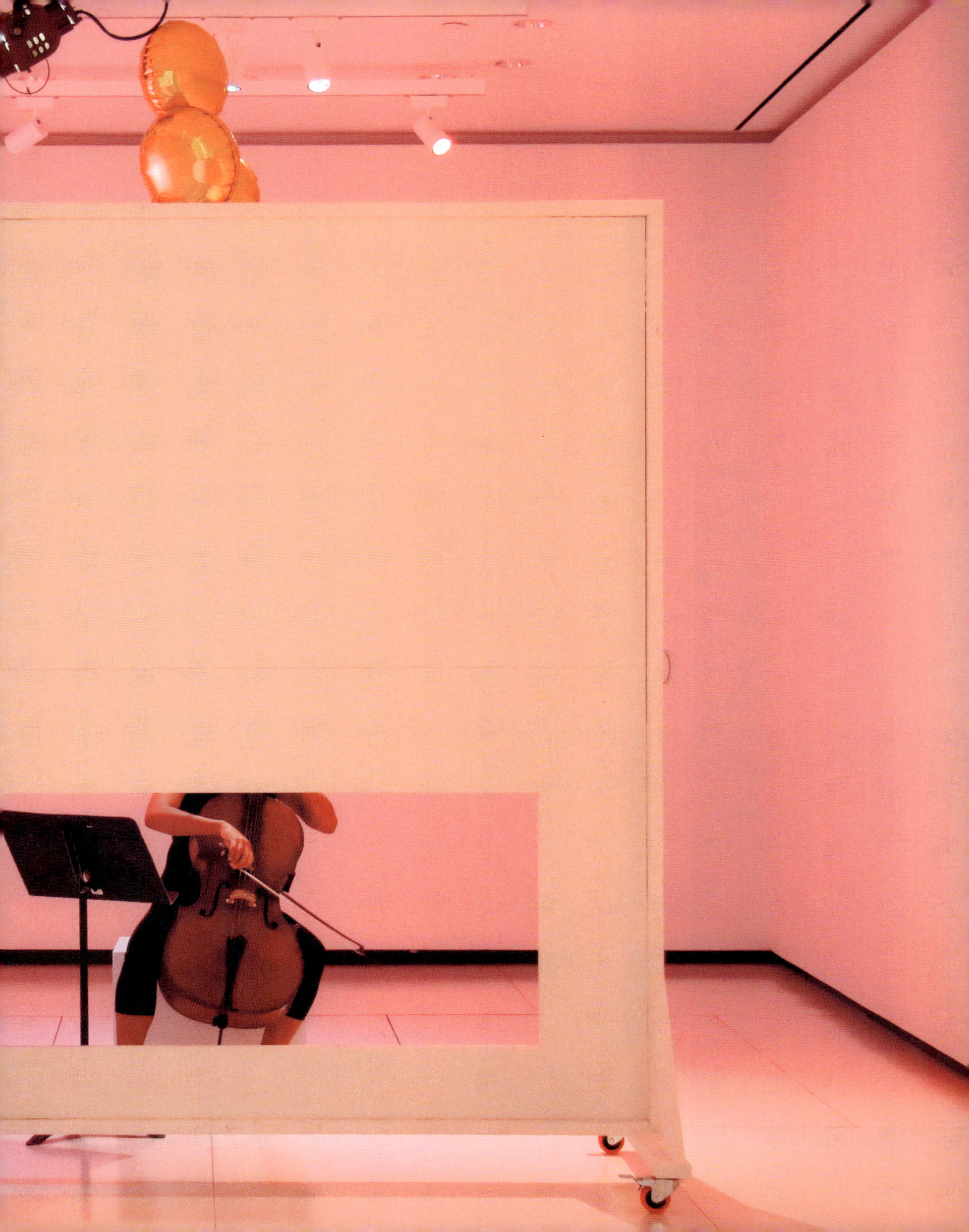

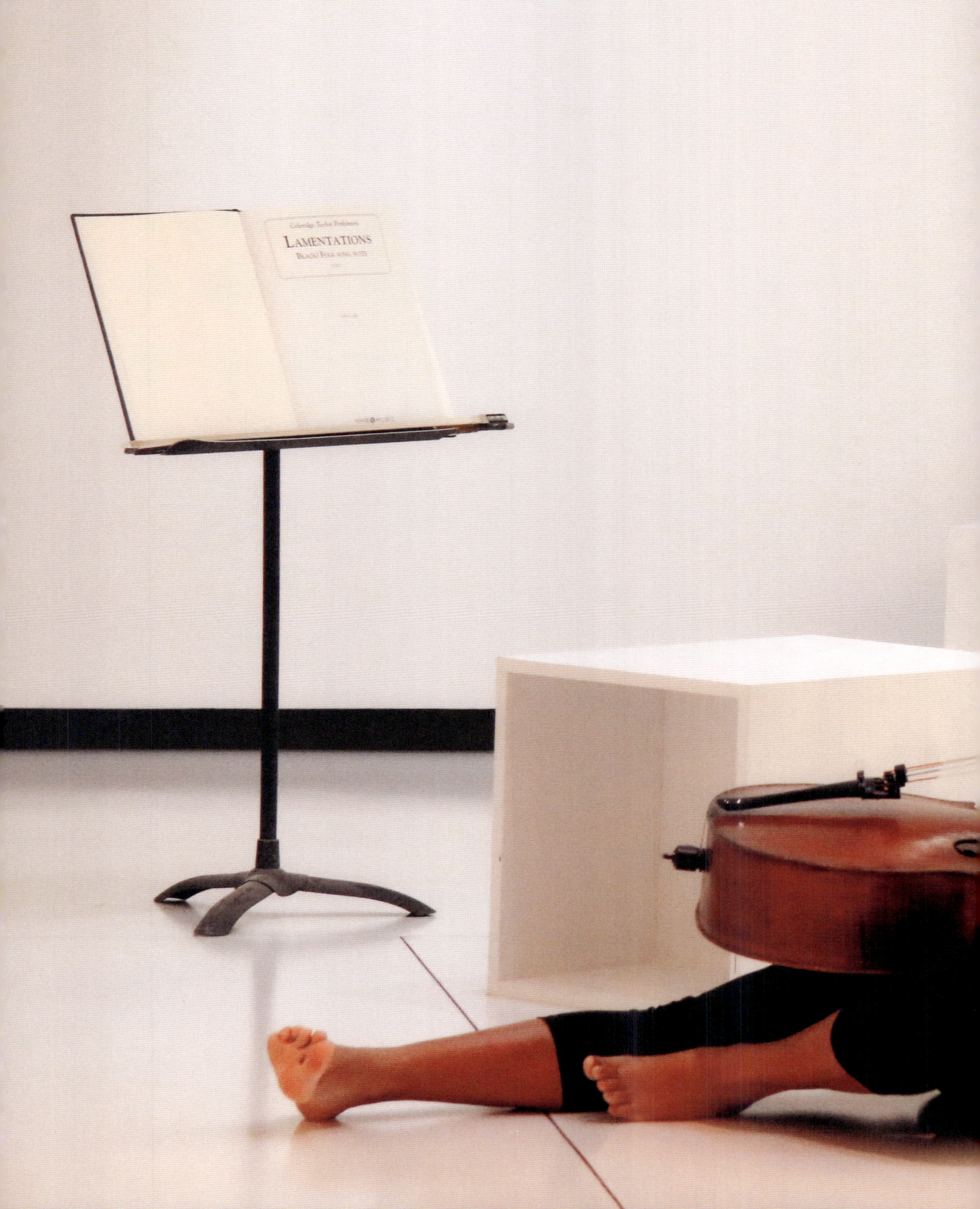
Coleridge-Taylor Perkinson's
LAMENTATIONS
BLACK/FOLK SONG SUITE

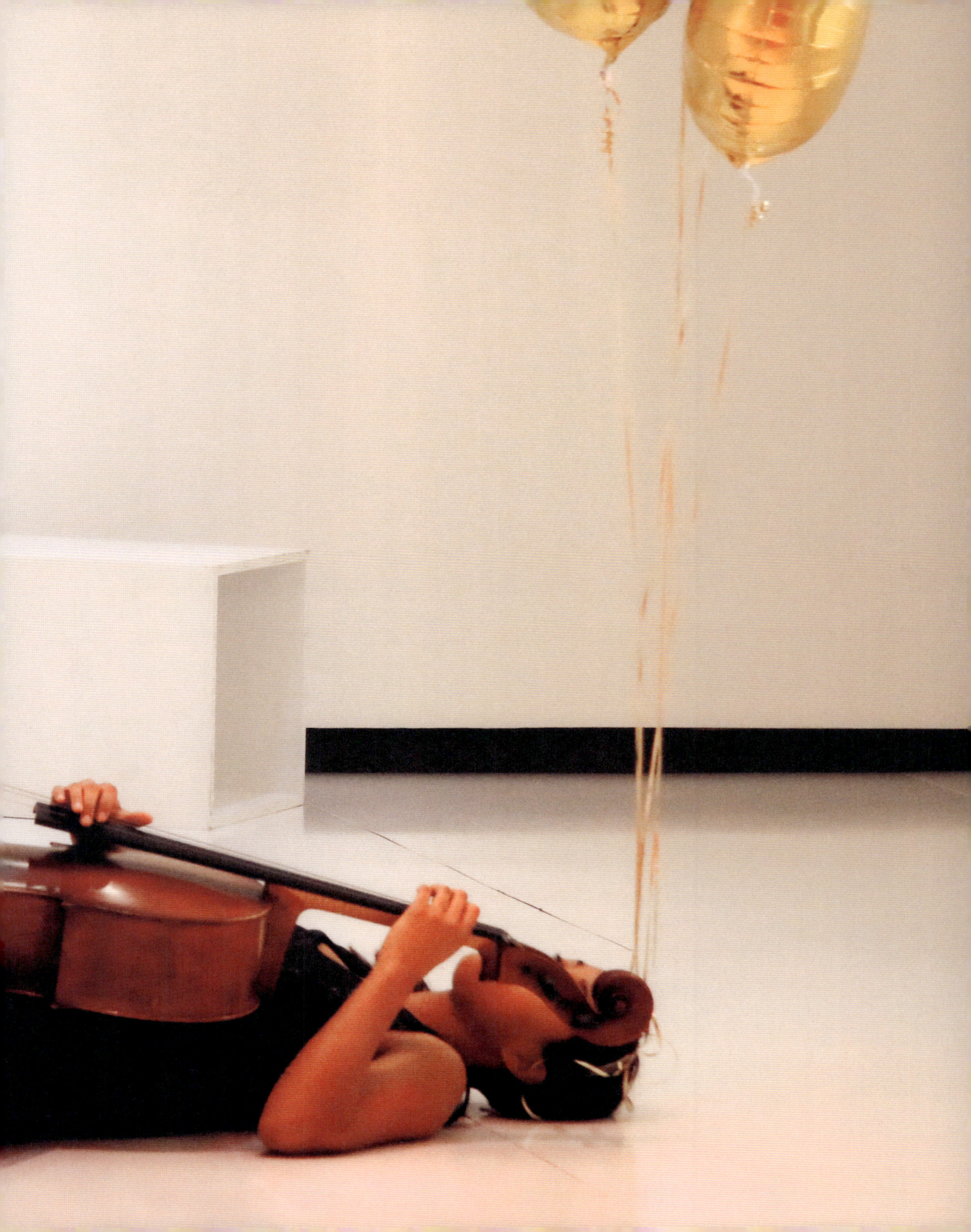

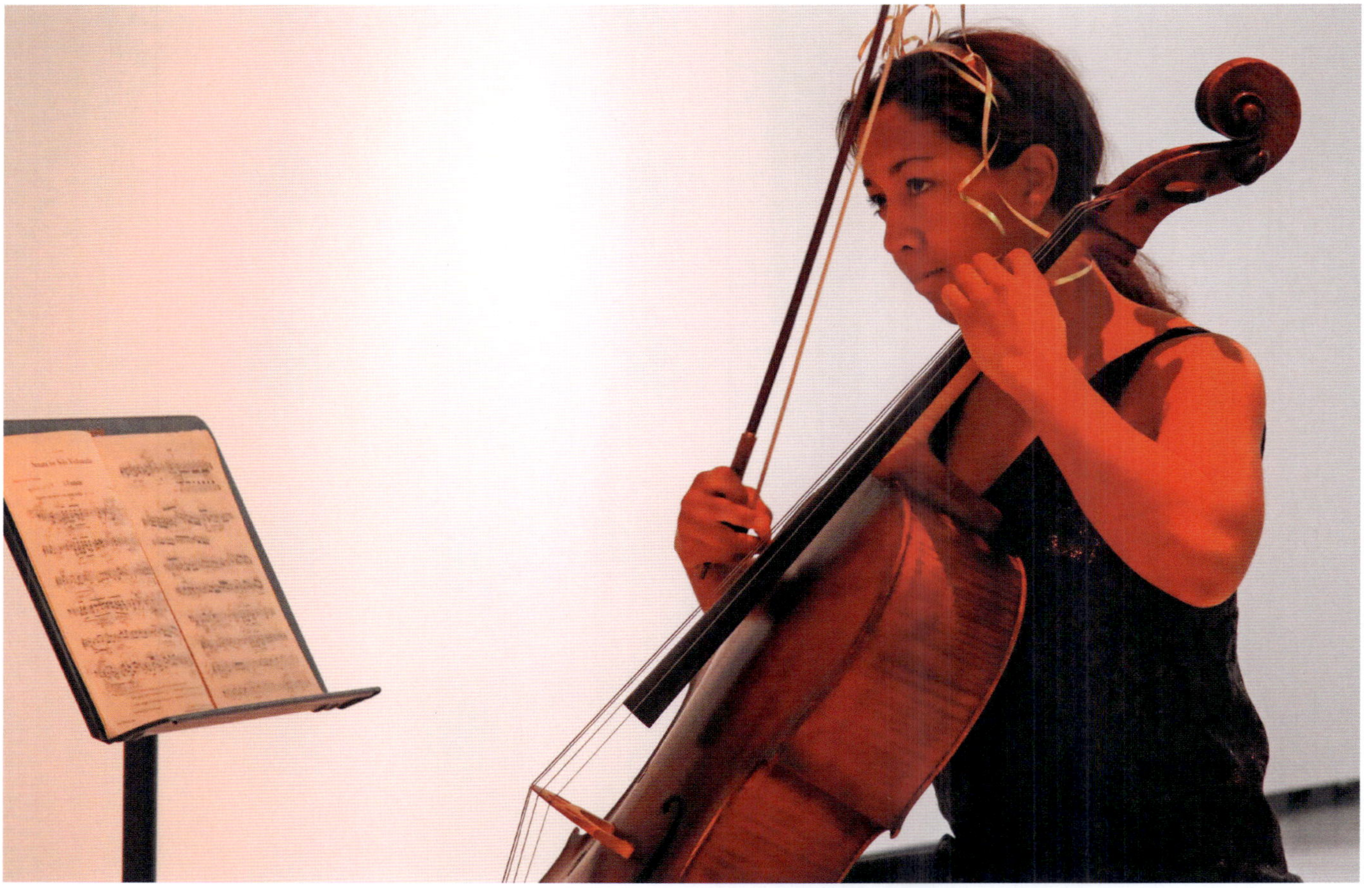

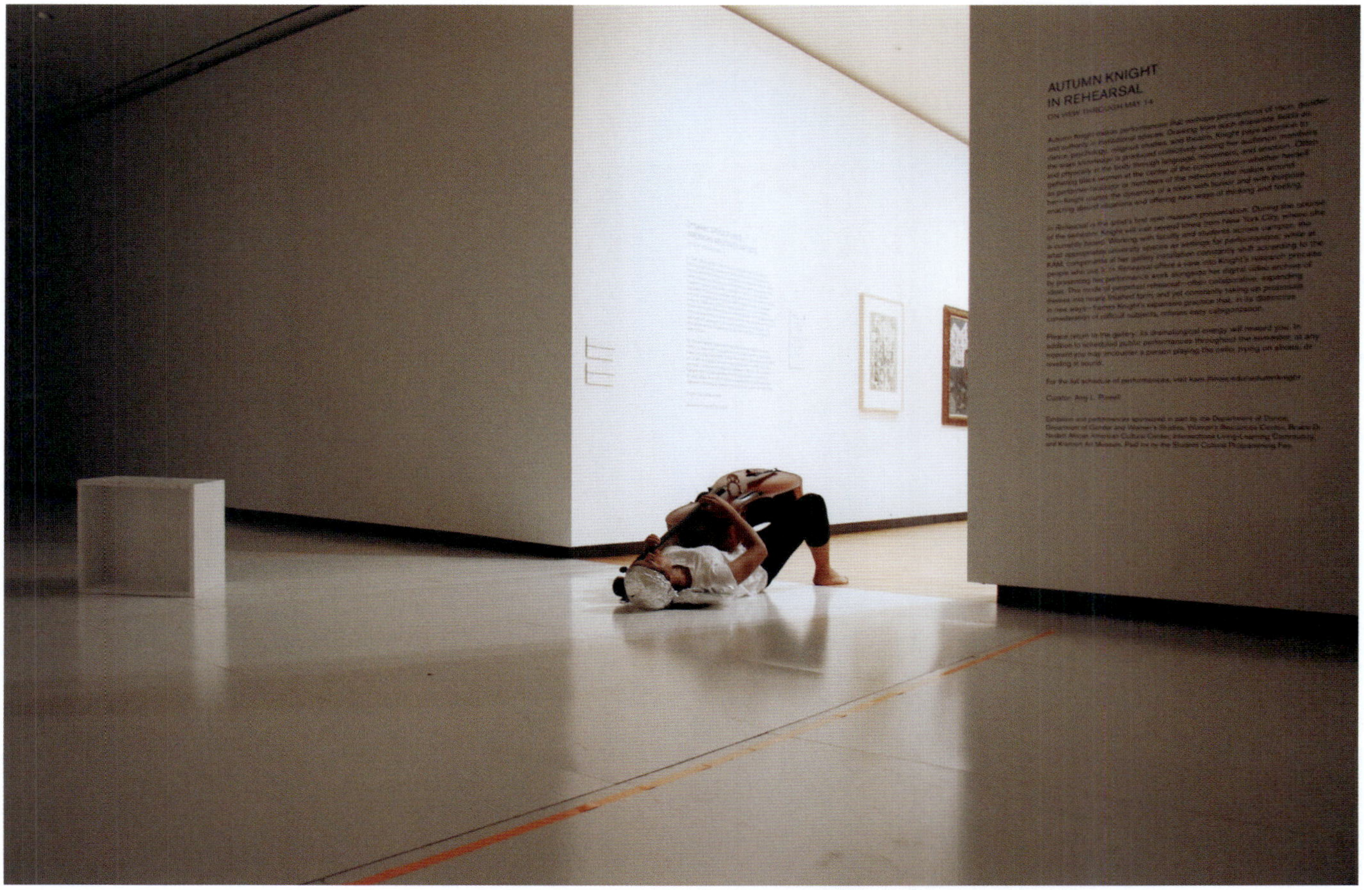

AUTUMN KNIGHT
IN REHEARSAL
ON VIEW THROUGH MAY 14

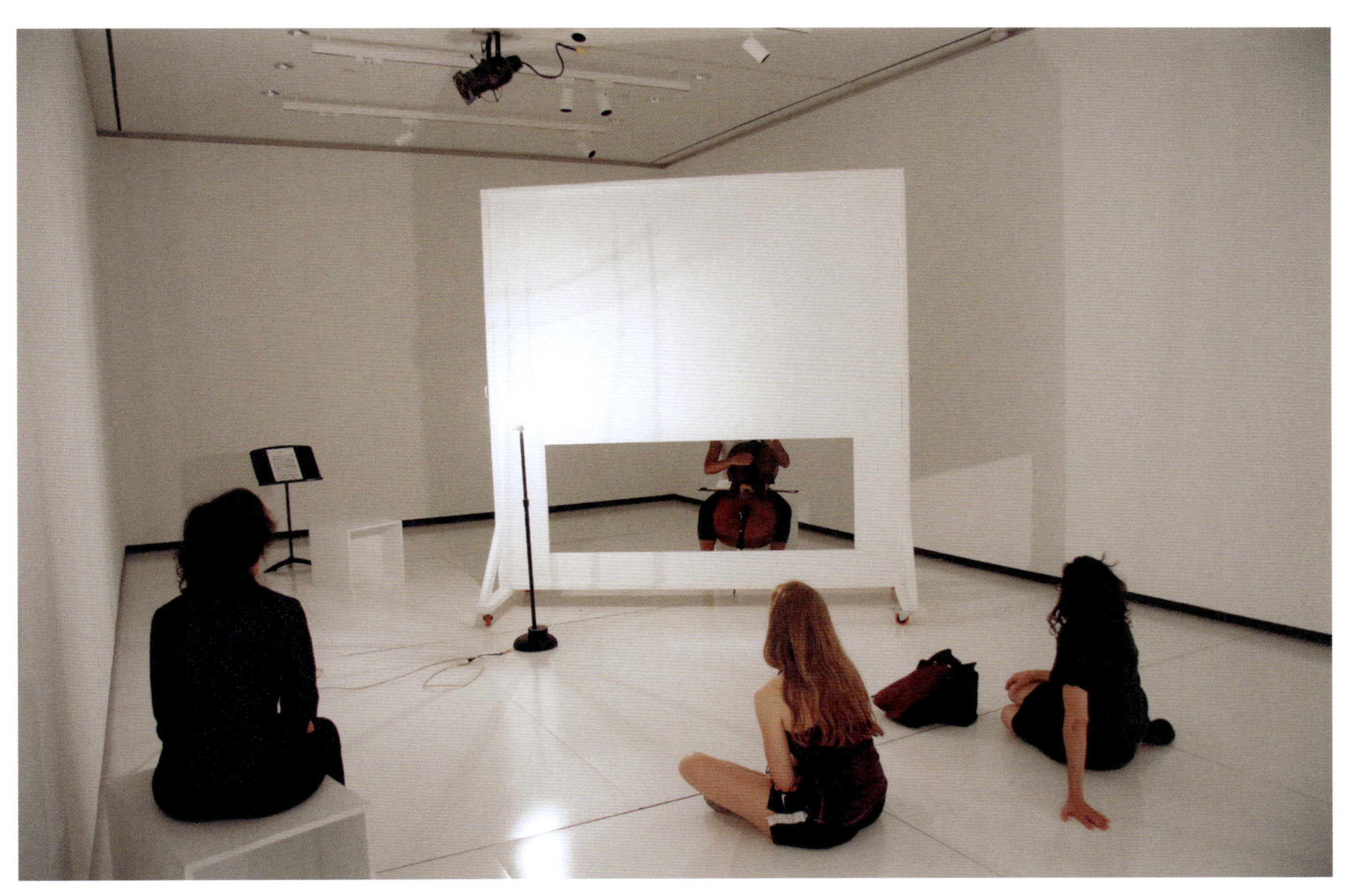

Pages 106–111: Performance scores for
Autumn Knight: In Rehearsal, with Holly
Garrett. Krannert Art Museum, Champaign,
April 5 and April 26, 2017

PERFORMANCE SCORES

RESEARCH

2   Keva: Facetime with Mekeva.
3   Walking back and forth.
4   ~~Having a phone conversation in the gallery. Who can you~~
~~call? Issues with public/private.~~
~~Who can you talk to for an hour? Can you set this up? We rare-~~
~~ly make time for a full phone conversation. Usually if~~
~~that happens, its an accident. Endulge. Dig in. Find out more~~
~~Reconnect. Be mundane. The hope/purpose is to slow down time.~~
5   What other sources of light can you bring into the museum?
Can you show?
6   Tell me your secrets.
7   ~~Stack things neatly. What can you get a hold of, that you~~
~~can stack over and over again? Recategorize and recategorize~~
~~until you can't anymore.~~
~~Color, texture, similarity, shape.~~
~~Can I dump out the contents of your bag and organize it?~~
(Bianca, every time she does something big, she cleans her
house first.)
8   ~~Filters. How to build filters. How to filter words.~~
9   ~~Restage a black play in the museum.~~
10 Give yourself a breast exam in the gallery. Print out
the directions for this exam. Read them aloud. Describe what
you feel during the exam. If you can, stick your breasts
in the different spaces of the walls, and examine your breast
through these spaces. Stand on top of the boxes and give
exams from there.
11 Perform in the dark. Turn off all the lights.
12 Give an hour-long lecture on water filtration, with a
PowerPoint presentation.
13 ~~Reading a text?~~
15 Watching something invisible.
16 Something with "hurt bae" but positive.
My own bae.

17 File nails on black clothes.
18 Dance: Get the FUCK Down. + 14. Endurance performance.
Bring headphones and music into the space. Dance
the whole time if you can. This will probably require
a playlist. Ideally you could create or access a
playlist that has a range of emotions associated with it.
An hour of your favorite songs. Filling you over
and over with memories, with gladness, with lust,
with motion.
19 Speak the Speech, I Pray You:
Speak one sentence or a few words in each language.
Communicate across these barriers. Last week you spoke
with your eyes. This week you will speak with your
mouth. Start with these languages. Then move to indeci-
pherable languages.

<u>Bianca speaks bits of other languages:</u>
Arabic
Swahili
French
Spanish
Japanese
Slang
Afrikaans

<u>Instruments:</u>
Clarinet
Trumpet
Bianca reads from her own published
dissertation and other texts.

Trump(et)
Raps/Sings

Bianca says she's never nervous.
Students visiting the museum drew the shapes she made
with the walls and blocks.
Bianca told a story about a baby with HIV.
Relating to students during the performance.
They were writing paragraphs about the performance for
an extra credit. Economics + Art students.

Futzing instructions: FUTZING INSTRUCTIONS:
Place on wall. Cardstock.

Call your mother. Make sure she has had scheduled
mammogram.

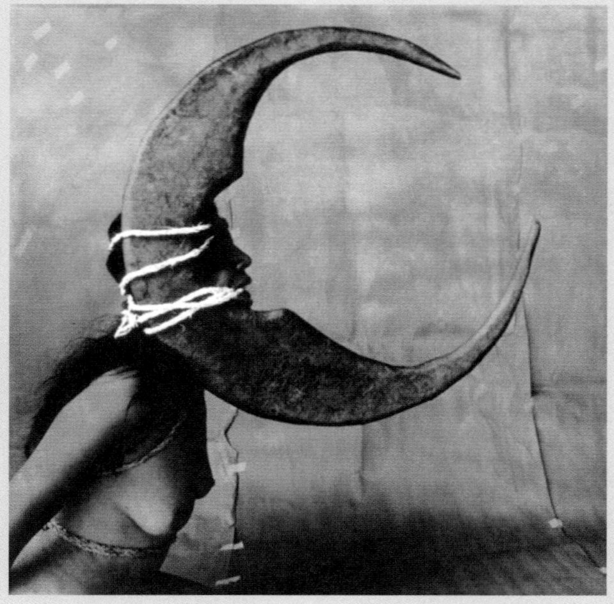

Then tell her to tell you something funny
about a family member.

Give a gift to the next person you see.

What would it take to ride your bike more?

What are the consequences of jealousy?

Prepare to do one thing on your bucket list.

Write a shopping list from the perspective of a prostitute.

Justify why you are here right now.

Stay here a bit longer than you should.

Call Sallie Mae right now: 1-888-2-SALLIE (888-272-5543).
Tell that person you appreciate their work.
Take a photo of yourself laughing and send to this email
address: autkni@gmail.com.

Make up a dance routine.

Leave one thing in the space you honestly do not need.

Let's learn another language together.

                    RESEARCH

General movement pattern notes: falling, popping up, dragging, falling apart, gasping, false hope, incredible bursts of hope. I've attached images of movement that are worth exploring. In terms of drawing on the present faculty for inspiration, I'm into the work of Tere O'Connor, Jennifer Monson, Becky Maybee-Ferrell (of course), and Cynthia Oliver (of course). I've got to look into others; these are the ones I got to first.

Movement 1: Chained
There are places along the perimeter of the seating where the animals are pinned. I thought we could use this for the opening. Images attached.
The space is so large and amazing. So much to play with (and ground to cover). Opening Movement:
https://www.youtube.com/watch?v=3hcUqoM2bqU (I'm interested in first two minutes of this video.)

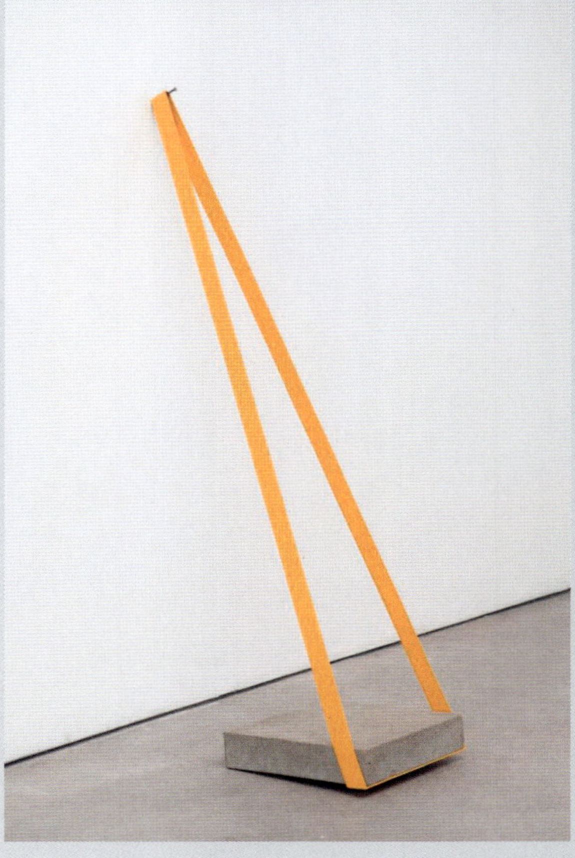

This is how I envision this might look, with Abijan's body as the block, in the middle of that space, pivoting from this point.

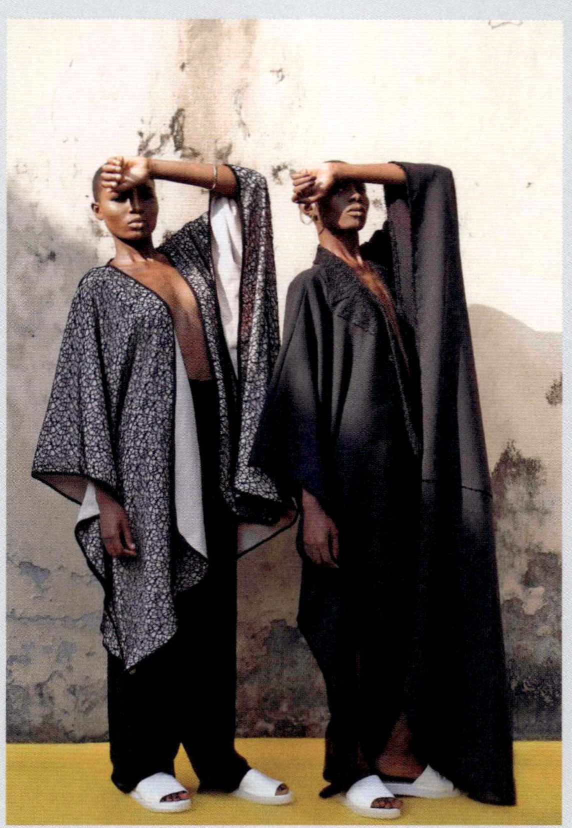

I like this one for the combination of contemporary dances
and the way they cover the floor space:
https://www.youtube.com/watch?v=9BKr3D-xQhO

Movement 3: A Moment of Release/Burst of Life
http://eloronegro.tumblr.com/post/156882694875
/californiadrian-Oz-cmooooon-raiden-ooohhhh

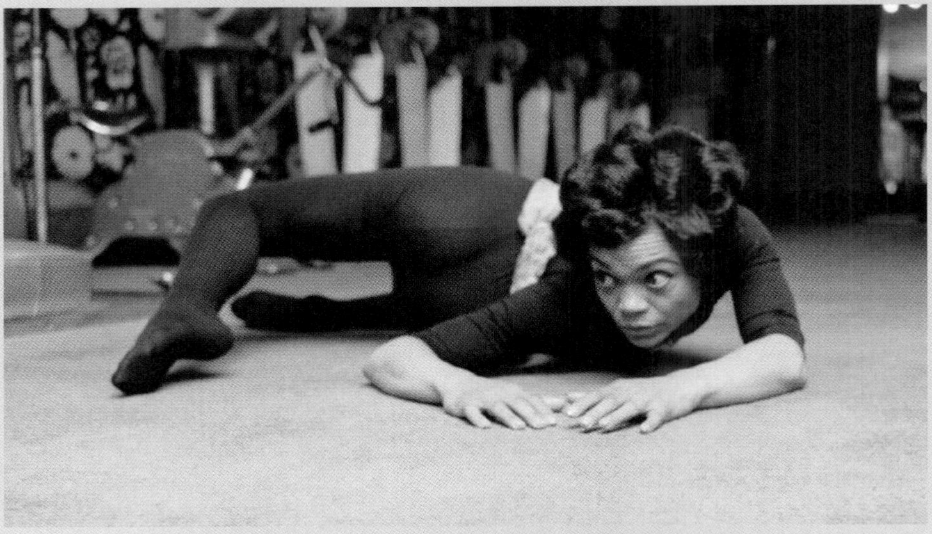

http://eloronegro.tumblr.com/post/128200437995
/knucklecartel-a-nice-clip-from-rosas-danst

http://eloronegro.tumblr.com/post/79101540572
/somethingtoseeorhear-hr-of-bad-brains

Movement 5: Wasting
This will more than likely be the moment where Abijan
moves fully into the water, which will be on from the
beginning. Moving more into the original choreography.

This is just to get started.
Thanks for your patience!
Looking forward to it!

Sound:
I'm still working on sound, but this is some of the
inspiration/audio from the first iteration of the
performance: https://soundcloud.com/trepverter/lonnies
-lament-john-coltrane

Can we still be talking about *Wall*?

Should there be an installation of a green room?
In one corner of the gallery.

Should the whole space be a rehearsal studio?

What can I get from my time in England?
Janice Kerbel.
What is it about lights, flexible spaces?
What is it about theatre, the process, the space, that keeps
me interested?
Can something be destructed over time?
White couch, lights/video can be projected onto this sur-
face. On a bunch of white surfaces. White table, etc. All
of these projected surfaces are the places that inspiration,
ideas, imagery comes from, emerges, and falls at the end
of the day.
One of the walls has a hole in it.
Raked area with humps on it. On one side of the gallery.

PERFORMANCE 1: El Diablo y Cristo Negro

Jesus as demure and evil

Cast:
2 queer male actors of color
Xavier Roe: from the South Side of Chicago
Chivas Michael

Looks:
Glitter beard
Long Jesus-wig: 22-inches
Lashes

Set:
El Diablo has ladder
Cristo Negro on scaffold has wheels

                              RESEARCH

Autumn Knight

Born in Houston, 1980
Lives in New York

Education

2016 — Skowhegan School of Painting and Sculpture, Skowhegan, ME

2010 — MA, Drama Therapy, New York University, New York

2003 — BA, Theatre Arts/Speech Communications, Dillard University, New Orleans

2002 — Certificate, Arts Management & Marketing, University of London

Solo Exhibitions, Performances, and Screenings

2018 — *Grand Opening/Grand Closing*, Marfa Contemporary, Marfa, TX
The La-a Consortium: Convening #3, Dwell in Other Futures: Art/Urbanism/Midwest, Pulitzer Arts Foundation, St. Louis
Sanity TV, Akademie Der Künste, Berlin

2017 — *In Rehearsal*, Krannert Art Museum, Champaign
Directions to Prairie View, whatsherface: IRL, The Hand, Brooklyn

2016 — *The La-a Consortium*, New Cities Future Ruins, Dallas

2015 — *She Think She Kawaii*, Artpace, San Antonio

2014 — *GYN*, Fresh Arts, Houston
My Son Quazaar, Afronaut(a) 2.0 Media Festival, Kelly-Strayhorn Theater, Pittsburgh
Yates vs. Wheatley, BOX 13 ArtSpace, Houston
Untitled, Lone Star Explosion International Performance Biennale, Houston

2013 — *Evilene: Upcycle Queen*, Art League Houston
Auditive Chamber, Alabama Song, Houston

2012–13 — Round 37 | *Futz: A Research Method*, Project Row Houses, Houston

Collaborative Performances and Screenings

2018 — *Instructions for a Fight* (with Chelsea Knight), Single Channel: Video Art Festival, Anthology Film Archives, New York

2017 — *READ (Cont.)* (with John Pluecker), The Poetry Project, New York
Instructions for a Fight (with Chelsea Knight), Volta Art Fair, New York
Mayday Mayday (with Chelsea Knight), Skowhegan, New York

2016 — *Clown and Dragon* (with Lisa E. Harris), Chale Wote Street Art Festival, Accra, Ghana
Derelicts Dish (with Chelsea Knight), Untitled Art Fair, Miami

2015 — *Knight + Knight Latencies* (with Chelsea Knight), Project Row Houses and DiverseWorks, Houston; Skowhegan and New Museum, New York
Eugene Howard Open Lecture Series, Project Row Houses, Alabama Song, and Art League Houston, Houston

2014 — *The Ghost of Robert Rauschenberg* (with Thomas Dougherty), Galveston Artist Residency
Flower Man Bike Parade (with Lisa E.

Harris and M'kina Tapscott),
CounterCurrent, Houston

2013 *You Completes Me* (with Steffani Jemison),
Studio Museum in Harlem and
University of North Carolina at
Chapel Hill
What Is Seen As It Is Seen (with John Pluecker),
DiverseWorks, Houston
Clown and Dragon (with Lisa E. Harris),
Marigny neighborhood, New Orleans
Sunday Social (with Robert Pruitt/MF
Problem), Sauer and McGowen
Streets, Houston
2012 *City Council Meeting* (with Aaron Landsman),
DiverseWorks, Houston
*Inter-Galactic Bodily Spatial Positioning
and Move-meant* (with Otabenga
Jones & Associates), Houston Museum
of African American Culture
2009 *The Sound and the Fury (April Seventh, 1928)*,
(with Elevator Repair Service),
Wiener Festwochen, Vienna, and
The Holland Festival, Amsterdam

Selected Group Exhibitions

2018 *Declaration*, Institute for Contemporary
Art, Virginia Commonwealth
University, Richmond
2017 *We Go As They: Artists In Residence
2016–2017*, Studio Museum in Harlem
I've Only Known My Own, Optica Centre for
Contemporary Art, Montreal
How Do I Say Her Name?, Art League
Houston
Post Election (with Chelsea Knight),
September Gallery, Hudson, NY
2016 *I've Only Known My Own*, Flex Space, Houston
2015–16 *Island Time: Galveston Artist Residency–
The First Four Years*, Contemporary Arts
Museum Houston
2015 *I perceive the other and lose myself*, She Works
Flexible, Houston
2014 *State of the Art: Discovering American
Art Now*, Crystal Bridges Museum,
Bentonville, AK
Artists in Residence Exhibition, Galveston

Artist Residency
Antena @ Blaffer, Blaffer Art Museum, Houston
Adding a Beat: Hirsch Library Project, Museum
of Fine Arts Houston
2013 *I Am Him*, The Community Artists' Collective,
Houston
do it: Houston, Alabama Song, Houston
*Coming Through The Gap in the Mountain
on an Elephant*, University Museum
at Texas Southern University, Houston
2011 *State Fair*, DiverseWorks, Houston

Residencies

2018 Triangle Arts Association, New York
Pioneer Works, Brooklyn
Creative Exchange Lab, Portland Institute
for Contemporary Art
The MacDowell Colony (with Chelsea Knight),
Peterborough, NH
2017 Denniston Hill, Monticello, NY
2016–17 Studio Museum in Harlem
2015–16 Dance Source Houston
2015 Yamaguchi Institute of Contemporary Art, Japan
Artpace, San Antonio
2014 Millay Colony for the Arts, Austerlitz, NY
In-Situ-In-Place, Pendle, England
2013–14 Galveston Artist Residency
2012 Taller Portobelo Norte, Panama City

Awards

2017 William H. Johnson Prize Finalist
National Performance Network (NPN) Creation
Fund Award
2015 Artadia Award
2014 The Idea Fund Grant, TX
2006 Theatre Communications Group New
Generations Fellowship

Selected Bibliography

2017 Hallie Ringle, Ian Alteveer, Rashida Bumbray,
Daniella Rose King, *We Go as They:
Artists in Residence 2016–17* exhibition

pamphlet (New York: Studio Museum in
    Harlem, 2017).
Rainey Knudson, "Autumn Knight:
    Directions to Prairie View," Glasstire
    (May 8, 2017), http://glasstire.com
    /2017/05/08/autumn-knight-directions
    -to-prairie-view/.
Nicole Burisch, *I've Only Known My Own*
    (Canada: Nicole Burisch, 2017)
Carrie Marie Schneider, "Emancipation Park,
    Emancipatory Art: Flipping the
    Gentrification Playbook," *OffCite* (June 19,
    2017), http://offcite.org/emancipation
    -park-emancipatory-art-flipping-the
    -gentrification-playbook/.

2016   Andy Campbell, "The Year in Performance,"
    Artforum International 55.4 (December
    2016): 117–118.

2015   Jessica Santone, "Otherness and Empathy:
    Performing Affective Pedagogy," *Gulf
    Coast: A Journal of Literature and Fine
    Arts* 27.1 (Winter/Spring 2015): 211–219.

2013   Carrie Marie Schneider, "A Collaborative
    Review of Futz: Autumn Knight's
    Experimental Research Method and
    Performance Series," *Temporary Art
    Review* (March 21, 2013), http://
    temporaryartreview.com/a-collaborative
    -review-of-futz-autumn-knights
    -experimental-research-method-and
    -performance-series/.

2011   Carrie Marie Schneider, "Autumn Knight's
    'Performance Prescriptions' at
    DiverseWorks' 'State Fair'," *Glasstire*
    (September 30, 2011), http://glasstire.com
    /2011/09/30/state-fair-at-diverseworks/.

Contributors

Ryan N. Dennis is curator and programs director at Project Row Houses (PRH) in Houston. She has organized many public art projects, including Round 47 | *The Act of Doing: Revitalizing, Preserving and Protecting Third Ward* (2017); Round 46 | *Black Women Artists for Black Lives Matter at Project Row Houses* (2017); and Round 40 | *Monuments: Right Beyond the Site* (2014). Her writing has appeared in *Prospect.3 Notes for Now* (2014), *Gulf Coast: A Journal of Literature and Fine Arts* (Winter/Spring 2015), and *Studio Magazine* (Winter/Spring 2014).

Jennifer Doyle is a professor of English at the University of California, Riverside. She is the author of *Campus Sex, Campus Security* (2015), *Hold It Against Me: Difficulty and Emotion in Contemporary Art* (2013), and *Sex Objects: Art and the Dialectics of Desire* (2006).

Cynthia Oliver is an award-winning choreographer and dance artist. Her performance, experimental, and scholarly essays have appeared in the anthologies *The Oxford Handbook on Dance and Politics* (2017), *Making Caribbean Dance: Continuity and Creativity in Island Cultures* (2010), and *Caribbean Dance From Abakua to Zouk: How Movement Shapes Identity* (2005); in exhibition catalogues for visual artists Bill Traylor (2005) and Kehinde Wiley (2015); and in *Women and Performance* (2004) and *Movement Research Journal* (2004). Oliver has danced with numerous independent choreographers and companies in the US, including David Gordon's Pick Up Performance Co., Ronald Kevin Brown's Evidence, A Dance Company, Bebe Miller Company, and Tere O'Connor Dance. A professor in the department of Dance at the University of Illinois at Urbana-Champaign, Oliver was recently appointed Associate Vice Chancellor for Research in the Humanities, Arts, and Related Fields.

Amy L. Powell is curator of modern and contemporary art at Krannert Art Museum (KAM), University of Illinois at Urbana-Champaign. In addition to *Autumn Knight: In Rehearsal*, her exhibitions at KAM have included *Basel Abbas and Ruanne Abou-Rahme: And yet my mask is powerful* (2018), *Attachment* (2015), *Time / Image* (2016), and *Zina Saro-Wiwa: Did You Know We Taught Them How to Dance?* (2016–2017). Powell's work has been supported by The Andy Warhol Foundation for the Visual Arts, the Smithsonian Institution, and the Institute for Research in the Humanities at the University of Wisconsin-Madison, where she completed a PhD in art history in 2012.

Sandra Ruiz is an assistant professor of Latina/Latino Studies and English at the University of Illinois at Urbana-Champaign. She has published in *Performance Matters* (2017), *Women & Performance: a journal of feminist theory* (2015, 2007), and *Small Axe: A Caribbean Journal of Criticism* (2015). Her book *Ricanness: Staging Time in Anticolonial Performance* (NYU Press) is due out in 2019, and she is currently working on a book project tentatively titled *Perilous Pedagogy: Crossing the Line & Forming Psychoanalytic Affections in Aesthetics*.

Acknowledgments

I first saw Autumn Knight perform in Houston in 2013. I knew about her work from friends and Facebook invitations. The performances were scheduled not too far in advance and were embedded in the community of artists that made Houston a rich place to live. Autumn's collaborators and most audience members were involved in the artist-centered spaces of Project Row Houses, DiverseWorks, Alabama Song, and the University Museum at Texas Southern University. Ryan Dennis's Round 37 exhibition at Project Row Houses dedicated one historic home-turned-installation space to Autumn's performances; *Futz: A Research Method* was vital to the planning of *In Rehearsal*. Each of those early performances was completely different from the last and genuinely evocative—unlike any work I had ever experienced—of the complex interrelations of race, gender, and sexuality. In part from my desire to work with performance, and primarily from my curiosity to see how Autumn's thinking would expand beyond Houston's orbit, I came to Champaign-Urbana in 2014 hoping that we could work together.

I am exceedingly proud of what we designed, which would not have been possible without many supporters and interlocutors. The effects are still resounding. Autumn and I worked for more than a year building connections with faculty, making site visits for possible performances, and brainstorming who might serve as performers, participants, and audiences for the exhibition. Warm thanks go to Ruth Nicole Brown, Lisa Dixon, Becky Ferrell, Patrick Hammie, Carla Hunter, Candice Jenkins, Brett Kaplan, Maryam Kashani, Prita Meier, Cynthia Oliver, Allyson Purpura, Stacey Robinson, Kristin Romberg, Sandra Ruiz, Siobhan Somerville, and Endalyn Taylor. Maryam Kashani and Sandra Ruiz organized their courses to include the exhibition, and I am thrilled that our performance interests continue to unfold along with Ruth Nicole Brown and Becky Ferrell. Lydia Khuri ensured the co-sponsorship of the University's Intersections Living-Learning Community, which provided housing for all guest performers. Many thanks to Doug Parrett for facilitating the Stock Pavilion as a venue for *Lament* and to Doug Boyer and Cody Demas at the Activities and Recreation Center for navigating our unusual request to have an artist perform in the outdoor pool. Susan Koshy made sure that Jennifer Doyle would have time to participate in *Here + Now*, and I am grateful to her and to Sandra Ruiz for making this thoughtful connection. Thanks as well to Tekita Bankhead, Pat Morey, Lovie Olivia, and Preetika Rajgariah. Becky Ferrell ensured invaluable time and space for rehearsal in the department of Dance, and I am grateful to her and to Jan Erkert and Natalie Fiol for their support. Video Services made fine productions of performance rehearsals: special thanks to Andrew Gleason, Anne Lukeman, Jack Maples, Emily Polk, and Todd Wilson. Special additional thanks to Allyson Purpura and Kristin Romberg for their insightful comments on my essay in this book.

My profound appreciation goes to the guest artists of *In Rehearsal*: S. Bianca Bailey, Becky Ferrell, Holly Garrett, Athanasia Giannetos, Kelley Hershman, Abijan Johnson, Chivas Michael, and Xavier Roe. The entire staff of Krannert Art Museum dedicated themselves to this exhibition, which is meaningful because live performance challenges the institution at every turn. Warm thanks to Kathleen Harleman for her support at the inception of this project and to Jon Seydl for seeing it to its conclusion. For their unwavering support of Autumn's work, I thank Rachel Cook, Ryan Dennis, John Pluecker, and Robert Pruitt. Jim Powell made this work possible in more ways than I can acknowledge, and my deep gratitude goes to him and to Gibson.

This exhibition and publication would not have been possible without generous funding from Krannert Art Museum, the College of Fine + Applied Arts, and The Andy Warhol Foundation for the Visual Arts. I am particularly grateful for Project Row Houses's continuing support of Autumn's work by supporting essay contributions in this book, with sincere thanks to Eureka Gilkey and Ryan Dennis. I am grateful to all of these supporters for making such ventures thinkable, much less feasible. In a similar vein, one could hope for no better senior curator than Allyson Purpura, whose support is without rival. Ryan Dennis, Jennifer Doyle, Cynthia Oliver, and Sandra Ruiz have fortified this book with their writing and conversation, which is beautifully framed by rockstar designers James Goggin and Shan James of Practise. I'm especially grateful to Maria Bailey for her copyediting and to Katie Koca Polite for her expert management of the publication.

My conversations with Autumn illuminate what motivates and sustains my work with contemporary art, and I count them among my most cherished experiences. Her performances convey a difficulty, humor, and urgency driven by her incredibly generous curiosity. For her consistent thinking across the breadth of her practice and her care and commitment to everything she does, all of my gratitude is reserved for Autumn.

Amy L. Powell

Thank you Amy Powell, Julia Kelly, Christopher Schaede, Carla Hunter, Maryam Kashani, Sandra Ruiz, Siobhan Somerville, Ruth Nicole Brown, Candice Jenkins, Becky Ferrell, Endalyn Taylor, Abijan Johnson, Cynthia Oliver, Bianca Bailey, Holly Garrett, Krannert Art Museum staff, Chivas Michael, Athanasia Giannetos, Kelley Hershman, Walter Wilson, Eric Lemme, Mitchell Oliver, Allyson Purpura, Prita Meier, Kristin Romberg, Patrick Earl Hammie, Stacey Robinson, Robert Pruitt, Gavin Kroeber, Anne Lukeman, and the University of Illinois at Urbana-Champaign for allowing me to play on your campus.

Autumn Knight

Image Credits

All works conceived and performed by Autumn Knight unless otherwise noted.

Works performed at Krannert Art Museum and other locations on the campus of the University of Illinois at Urbana-Champaign took place in Champaign or Urbana, IL.

Images from Krannert Art Museum are © and courtesy the University of Illinois and Autumn Knight, with all other venues © and courtesy Autumn Knight, unless otherwise indicated.

Front cover: Rehearsal view of *El Diablo y Cristo Negro*, Krannert Art Museum, photo: Julia Nucci Kelly; **Inside front cover:** Rehearsal view of *Lament*, University of Illinois Stock Pavilion, photo: Robert Pruitt; **Page 1:** *An experimental freezing of a room through metaphorical means*, University of Illinois Activities and Recreation Center, photo: Julia Nucci Kelly; **2–3:** Installation view of *Autumn Knight: In Rehearsal*, Krannert Art Museum, photo: Katie Koca Polite; **10:** Performance score, Krannert Art Museum, photo: Amy L. Powell; **13:** *Direct from Broadway* © Whoopi Goldberg; *Sesame Street* © Sesame Street Workshop; *Tampopo* © Itami Productions; **14:** *Performance Prescriptions*, DiverseWorks, Houston, photo: Robert Pruitt; **15:** Rehearsal view of *El Diablo y Cristo Negro*, Krannert Art Museum, photo: Amy L. Powell; **21:** Rehearsal view of *El Diablo y Cristo Negro*, Krannert Art Museum, photo: Julia Nucci Kelly; **23–29:** *El Diablo y Cristo Negro*, Krannert Art Museum, photos: Julia Nucci Kelly; **30–31:** *El Diablo y Cristo Negro*, Project Row Houses, Houston, photos:

Robert Pruitt; **32–33:** Round 37 | *Futz: A Research Method,* Project Row Houses, Houston, photo: Autumn Knight; **35:** *Roach Dance*, Project Row Houses, Houston, photos: Claudia Casbarian; **36:** *Hands in Your Lap*, Project Row Houses, Houston, photos: Robert Pruitt; **38:** *Flower Man Bike Parade*, Houston, photo: Stephen Wilson; **40, 42–45, 47:** *Here + Now*, Krannert Art Museum, photos: Julia Nucci Kelly; **48–49:** *Here + Now*, Project Row Houses, Houston, photos: Dean Liscum; **51:** Installation view of *Here + Now*, Krannert Art Museum, photo: Julia Nucci Kelly; **54:** Performance score, Krannert Art Museum, photo: Amy L. Powell; **56:** Sandra Ruiz's class, "A Lover's Discourse: Literature, Theory, and Performance," University of Illinois Department of Latina/Latino Studies, photos: Autumn Knight; **61–66:** *Lament*, University of Illinois Stock Pavilion, photos: Natalie Fiol; **67:** *Lament*, Project Row Houses, Houston, photos: Autumn Knight; **68–69, 72–73:** Video stills from *Lament*, 2017, courtesy Video Services | Public Affairs at Illinois and Autumn Knight; **77, 79–85:** *An experimental freezing of a room through metaphorical means*, University of Illinois Activities and Recreation Center, photos: Julia Nucci Kelly; **86–87** *An experimental freezing of a room through metaphorical means*, Alabama Song, Houston, photos: Robert Pruitt; **95:** (top) Cynthia Oliver, *Virago-Man Dem*, BAM (Brooklyn Academy of Music), Brooklyn, photo: Julieta Cervantes; (bottom) Autumn Knight, *Grand Opening/Grand Closing*, Marfa Contemporary, Marfa, TX, photo: Stephanie Huang; **99–103:** Performance scores, Krannert Art Museum, photos: Amy L. Powell; **106–111:** Performance scores, Krannert Art Museum, photos: Amy L. Powell;

127: Rehearsal view of *El Diablo y Cristo Negro*, Krannert Art Museum, photo: Amy L. Powell; **Inside back cover:** Rehearsal view of *Lament*, University of Illinois Stock Pavilion, photo: Robert Pruitt; **Back cover:** *El Diablo y Cristo Negro*, Krannert Art Museum, photo: Julia Nucci Kelly.

Every effort was made to secure copyright credit for images contained within.

Page 127: Rehearsal view of *El Diablo y Cristo Negro*, with Chivas Michael and Xavier Roe. Krannert Art Museum, Champaign, January 25, 2017

Krannert Art Museum Staff

Jackson Bird, Security Guard
Claudia Corlett-Stahl, Associate Director
Tim Fox, Design and Installation Specialist
Kamila Glowacki, Education Coordinator
David Holzner, Security Supervisor
Julia Nucci Kelly, Communications and
     Marketing Coordinator
Kathryn Koca Polite, Assistant Curator and
     Publications Specialist
Brenda Nardi, Director of Development
John Parks, Building Maintenance
Amy L. Powell, Curator of Modern and Contemporary Art
Allyson Purpura, Senior Curator and Curator of
     Global African Art
Trish Rountree, Security Guard
Christine Saniat, Museum Registrar and
     Exhibitions Director
Anne Sautman, Director of Education
Chris Schaede, Office Manager
Aimee Schneider, Giertz Education Center Coordinator
Jon L. Seydl, Director
Kim Sissons, Collection Manager
Maureen Warren, Curator of European and American Art
Walter Wilson, Design and Installation Specialist

Inside back cover: Rehearsal view of *Lament*, with
Autumn Knight. University of Illinois Stock Pavilion,
Urbana, April 11, 2017

Back cover: *El Diablo y Cristo Negro*, with Autumn Knight,
Chivas Michael, and Xavier Roe. Krannert Art Museum,
Champaign, January 26, 2017

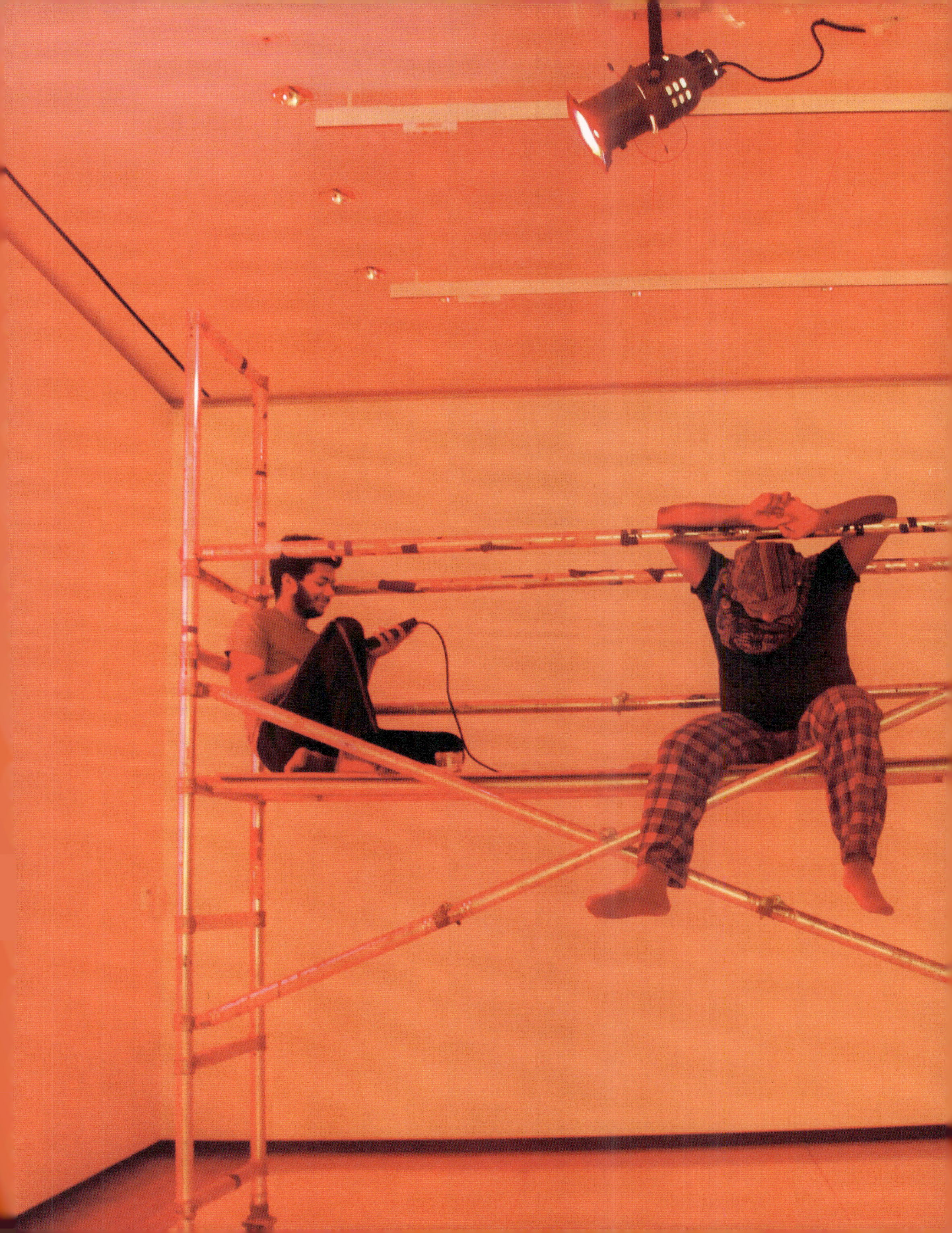